The

Good Soldiers

The
Good
Soldiers

David Finkel

Douglas & McIntyre
D & M PUBLISHERS INC.
Vancouver/Toronto

Published by arrangement with Sarah Crichton Books,
an imprint of Farrar, Straus and Giroux, LLC, New York.

Portions of this book originally appeared,
in different form, in *The Washington Post*.

Published in Canada by
Douglas & McIntyre
An imprint of D&M Publishers Inc.
2323 Quebec Street, Suite 201
Vancouver BC Canada v5t 4s7
www.douglas-mcintyre.com

Cataloguing data available from Library and Archives Canada
ISBN 978-1-55365-516-9 (cloth)
ISBN 978-1-55365-548-0 (pbk.)

Design by Abby Kagan
Cover photograph courtesy of David Finkel
Top photograph on page 108 courtesy of the U.S. Army
All other photographs courtesy of David Finkel
Printed and bound in Canada by Friesens
Text printed on acid-free, 100% post-consumer paper

To Lisa, Julia, and Lauren

CONTENTS

The

Good Soldiers

1

APRIL 6, 2007

Many listening tonight will ask why this effort will succeed when previous operations to secure Baghdad did not. Well, here are the differences . . .
—GEORGE W. BUSH, *January 10, 2007, announcing the surge*

His soldiers weren't yet calling him the Lost Kauz behind his back, not when this began. The soldiers of his who would be injured were still perfectly healthy, and the soldiers of his who would die were still perfectly alive. A soldier who was a favorite of his, and who was often described as a younger version of him, hadn't yet written of the war in a letter to a friend, "I've had enough of this bullshit." Another soldier, one of his best, hadn't yet written in the journal he kept hidden, "I've lost all hope. I feel the end is near for me, very, very near." Another hadn't yet gotten angry enough to shoot a thirsty dog that was lapping up a puddle of human blood. Another, who at the end of all this would become the battalion's most decorated soldier, hadn't yet started dreaming about the people he had killed and wondering if God was going to ask him about the two who had been climbing a ladder. Another hadn't yet started seeing himself shooting a man in the head, and then seeing the little girl who had just watched him shoot the man in the head, every time he shut his eyes. For that matter, his own dreams hadn't started yet, either, at least the ones that he would remember—the one in which his wife and friends were in a cemetery, surrounding a hole into which he was suddenly falling; or the one in which everything around him was exploding and he was trying to fight back with no weapon and no ammunition other than a bucket of old bullets. Those dreams would be along

Ralph Kauzlarich, Fort Riley, Kansas

soon enough, but in early April 2007, Ralph Kauzlarich, a U.S. Army lieutenant colonel who had led a battalion of some eight hundred soldiers into Baghdad as part of George W. Bush's surge, was still finding a reason every day to say, "It's all good."

He would wake up in eastern Baghdad, inhale its bitter, burning air, and say it. "It's all good." He would look around at the fundamentals of what his life had become—his camouflage, his gun, his body armor, his gas mask in case of a chemical attack, his atropine injector in case of a nerve gas attack, his copy of *The One Year Bible* next to his neat bed, which he made first thing every morning out of a need for order, his photographs on the walls of his wife and children, who were home in Kansas in a house shaded by American elm trees and with a video in the VCR of him telling the children the night before he left, "Okay. All right. It's time to start the noodles. I love you. Everybody up. Hut hut"—and say it. "It's all good." He would go outside and immediately become coated from hair to boots in dirt, unless the truck that sprayed sewage water to keep the dirt under control had been by, in which case he would walk through sewage-laden goop, and say it. He would go past the blast walls, the sandbags, the bunkers, the aid station where the wounded from other battalions were treated, the annex where they assembled the dead, and say it. He would say it in his little office, with its walls cracked from various explosions, while reading the morning's e-mails. From his wife: "I love you so much! I wish we could lay naked in each other's arms . . . bodies meshing together, perhaps a little sweat :-)." From his mother, in rural Washington state, after some surgery: "I must say, the sleep was the best I have had in months. Everything turned out to be normal, goody, goody. Rosie picked me up and brought me back home because that was the morning our cows were butchered and your Dad had to be there to make sure things were done right." From his father: "I have laid awake many nights since I last saw you, and have often wished I could be along side you to assist in some way." He would say it on his way to the chapel, where he would attend Catholic Mass conducted by a priest who had to be flown in by helicopter because a previous priest was blown up in a Humvee. He would say it in the dining facility, where he always had two servings of milk with his dinner. He would say it when he went in his

5

Humvee into the neighborhoods of eastern Baghdad, where more and
more roadside bombs were exploding now that the surge was under way,
killing soldiers, taking off arms, taking off legs, causing concussions, exploding ear drums, leaving some soldiers angry and others vomiting and
others in sudden tears. Not his soldiers, though. Other soldiers. From
other battalions. "It's all good," he would say when he came back. It could
seem like a nervous tic, this thing that he said, or a prayer of some sort.
Or maybe it was a declaration of optimism, simply that, nothing more,
because he *was* optimistic, even though he was in the midst of a war that
to the American public, and the American media, and even to some in the
American military, seemed all over in April 2007, except for the pessi-
mism, the praying, and the nervous tics.

But not to him. "Well, here are the differences," George W. Bush had
said, announcing the surge, and Ralph Kauzlarich had thought: We'll be the
difference. My battalion. My soldiers. Me. And every day since then he
had said it—"It's all good"—after which he might say the other thing he often said, always without irony and utterly convinced: "We're winning." He
liked to say that, too. Except now, on April 6, 2007, at 1:00 a.m., as someone banged on his door, waking him up, he said something different.

"What the fuck?" he said, opening his eyes.

The thing is, he and his battalion weren't even supposed to be here, and
that's one way to consider everything that was about to happen as Kauzlarich, awake now, dressed now, made the short walk from his trailer to the
battalion's operations center. The March rains that had turned the place
sloppy with mud were thankfully over. The mud had dried. The road was
dusty. The air was cold. Whatever was happening was only a mile or so
away, but there was nothing for Kauzlarich to see, and nothing for him to
hear, other than his own thoughts.

Two months before, as he was about to leave for Iraq, he'd sat in his
kitchen in Fort Riley, Kansas, after a dinner of ham and double-baked
potatoes and milk and apple crisp for dessert, and said, "We are America.
I mean, we have all of the resources. We have a very intelligent population. If we decide, just like we did in World War Two, if we all said, 'This

is our focus, this is our priority, and we're going to win it, we're going to do everything that we have to do to win it,' then we'd win it. This nation can do anything that it wants to do. The question is, does America have the will?"

Now, as he entered the operations center a few minutes after 1:00 a.m., the war was in its 1,478th day, the number of dead American troops had surpassed 3,000, the number of injured troops was nearing 25,000, the American public's early optimism was long gone, and the miscalculations and distortions that had preceded the war had been exposed in detail, as had the policy blunders that had been guiding it since it began. Four injured, he was told. One slightly. Three seriously. And one dead.

"Statistically, there's probably a pretty good chance I'm going to lose men. And I'm not quite sure how I'm going to deal with it," he had said at Fort Riley. In nineteen years as an army officer, he had never lost a soldier under his direct command.

Now he was being told that the dead soldier was Private First Class Jay Cajimat, who was twenty years and two months old and who might have died immediately from the blast of the explosion, or a little more slowly in the resulting fire.

"This is probably going to change me," Kauzlarich had said at Fort Riley, and when he wasn't around to overhear, a friend had predicted what the change was going to be: "You're going to see a good man disintegrate before your eyes."

Now he was being told that the soldiers at the Mortuary Affairs collection point were being alerted to get ready for remains, as were the soldiers at the collection point called Vehicle Sanitization.

"I mean, bottom line, if we lose this war, Ralph Kauzlarich will have lost a war," Kauzlarich had said at Fort Riley.

Now, as more details came in, he tried to be analytical rather than emotional. Instead of thinking how Cajimat was one of the first soldiers he had been assigned when he was forming the battalion, he sifted through the sounds he had heard as he was going to sleep. At 12:35 there had been a boom in the distance. A soft boom. That must have been it.

They were going to go to Afghanistan. That had been the first rumor. Then Iraq. Then nowhere at all. They were going to stay in Fort Riley and miss the war entirely. So many twists and turns had gotten the battalion that was going to win the war in the position to do it:

In 2003, when the war began, the battalion didn't even exist, except on some chart somewhere that had to do with the army's eternal reorganization of itself. In 2005, when it did come into existence, it didn't even have a name. A unit of action—that's how it was referred to. It was a brand-new battalion in a brand-new brigade that began with no equipment other than Kauzlarich's and no soldiers other than him.

Worse, as far as Kauzlarich was concerned, was the place where the battalion was going to be based: Fort Riley, which unfairly or not suffered from a reputation as one of the armpits of the army. Kauzlarich, who was about to turn forty years old, had attended West Point. He had become an Army Ranger, perhaps the defining experience of his life as a soldier. He had fought in Operation Desert Storm in 1991. He had been in Afghanistan in the early days of Operation Enduring Freedom. He had been on a couple of missions in Iraq, had jumped out of airplanes eighty-one times onto mountains and into woods, and had lived in the wilderness for weeks at a stretch. But Fort Riley, to him, felt like the most remote place he had ever been. From the very first he felt like an outsider there, a feeling that only deepened in the days leading up to the surge, when reporters descended on Fort Riley looking for soldiers to talk to and were never directed to him. Even if they were looking for officers, his name wasn't mentioned. Even if they were specifically looking for officers who were battalion commanders, his name wasn't mentioned. Even if they were looking for *infantry* battalion commanders, of which there were only two.

There was just something about him that the army resisted even as it continued to promote him. He was not their smooth-edged, cookie-cutter officer. There was an underdog quality to him, which made him instantly likeable, and a high-beam intensity to him, which at times would emanate from him in waves. And if there were things the army resisted in him, there were things about the army that he resisted as well—insisting, for example, that he would never want a posting that would put him inside the Pentagon, because those postings often went to sycophants rather than to true soldiers, and he was a true soldier through and through. It was an insistence that struck some of his friends as noble and others as silly, both of which were part of his complicated soul. He was kind. He was egotistical. He was humane. He was self-absorbed. Growing up in Montana and the Pacific Northwest, he had been a skinny boy with jutting ears who had methodically re-created himself into a man who did the most push-ups, ran the fastest mile, and regarded life as a daily act of will. He took pride in his hard stomach and his pitch-perfect ability to recall names and dates and compliments and slights. He had precise and delicate handwriting, almost like calligraphy. He attended Mass every Sunday, prayed before eating, and crossed himself whenever he got on a helicopter. He liked to say, "Let me tell you something," and then tell you something. He could be honest, which worked in his favor, and blunt, which sometimes didn't. Once, when he was asked by a journalist about an investigation he had done into the death of Pat Tillman, the professional football player who became an Army Ranger in Kauzlarich's regiment and was killed by friendly fire in Afghanistan, he suggested that the reason Tillman's family was having difficulty finding closure might have to do with religious beliefs. "When you die, I mean, there is supposedly a better life, right? Well, if you are an atheist and you don't believe in anything, if you die, what is there to go to? Nothing. You are worm dirt," he had said. So, blunt. And maybe insensitive, too. And crude on occasion. "It's hot as balls" seemed to be his favorite weather report.

But beyond all of that was the fact that he was, at his core, a good leader. When people were around him, they wanted to know what he thought, and if he told them to do something, even if it was dangerous, they did it not out of intimidation but because they didn't want to let him down. "Ask anybody," his executive officer, Major Brent Cummings, said. "He has this dynamic personality about himself that people want to be led by him." Or, as another of his soldiers put it, "He's the kind of guy you follow to hell and back. He's that kind of leader." Even the big, bloated, political army could see this, and so, in 2005, Kauzlarich was made a battalion commander, and in 2006 he was notified that his unit was being given the dusted-off name of a dormant battalion called the 2-16, which was short for the Second Battalion, Sixteenth Infantry Regiment of the Fourth Infantry Brigade Combat Team, First Infantry Division.

"Holy shit. You know what the nickname is?" Brent Cummings said when Kauzlarich told him. "The Rangers."

Kauzlarich laughed. He pretended to smoke a victory cigar. "It's destiny," he said.

He meant it, too. He believed in destiny, in God, in fate, in Jesus Christ, and in everything happening for a reason, although sometimes the meaning of something wasn't immediately clear to him. That was the case at the end of 2006, when he was at last informed of his mission, that he and his battalion would be deploying to western Iraq to provide security for supply convoys. He was stunned by this. He was an infantry officer in charge of an infantry battalion, and the assignment he'd drawn in the decisive war of his lifetime was to guard trucks carrying fuel and food as they moved across the flat, boring lonesomeness of western Iraq for twelve boring months? What, Kauzlarich wondered, could be the meaning of this? Was it to humble him? Was it to make him feel like a loser? Because that was precisely how he was feeling on January 10, 2007, as he dutifully turned on the TV to watch George W. Bush, who was in the deepening sag of his presidency, announce his newest strategy for Iraq.

A loser watching a loser: On January 10, it was hard to see Bush any other way. At 33 percent, his approval rating was the lowest yet of his presidency, and as he began to speak that night, his voice, at least to the 67 percent who disapproved of him, might have sounded more desperate than resolute, because by just about any measure, his war was on the verge of failure. The strategy of winning an enduring peace had failed. The strategy of defeating terrorism had failed. The strategy of spreading democracy throughout the Middle East had failed. The strategy of at least bringing democracy to Iraq had failed. To most Americans, who polls showed were fed up and wanted the troops brought home, the moment at hand was of tragedy, beyond which would be only loss.

In that moment, what Bush then announced seemed an act of defiance, if not outright stupidity. Instead of reducing troop levels in Iraq, he was increasing them by what would eventually be thirty thousand. "The vast majority of them—five brigades—will be deployed to Baghdad," he said, and continued: "Our troops will have a well-defined mission: to help Iraqis clear and secure neighborhoods, to help them protect the local population, and to help ensure that the Iraqi forces left behind are capable of providing the security that Baghdad needs."

That was the heart of his new strategy. It was a counterinsurgency strategy that the White House initially called "the New Way Forward," but that quickly became known as "the surge."

The surge, then. As far as the majority of the American public was concerned, those additional troops would be surging straight into the tragic moment of the war, but as Bush finished speaking, and rumors about the identities of the five brigades began circulating, and their identities started becoming public, and the official announcement came that one would be a brigade that was about to deploy from Fort Riley, Kansas, Kauzlarich saw it differently.

A battalion commander in the thick of the war: that was who he was going to be. Because of strategic disasters, public revulsion, political consequences, and perfect timing, he and his soldiers weren't going to be protecting supply convoys. They were going to Baghdad. Meaning restored, Kauzlarich closed his eyes and thanked God.

Three weeks later, his departure now a few days away, his hand a bit sore from being grabbed so many times by people shaking it and hanging on to it and looking in his eyes as if they were already trying to remember the last time they saw Ralph Kauzlarich, Kauzlarich sat down in his house to fill out a booklet called the Family Contingency Workbook.

I want to be buried / cremated.

"Buried," he wrote.

Location of cemetery:

"West Point," he wrote.

Personal effects I want buried with me:

"Wedding band," he wrote.

In came his wife, Stephanie, who had been in another part of the house with their three young children. They had met twenty years before, when both were at West Point, and he had sensed immediately that this tall, athletic, chin-out woman suddenly in front of him was someone who would be able to hold her own against him. She was a catch, and he knew it. He considered himself one, too, and his very first words to her, spoken with utter confidence, were, "You can call me The Kauz." The Kauz—to him, it sounded so much better than Ralph, and so much better than his full last name, which some people properly pronounced as KAUZ-la-rich, and some people mispronounced. Now, so many years later, years in which Stephanie had never, not even once, called him The Kauz, she looked at what he had written down and said, "That's all you want to be buried with?"

"Yes," he said, continuing.

Type of headstone:

"Military," he wrote.

Scripture you want read:

"Psalm 23," he wrote.

Music you want played:

"Something upbeat," he wrote.

"Ralph, upbeat music?" Stephanie asked.

Meanwhile, in other parts of Fort Riley, the other soldiers were getting ready, too. Finishing wills. Designating powers of attorney. Working their way down final medical checklists. Hearing. Heart rate. Blood pressure. Blood type. They went to health briefings and were told: Wash your hands. Drink bottled water. Wear cotton underwear. Watch out for rats. They put on their body armor and stood outside in a zero-degree wind chill for inspection and were told that the straps weren't tight enough, the ceramic plates intended to stop high-powered sniper bullets were an inch off, their compression bandages and tourniquets were stored in the wrong place, they were effectively dead men. They went to a briefing on stress management and suicide prevention and were told by a chaplain, "This is important. If you are not ready to die, you need to get there. If you are not ready to die, you need to be. If you are not ready to see your friends die, you need to be."

And were they ready? Who knew? For most of them, this would be their first deployment, and for many it would be their first time away from the United States. The average age in the battalion was nineteen.

Could a nineteen-year-old be ready? What about a nineteen-year-old soldier named Duncan Crookston, who was in his little apartment with his mother and father and new, nineteen-year-old wife, packing his things, when the phone rang? "Buried," he said. "Battle Hymn of the Republic," he said. Ten minutes later he hung up. "Just planned my funeral," he nonchalantly told his curious parents and new wife, and was Duncan Crookston ready?

What about the youngest soldier in the battalion, who was only seventeen? "Roger that," he said, whenever he was asked if he was ready, but when rumors about the deployment first began to circulate, he had taken aside his platoon sergeant, a staff sergeant named Frank Gietz, to ask how he'd be able to handle killing someone. "Put it in a dark place while you're there," Gietz had said.

So was a seventeen-year-old ready?

For that matter, was Gietz, who had been to Iraq twice, was one of the oldest soldiers in the battalion, and knew better than anyone the meaning of "a dark place"?

Was Jay Cajimat, who in ten weeks was going to be remembered by his mother in the local paper as a "soft-hearted boy"?

Didn't matter. They were going.

They packed ammunition and photographs and first-aid kits and candy. They went into town for the last time and in a few cases drank too much, in a few other cases went AWOL to see girlfriends, and in at least one case got married. Five days before departure, Kauzlarich studied a list of soldiers who wouldn't be able to go. Seven needed some sort of surgery. Two were about to become fathers. One had an infant in intensive care. Two were in jail. Nine were, for various reasons, as Kauzlarich put it, "mentally incapable of doing what we're about to do." But most were eager to do what they were about to do, were impatient, even, and said so with certainty. "It's the decisive point of the fight," one soldier explained, foot tapping, head nodding, practically vibrating. "This is the chance to win it."

Four days until departure:

Kauzlarich gathered the battalion in a field behind headquarters to explain where in Baghdad they would be based. It had snowed, and it was cold, and the sun was going down as he said that they soon would be near Sadr City, Baghdad's infamous slum and a center of the insurgency. The soldiers ringed him and pressed closer to hear, and as he raised his voice and said the words "a nice, little, mean, nasty area," they echoed off the ice and the surrounding buildings, making this place feel even chillier than it was.

"Now, it's not a game, guys," he said. "You are going to see some horrific things in the next year. You are going to see some things you are not going to understand . . . It's down to nut-cutting time, and we're going to get some, but we're going to do it in a disciplined manner, like we do everything . . . I am absolutely confident in your abilities, absolutely confident . . . The bottom line is this weekend's your last, okay? So call your parents, love your families, stay focused on them for this weekend. Not later than Tuesday night, as soon as you get on that airplane and that airplane takes off, your sole focus is going to be winning our nation's war."

There was a pause, just long enough for the word *war* to finish echoing, and then the soldiers began to cheer, lustily and for a long while, after which they headed inside, filling the room with the wintry smell of boys who have been out in the snow.

One day until departure:

In the Kauzlarich house, the children were running around with stuffed animals purchased over the weekend, each with a memory chip containing a quick-recorded message from their father for them to play over the coming year. "Hi Jacob. I love you." "Hi Garrett. I sure do love you." "I love you, Allie-gator." Allie was seven-year-old Alexandria Taylor Kauzlarich, a name chosen because the initials were ATK, which reminded her father of the word *attack*. The oldest of the three children, she was also the most sensitive to what was at hand. "I don't want you to leave," she said at one point, and when her father told her, "I'll be okay, and if I'm not okay, you'll be okay, because I'll be checking on you," she said, "Then I'll kill myself so I can be with you." She climbed onto his lap, and meanwhile, Jacob, five, and Garrett, three, both too young for such sensitivities, continued to run around the house clobbering each other with their stuffed animals, while Stephanie had her own images to contend with. "Gray. Dismal. A very sad place to live," is how she envisioned the place her husband was going. She had done her time in the army after graduating from West Point and had learned to guard against too much sentimentality, but now came a new image, that of a freshly dead soldier. Meanwhile, Kauzlarich looked at his family and, giving into that sentimentality a bit, said, "I mean, this is a very complex war. The end state, in my opinion, the end state in Iraq would be that Iraqi children can go out on a soccer field and play safely. Parents can let their kids go out and play, and they don't have a concern in the world. Just like us. Being able to go out and do what we want to do and not being concerned about being kidnapped, accosted, whatnot. I mean, that's the way the whole world should be. Is that possible?"

Departure day:

The soldiers were due in the battalion parking lot at 1:00 p.m., and by 12:42 the first hug between a soldier and his family was under way, a tangle of moving arms that was still going strong at 12:43. By 12:45, tears had begun in several places, including inside a car where a woman sat motionless against the door, head in her hands, while outside the car a soldier leaned against the trunk and smoked; and so it continued as the afternoon progressed.

The soldiers smoked cigarettes. They lined up their body armor. They signed out their weapons from lockup. They waited with wives, girlfriends, children, parents, and grandparents, and constantly checked their watches. One soldier couldn't stop kissing a young woman who was up on her tiptoes, while Gietz told his platoon to start wrapping up the goodbyes already, while another soldier loaded his parents' car with the things he wouldn't be taking, including a pair of cowboy boots whose top halves had been dyed a beautiful blue. Midafternoon now, and Kauzlarich arrived with Stephanie and the children. "This day sucks," he said, and when Allie started to cry, that only made things seem worse. He said goodbye to his family in his office. He said goodbye again when he put them in the car. He said goodbye again when they didn't leave right away, just stayed in the car, and then he went back into his office and into the final hours.

Family photo: packed. Extra tourniquet: packed. Extra compression bandage: packed. He looked out the window. The family car was gone. He turned out the lights, shut the door, went outside, and made his way with his soldiers to a nearby gymnasium to wait for buses that would carry them to the airfield.

Nighttime now.

Here came the buses.

The soldiers stood and moved forward, and Kauzlarich clapped their backs as they funneled by.

"Ready?" he asked.

"Yessir."

"Good?"

"Yessir."

"Ready to be a hero?"

"Yessir."

Out they went, one after another, until there was only one soldier left for Kauzlarich to speak with. "Are we ready for war?" he asked himself, and out he went, too.

A bus to a plane. A plane to another plane. Another plane after that to some helicopters, and at last they arrived at the place where they were to spend the next year, which wasn't the Green Zone, with its paved roads and diplomats and palaces, and wasn't one of the big army bases that members of Congress would corkscrew into just long enough to marvel at the Taco Bell before corkscrewing out. It was the place Congress and Taco Bell never got to, a compact forward operating base called FOB Rustamiyah, which some of the soldiers first got a sense of back in the United States by looking at maps. There was Iraq. There was Baghdad. There, marking the eastern edge of Baghdad, was the Diyala River. And there, next to a raggedy U-turn in the river, which to laughing nineteen-year-olds looked like something dangling from the rear end of a dog, was their new home.

Now that they had arrived, jamming in among 1,500 other soldiers from several other battalions, the descriptions would only get worse. Everything in Rustamiyah was the color of dirt, and stank. If the wind came from the east, the smell was of raw sewage, and if the wind came from the west, the smell was of burning trash. In Rustamiyah, the wind never came from the north or the south.

They began learning this as soon as they landed. The air caught in their throats. Dirt and dust coated them right away. Because they arrived in the dead of night they couldn't see very much, but soon after sunrise, a few soldiers climbed a guard tower, peeked through the camouflage tarp, and were startled to see a vast landscape of trash, much of it on fire. One thing they had been told before they arrived was that the biggest threat in their part of Baghdad would be from homemade roadside bombs, which were referred to as improvised explosive devices or, more simply, IEDs. They had also been told that IEDs were often hidden in piles of trash. At the time it didn't overly worry them, but now, as they looked out from the guard tower at acres of trash blowing across dirt fields and ashes from burned trash rising in smoke columns, it did.

"We ain't ever gonna be able to find an IED in all this shit," a soldier named Jay March said. Twenty years old and eager to fight, he could have been any soldier in the battalion. He said this quietly, and he said it nervously, too.

Several days later, their nervousness deepening, the entire battalion was ordered to gather before sunrise for its first operation: a day-long walk through the sixteen-square-mile area of operations they'd been assigned to bring under control. It was Kauzlarich's idea. He'd wanted a dramatic way to announce to eastern Baghdad that the 2-16 had arrived, and he'd also wanted a dramatic way to get his soldiers off of the FOB and into their area of operation, or AO, so they would realize that they had nothing to fear. "To pop everybody's cherry," as he put it.

"Operation Ranger Dominance" was the name he chose for the walk. "The Kauzlarich Death March" was what his soldiers were calling it.

"Hey, Two-sixteen," a soldier from a different battalion on the FOB scrawled on their bathroom wall the day before the operation. "Good luck on your Ranger Dumbass walk tomorrow."

In full body armor, they assembled at 5:00 a.m. near the FOB's main gate. Humvees would be interspersed here and there in case a soldier needed to be evacuated, but the point of the operation was to walk, to see and to be seen in some of Baghdad's most hostile neighborhoods, and so the soldiers made sure their ceramic plates were perfectly in place. They put on Kevlar helmets, bullet-resistant glasses, and heat-resistant gloves. They strapped on knee pads and elbow pads in case they had to hit the dirt. Each soldier packed a tourniquet in one pants pocket and first-aid bandages in another pocket, and grenades and 240 rounds of ammunition in pouches attached to their body armor. All carried an M-4 assault rifle, some carried full machine guns, some carried nine-millimeter handguns, some carried good-luck charms, and all were carrying at least sixty extra pounds of weaponry and bulletproofing as they walked out of the FOB to make their first impression on 350,000 people who surely were just waiting to blow the dumbasses up.

As they walked out of the gate, some of the soldiers were visibly shaking. Step by step, however, as they passed people who regarded them quietly, they began to relax, and by the time they got back to the FOB ten hours later, just as Kauzlarich had intended, they felt, if not fearless, then at least a little smarter about things. One platoon had found an unexploded mortar shell sticking out of the ground, with Iranian markings on the fins. A lesson, perhaps, in who they would be fighting.

Another platoon had been approached by a frantic woman carrying something bundled in a blanket, and when she didn't halt, they could have been forgiven for assuming she was a suicide bomber. But now, as she reached them, they saw that she was holding a badly burned little boy with open eyes and blistering skin, and as they knelt to wrap him in clean bandages, the mother they might have shot was instead thanking them in tears.

A lesson, then, in restraint.

And a third platoon got a lesson in stupidity and luck after a soldier said that a piece of foam block on the side of a street looked weird to him, a second soldier went over and gave it a nudge with his foot, and a third picked it up to have a look and saw a hole with wiring inside. Back on the FOB now, astonished, relieved, knowing that it had been an IED packed with nuts and bolts, they still couldn't believe it hadn't exploded.

But it hadn't, and as the first weeks of the deployment went by, that bit of good fortune seemed to set the pattern for them.

They were finding stockpiles of weapons before the weapons could be used against them. They were getting shot at but not hit. Training and standards, Kauzlarich said—that was the difference. Other battalions were getting rocked by IEDs, but not them, and Kauzlarich kept saying, "It's all good," and that's who they had become as March moved into April. They were the good soldiers.

On the FOB, they were the only ones who wore gloves as they walked around, always ready for the just-in-case, and whenever a convoy rolled out of the wire, as one did now on April 6, at ten minutes past midnight, the soldiers always drove slower than fifteen miles per hour, because slower improved the chances of finding an IED. Other soldiers in other battalions who had been around longer sped; but not them. They crept along encased in the very best body armor, eye protection, ear protection, throat protection, groin protection, knee protection, elbow protection, and hand protection available, as well as in the very best Humvees the army had ever built, with armoring so thick that each door weighed more than four hundred pounds.

Slowly, deliberately, they rolled into a neighborhood called Mualameen. They passed darkened apartment buildings. They passed the silhouette of a mosque. They drove with headlights off and night-vision goggles on, which at 12:35 a.m. flared into sudden blindness.

Here came the explosion. It came through the doors. It came through the body armor. It came through the good soldiers. It was perfectly aimed and perfectly timed, and now one of the good soldiers was on fire.

This was Cajimat, who in February had been gung ho to go, who in March had already seen enough to write in an online posting: "I just need some time to think this through," and who in April was driving the third Humvee in a convoy of six, which was the one chosen by someone hiding in some shadow with a trigger in his hand.

A wire ran from the trigger to another shadow, this one at the edge of the road. Almost certainly the man couldn't see the actual IED, but he'd lined it up beforehand with a tall, tilting, broken, otherwise useless light pole on the far side of the road, which he could use as an aiming point. The first Humvee arrived at the aiming point, and, for whatever reason, the man didn't push the trigger. The second Humvee arrived, and again he didn't push. The third Humvee arrived, and, for whatever reason, now he did push, and the resulting explosion sent several large steel discs toward the Humvee at such high velocity that by the time they reached Cajimat's door, they had been reshaped into unstoppable, semi-molten slugs. At most, the IED cost $100 to make, and against it the $150,000 Humvee might as well have been constructed of lace.

In went the slugs through the armor and into the crew compartment, turning everything in their paths into flying pieces of shrapnel. There were five soldiers inside. Four managed to get out and tumble, bleeding, to the ground, but Cajimat remained in his seat as the Humvee, on fire now, rolled forward, picked up speed, and crashed into an ambulance that had been stopped by the convoy. The ambulance burst into flames as well. After that, a thousand or so rounds of ammunition inside the Humvee began cooking off and exploding, and by the time the Humvee was transported back to Rustamiyah toward sunrise, there wasn't much left to see. As the battalion doctor noted on Cajimat's death report: "Severely burned," and then added: "(beyond recognition)."

Nonetheless, there were procedures to follow in such circumstances, and Kauzlarich now got to learn precisely what those involved.

They began when the Humvee was unloaded at Vehicle Sanitization, a tarped-off area with decent drainage just inside a side gate. There, hidden from view, photographs were taken of the damage, the holes in the door were measured and analyzed, and soldiers did their best to disinfect what was left of the Humvee with bottles of peroxide and Simple Green. "I mean, it's clean. It's cleaner than when it comes off the assembly line," the officer in charge told Kauzlarich of what his soldiers usually accomplished—but in this case, he said, "You're more consolidating it and getting it ready for shipment, because you can't really clean that."

At the same time, Cajimat's remains were being prepared for shipment behind the locked doors of a little stand-alone building in which there were sixteen storage compartments for bodies, a stack of vinyl body bags, a stack of new American flags, and two Mortuary Affairs soldiers whose job was to search the remains for anything personal that a soldier might have wanted with him while he was alive.

"Pictures," one of the soldiers, Sergeant First Class Ernesto Gonzalez, would say later, describing what he has found in uniforms of the bodies he has prepared. "Graduation pictures. Baby pictures. Standing with their family. Pictures of them with their cars."

"Folded flags," said his assistant, Specialist Jason Sutton.

"A sonogram image," Gonzalez said.

"A letter that a guy had in his flak vest," Sutton said, thinking of the first body he worked on. "'This is to my family. If you're reading this, I've passed away.'"

"Hey, man. Don't read no letters," Gonzalez said.

"It was the only time," Sutton said. "I don't read the letters. I don't look at the pictures. It keeps me sane. I don't want to know anything. I don't want to know who you are. I want the bare minimum. If I don't have to look at it, I won't. If I don't have to touch it, I won't."

Meanwhile, the Explosive Ordnance Disposal team was finishing its report about the explosion:

"Blast seat measured 8' x 9' x 2.5' and was consistent with 60–80 lb of unknown explosives."

The platoon leader was writing a statement about what had happened:

"PFC Cajimat was killed on impact and was not able to be pulled from the vehicle."

The platoon sergeant was writing a statement, too:

"PFC Diaz came running out of the smoke from the explosion. Myself and CPL Chance put him in the back of my truck where CPL Chance treated his wounds. I then saw to the left of the HUMV three soldiers, one being pulled on the ground. I ran to the soldiers and saw it was CPL Pellecchia being dragged, screaming he couldn't get PFC Cajimat out of the vehicle."

The battalion doctor was finishing his death report:

"All four limbs burned away, bony stumps visible. Superior portion of cranium burned away. Remaining portion of torso severely charred. No further exam possible due to degree of charring."

The Pentagon was preparing a news release on what would be the 3,267th U.S. fatality of the war:

"The Department of Defense announced today the death of a soldier who was supporting Operation Iraqi Freedom."

And Kauzlarich, back in his office now, was on the phone with Cajimat's mother, who was in tears asking him a question:

"Instantly," he said.

Several days later, Kauzlarich walked to a far corner of FOB and went into a building that was indistinguishable from all the other buildings except for a sign on a blast wall that read, CHAPEL. One last thing to do.

Inside, soldiers were preparing for that night's memorial service. A slide show of Cajimat was being shown on a screen to the left of the altar. In the center, a few soldiers were making a display out of his boots, his M-4, and his helmet. Sad, sentimental music was playing, something with bagpipes, and Kauzlarich listened in silence, his expression betraying nothing, until Cajimat's platoon wandered in and took seats.

Diaz, the one who'd come running out of the smoke, his lower leg now filled with shrapnel, was among them, on crutches, and when he took a seat, Kauzlarich sat next to him and asked how he was.

"Yesterday I put on a tennis shoe for the first time," he said.

"We'll get you out in the fight again ricky tick," Kauzlarich promised him, slapping him on the good leg, and when he got up and moved on, Diaz closed his eyes for a moment and sighed.

He next made his way to John Kirby, the staff sergeant who had been in the right front seat of the Humvee, just a foot or so from Cajimat, and whose eyes suggested he was still there.

"How are the burns?" Kauzlarich asked.

"All right," Kirby said, shrugging as he gave the good soldier's answer, and then, willing his eyes to be still, he looked directly at Kauzlarich and said, "I mean, it sucks."

Up on the screen, the pictures of Cajimat continued to rotate.

There he was smiling.

There he was in his body armor.

There he was smiling again.

"I love that picture," one of the soldiers said, and they were all watching now, chewing gum, picking at fingernails, saying nothing. It was late morning, and even though the chapel was surrounded by blast walls, a few rays of gray light managed to find their way in through the windows, which helped.

That night, though, when the memorial service began, it was different. The light was gone. The chapel was dark. The air didn't move. Several hundred soldiers sat shoulder to shoulder, and some were crying as the eulogies began. "He was always happy. He had a heart bigger than the sun," said one soldier, and if that wasn't sad enough to hear from a nineteen-year-old who ten weeks before had been hollering in some Kansas snow, another said, "He was always there for me. I wish I could have been there for him. I'm sorry."

Through it all, Kauzlarich sat quietly, waiting for his turn, and when it came, he walked to the lectern and looked in silence at his soldiers, all of whom were looking at him. In this moment, he wanted to say something that would describe Cajimat's death for them as more than grievous. He had been thinking for several days about what to say, but while it was easy enough to sit in Kansas filled with ham and apple crisp and talk about change with a detached curiosity, now they had lost their first soldier. Their cherries had been popped. As had his.

So he decided to call it what he believed it to be, a rallying point as much as a loss, the point from which to measure everything to come, and said so to the soldiers. "Tonight," he said, "we take the time to honor Task Force Ranger's first loss, an unfortunate loss that in a special way made us as an organization whole."

That's how he characterized the subtraction of a soldier—as making the 2-16 whole—and the word seemed to hover in the air for a moment before settling onto the quiet men. Among them was Diaz, and as he sat there with shrapnel in his leg, did he believe that, too? Did Kirby, with his twitchy eyes? Did the other two soldiers who'd been in the Humvee, who were both on their way back to the United States with injuries so serious that they would be out of the fight for good?

Did all of them?

Didn't matter. Of course they did.

That's what their commander said, and that's what their commander believed. For two months the soldiers had thought they were in the war, but now they really were in it, Cajimat was the proof, Cajimat was the validation, and as soon as the memorial ended, Kauzlarich hurried back to his office to see what would come next.

He turned on his computer. A fresh e-mail was waiting for him. It was from army headquarters, and it was informing him that in order to better accomplish the strategy of the surge, the 2-16's deployment was being extended from twelve months to fifteen months.

"That's okay," he said.

He read it again.

"More time to win," he said.

Again.

"It's all good," he said, and went into the next room to tell the news to Major Cummings, who was at his desk, lost in thought, a little homesick, and Michael McCoy, his command sergeant major, who was tracking a fly that was crawling across the battalion's American flag. Red stripe. White stripe. Red stripe. White stripe. Now McCoy reached toward a stack of programs left over from Cajimat's memorial and grabbed a dirty fly swatter that was resting on top of them. Kauzlarich paused. The fly fell. Then the surge resumed.

2

APRIL 14, 2007

Violence in Baghdad, sectarian violence in Baghdad, that violence
that was beginning to spiral out of control, is beginning to subside.
And as the violence decreases, people have more confidence, and
if people have more confidence, they're then willing to
make difficult decisions of reconciliation necessary for Baghdad
to be secure and this country to survive and thrive as a democracy.
—GEORGE W. BUSH, *April 10, 2007*

The building that Kauzlarich got for his headquarters was the one on the FOB that none of the other battalions had wanted, a two-story box that was being used for storage until the 2-16 took it over. It had deep cracks in several walls from earlier rocket attacks, and whenever a rocket landed nearby, dust clouds would come flying inside. Other battalion commanders on the FOB had offices big enough for sofas and conference tables; Kauzlarich's office had just enough room for his desk and three metal folding chairs. It wasn't even an office, really, but a section of an existing room that soldiers had walled off with spare plywood. He squeezed into the space on one side of the plywood, and on the other side were McCoy, Cummings, and four items whose importance would shift back and forth during the course of the deployment.

One was the fly swatter. One was a tape dispenser. One was a book called *Counterinsurgency FM 3-24*. And one was a large cardboard box filled with dozens of deflated soccer balls.

Views from the right rear window of a Humvee, Baghdad, Iraq

For now, Kauzlarich thought that giving soccer balls to Iraqi children who would run up to his Humvee screaming, "Mister, mister," was having an effect. A child would take home a soccer ball; his parents would ask where it came from; he would say, "the Americans"; the parents would be delighted; their confidence would increase; they would be more willing to make the difficult decisions of reconciliation; Baghdad would become secure; democracy in Iraq would thrive; the war would be won. Eventually, Kauzlarich would give up on soccer balls.

For now, no one touched the tape dispenser. Eventually, Cummings would begin swatting flies just hard enough to stun them, stick them to a piece of tape, and drop them alive into his trash can, which would be something that *did* have an effect. "I *hate* flies," he would say each time he did this.

Eventually, the book would become covered with dust. But in these days after Cajimat, it was still something that was referred to, enough so that Cummings had bookmarked page 1-29 with a piece of paper on which he had written: "Are We Winning Table."

The book, released just before the 2-16 deployed, was the military's first update to its counterinsurgency strategy in twenty years. When he announced the surge, Bush had made it clear that counterinsurgency was now what the war was about, and to the extent that a war could have an instruction book, that's what the field manual was. It was 282 pages of lessons, all urging soldiers to "focus on the population, its needs, and its security" as the best way to defeat the enemy, rather than by killing their way to victory. Control the population, win the war. Win the people, win the war. To the soldiers of the 2-16, this was an interesting turn of events. "Remember, we are an infantry battalion," Cummings said one day. "Our task and purpose is to close with and destroy the enemy. We are the only force designed for this. Armor stands off and they kill from a distance. Aviation kills from a distance. The infantryman goes in and kills with his hands, if necessary." The manual got even more interesting under the section called "Paradoxes of Counterinsurgency," which sounded suspiciously Zen-like. "Sometimes, the more force is used, the less effective it is." "Some of the best weapons for counterinsurgents do not shoot." "Sometimes, the more you protect your force, the less secure you may be."

Privately, Cummings wondered whether this was the type of war Kauzlarich would want to fight. "He's a soldier. All he is *is* a soldier. He's an instrument of war, and he's looking for that fight, and that's why I think he is somewhat frustrated in the fact that he's not in the clean war, where he can be the leader up front—'Follow me, men'—because this war doesn't dictate it. This war dictates drinking *chai*, handshaking, being political. And I think that's where he's a little uncomfortable. Because he's the guy at the front of the formation who can run the battalion into the ground, if necessary. Literally: 'Follow me.'"

But Kauzlarich, at least at this point, insisted that he loved being part of the strategy. "You know what's funny? This is what I always wanted to do. I always wanted to be a soldier and statesman together," he said one day. He was in his office, looking at a wall map that showed the 2-16's AO. Some people called the area New Baghdad. Some called it Nine Nissan, for the ninth of April, the day Baghdad fell. Kauzlarich had his own name for it. "This place is a shithole," he said, "but it has so much potential. I've often thought, let's take Fedaliyah"—he pointed to one of the worst neighborhoods in the AO—"and let's bulldoze the whole town. In six months, I could have an entire city rebuilt. It would have electricity. It would have running fresh water. It would have sewerage. It would have new schools. It would have houses that were built to some sort of safety code. And then we move to Kamaliyah and do the same thing there. Rebuild the whole darn place."

The map he was looking at, composed of satellite imagery, was extraordinary in its detail. It showed Fedaliyah, Kamaliyah, Mualameen, Al-Amin, Mashtal, and every other neighborhood in the AO, building by building and street by street, each of which had been given an American name. That wide street with the waterway running down the middle of it, which Iraqis called Canal Road, was, to the Americans, Route Pluto; the busy road it intersected with, which was constantly being seeded with hidden bombs, was Route Predators; the one where Cajimat died was Route Denham; and the skinny one that soldiers tried to avoid because of its ambush possibilities was Dead Girl Road.

Where did the names come from? Who had the dead girl been? How had the dead girl died? This far into the war, no one seemed to care. Sometimes anything more than an assumption is a waste of time in Iraq; and anyway, the names were fixed now, not just in 2-16's AO but throughout all of Baghdad, which the map showed as well. Neighborhood by neighborhood, there was Baghdad in its entirety for Kauzlarich to consider—the east side, which was largely Shi'a after several years of violent ethnic and religious cleansing that had been brought on by the war; and the west side, which was largely Sunni. The west side contained elements of al Qaeda, and the east side contained the insurgent armies of the radical cleric Muqtada al-Sadr, called the Jaish al Mahdi, or, in American-speak, JAM. The west side had suicide bombers killing American troops, and the east side had a particularly lethal type of IED called an explosively formed penetrator, or EFP, which was the type of bomb that had so easily penetrated Cajimat's Humvee. The east side was the 2-16's side, and every day that Kauzlarich looked at the map it got uglier and uglier, especially the way the Tigris River, which runs north–south and divides the city in half, curves to the west at one point and then curves back to the east, creating an elongated peninsula that is politely referred to as "teardrop shaped." Kauzlarich wasn't always polite, though. "It's the perfect metaphor for this place," he said, staring at the way the peninsula seemed to be inserting itself into the west side of the city. "Iraq fucking itself."

His war, then, would be to take all of this on—the JAM, the EFPs, the mounds of garbage, the running sewage, the whatever else—and fix it. So far, no one had been able to do this, but he seemed so confident that he made a prediction. "Before we leave, I'm going to do a battalion run. A task force run. In running shorts and T-shirt." He traced the route he had in mind on the map. Up Pluto, along First Street, up toward Denham, over toward Predators, and back.

"That's my goal—without taking any casualties," he said, and to that end, he was willing to try anything that might fall under counter-insurgency strategy, including one highlighted on page 1-29 of the field manual, which read, "Conduct effective, pervasive, and continuous information operations." Hidden away on the FOB was a U.S.-funded radio station, and that's where Kauzlarich headed late one afternoon, to speak to the residents of his nice, little, mean, nasty area via PEACE 106 FM.

The air was dusty as usual, and the wind, from the west, carried the scent of burning plastic as he walked past a latrine trailer, under which lived a feral cat with grossly swollen testicles. The fact that the cat was alive at all surely said something about resiliency in a country where life was down to the survival level. There were plenty of mice and rats on the FOB to kill, but there were things that wanted to kill the cat, too, such as a fox that could be seen from time to time trotting by with something writhing in its mouth and at other times standing with its teeth showing as it watched soldiers entering and exiting the latrines.

Next he walked past the mooring site for a bright white blimp called an aerostat, which floated high above the FOB with a remote-controlled camera that could be focused on whatever might be happening a thousand feet below. Day or night, the aerostat was up there, looking down and around, as were pole-mounted cameras, pilotless drones, high-flying jets, and satellites, making the sky feel at times as if it were stitched all the way up to the heavens with eyes. There were helicopters, too, armed with thirty-millimeter cannons and high-resolution cameras that could focus tightly on whatever was about to be shot, which one day was a dead water buffalo that had been spotted on its side with wires sticking out of its rear end. Concerned that an IED had been hidden inside the water buffalo's rectum, the helicopter moved in for a closer look as its camera recorded what came next. There was the water buffalo. There were the wires. There was a dog trotting up to the water buffalo's rear. "Be advised, there's a dog licking the IED," the pilot said, and then he opened fire.

Next Kauzlarich walked past the PX, which would soon have to close temporarily after a rocket crashed through the roof and exploded next to a display rack of *Maxim* magazines, and then he entered a ruined, four-story building that once had been a hospital.

The studio was on the top floor, up where the workers lived, those who had come to Rustamiyah from Nepal and Sri Lanka to clean the latrines, sweep up the endless dust, sleep six to a room, and listen to mournful songs on tinny speakers purchased from the sad little shops on the hospital's first floor. The doors to these rooms were splintered and scuffed, and behind one of them was the radio staff. One of them was a local Iraqi whom the military was paying $88,000 a year to run the radio station. He introduced himself as Mohammed and then confided that Mohammed was a fake name he used to shield his identity. The other man was Mark, an interpreter, also from Baghdad, who confided that his name wasn't really Mark.

"Dear listeners. Welcome to a new show," Mohammed, or whoever he was, said to whoever might have been out there listening to PEACE 106 FM, and that's how the first of what would be dozens of radio shows began. It was a complicated process. In Arabic, Mohammed said to his listeners, "Our first question to Colonel Kauzlarich is about the situation nowadays in New Baghdad," which Mark then translated into English, to which Kauzlarich said in Arabic, "*Shukran jazilan*, Mohammed"— "Thank you very much, Mohammed"—and in English went on from there:

"Approximately eight weeks ago there was a great deal of crime," he said. "There was sectarian violence. There were numerous murders. There were many bombs going off, roadside bombs, IEDs, EFPs, and also car bombs that were killing many innocent civilians. Today that does not exist. Crime is down by over eighty percent. The people of Nine Nissan are beginning to feel safe."

He waited for Mark, or whoever Mark was, to translate what he'd said, and then continued: "My organization is known as Task Force Ranger, which is approximately eight hundred of the finest American soldiers. Everything that they do is in a controlled and disciplined manner. And one of the things I stress that they do as their commander is to go out and talk to the Iraqi people and determine what their feelings are, what their greatest fears are, and how we can best assist them and the Iraqi Security Forces in developing a very secure environment for them to live in."

Again he waited for Mark to translate, and continued: "Bottom line is, the current situation is good—but it's not as good as it's going to

31

be . . ." and on he went for thirty-six minutes until he said, seeking to win over the people, *"Shukran jazilan,"* and Mohammed said, *"Shukran jazilan,"* and Kauzlarich said, *"Ma'a sala'ama, sadiqi,"* and Mohammed said, *"Ma'a sala'ama."*

This was war fighting as counterinsurgency, just as it was when, in an attempt to "expand and diversify the host-nation police force," Kauzlarich met with an Iraqi army officer who was living in an elementary school that the Iraqis had taken over not far from the FOB. The walls were pink. They were decorated with Tweety Bird cutouts. There was a single cot and a small TV hooked up to a satellite dish, and the Iraqi had just brought Kauzlarich an orange soda when from the TV there came some kind of roar.

"Tomorrow, you're going to begin doing clearance operations?" Kauzlarich asked, ignoring the sound.

"Yes," said the Iraqi, shifting his eyes from Kauzlarich to the TV, where a movie was playing that showed American soldiers being shot.

"What is your personal assessment of the attitude of the Iraqi people in Baghdad al-Jadida?" Kauzlarich continued.

"Most of the people are from Sadr City," the Iraqi said, as blood spurted in slow motion, guns blazed in slow motion, and the actor Mel Gibson moved in slow motion. "Every time the Americans put pressure on Sadr City, they run here."

"What area do you think we should clear next?" Kauzlarich asked, shifting his attention to the TV, too, and then falling silent as he realized the movie was about a famous battle in the Vietnam War that had taken place just a few weeks after he had been born. In so many ways, that was the war that had made him want to be a soldier in this war. It had been the background scenery of his childhood from the day he was born, on October 28, 1965, when the number of dead American troops was at 1,387, to the end of the war in April 1975, when 58,000 were dead and he was nine and a half years old and thinking he would like to be in the army. It wasn't the deaths or politics that had affected him, but rather a boy's romanticized visions of courage and duty, especially the scenes he had watched on TV of released POWs in the embrace of weeping families. But even more than those scenes was the Battle of Ia Drang, which began when an outnumbered army battalion was airdropped into the midst of two thousand North Vietnamese soldiers and ended up in a face-to-face fight to the death. Years later, in the army now and studying the mistakes of Vietnam, Kauzlarich had also studied the heroics of Ia Drang, and when the battle was memorialized in a book called *We Were Soldiers Once . . . and Young*, he had a copy of it in hand when he one day met the commander of the battalion, Hal Moore, and asked him for advice. "Trust your instincts," Moore had scribbled in the book. Ever since, Kauzlarich had tried to do just that, and now, how strange, here he was: a battalion commander just as Moore had been, in Iraq watching the movie version of the book about the battle that had helped turn him into what he had become.

"This is one of my favorite movies," he said to the Iraqi.

"I like the way they fight," the Iraqi said.

"That's how I fight," Kauzlarich said.

"What's the name of the actor?" the Iraqi said.

"That's Mel Gibson," Kauzlarich said.

"He acts like a leader," the Iraqi said.

Now neither said anything, just watched until Gibson, the battle over, said inconsolably, "I'll never forgive myself—that my men died, and I didn't."

"Tsk tsk," the Iraqi said.

"He's very sad," Kauzlarich said.

"Tsk tsk," the Iraqi said again.

"He was the first guy to tell me to trust my instincts," Kauzlarich said. "Hal Moore."

The Iraqi got up and returned with a vanilla ice-cream cone that Kauzlarich began licking as Gibson, home now, fell into the arms of his wife—at which point the electricity went out, the TV went dead, and the movie came to a sudden end.

"Whoops," Kauzlarich said.

Both waited in vain for the electricity to come back.

"So, how are we going to fix this?" Kauzlarich said, meaning the war.

The Iraqi continued to look at the TV and shrugged.

"How are we going to get this to stop?" Kauzlarich tried again.

"We need God's help," the Iraqi said, and Kauzlarich nodded, finished his ice-cream cone, and after a while excused himself to return to the FOB.

Hours later, as the sun set, the sky took on its nightly ominous feel. The moon, not quite full, rose dented and misshapen, and the aerostat, a gray shadow now rather than the bright white balloon it had been in daylight, loomed over a landscape of empty streets and buildings surrounded by sandbags and tall concrete blast walls.

Inside some of those buildings were Kauzlarich's soldiers, all of whom had been trained not in counterinsurgency, but, as Cummings had put it, to close with and destroy the enemy. A week after Cajimat's death, they were passing time between missions like they usually did, by playing video games on their computers or videochatting over the Internet. Or lifting weights, or watching bootleg DVDs that they could buy at the hospital for a dollar. Or drinking Red Bulls or Mountain Dews or water mixed with high-protein powder. Or stuffing themselves with tubs of Corn Pops at the dining facility. Or flipping through magazines that came as close as possible to violating the army's ban on pornography. Such was life on the FOB for the eight hundred of the finest, whose behavior could be explained simply by the fact that so many of them were nineteen, or by the more complicated fact suggested by the ubiquitous blast walls that they did all of these things behind.

Blast walls surrounded their barracks.

Blast walls surrounded their dining facility.

Blast walls surrounded their chapel.

Blast walls surrounded their latrines.

They ate behind blast walls, prayed behind blast walls, peed behind blast walls, and slept behind blast walls, and now, on April 14, as the sun rose and the dented moon disappeared, they emerged from those blast walls and got in their Humvees wondering if this would be the day that they were now dreaming of behind the blast walls, the one in which, like Cajimat, they would get blasted.

"And we're off," Kauzlarich said.

He was in his usual spot—left rear seat, third Humvee from the front. There were always at least four vehicles in a convoy; this one happened to have five. Nate Showman, a twenty-four-year-old lieutenant whose belief in the war and optimism about it matched Kauzlarich's, was in the front right seat. There was no junior officer in the battalion with more promise than Showman, and Kauzlarich had selected him to be in charge of his personal security detail.

Out they went through the heavily guarded main gate of the FOB and were instantly on the front lines of the war. In other wars, the front line was exactly that, a line to advance toward and cross, but in this war, where the enemy was everywhere, it was anywhere out of the wire, in any direction: that building, that town, that province, the entire country, in 360 degrees.

In such a war, and in an area seeded with EFPs, what was the safest seat? The soldiers discussed it constantly. Kauzlarich didn't discuss it, but he thought about it, too. The lead truck in a convoy was the one that got hit the most, but lately insurgents had been aiming at the second in line, or the third, which had been Cajimat's, or sometimes the fourth or fifth. And while most EFPs had been coming from the right side, Cajimat's had come from the left.

So there was no sure thing to rely on, only precautions to be taken. The Humvees were fitted with jamming devices to defeat EFPs armed with infrared triggers, but the devices weren't always effective, which was why one Humvee also had a good-luck horseshoe wired to the front grille.

Every soldier had his own version of this. Showman carried a small cross knitted in army colors by someone in his parents' church in Ohio. The gunner tried to stand in a particular way, with one foot in front of the other, so that if an EFP slug came roaring in, he might only lose one foot instead of two, and for similar reasons Kauzlarich sometimes tucked his hands inside of his body armor as he looked out the window and wondered how aware he would be if the explosion came. "Instantly," he had told Cajimat's mother, but was that really the way it happened? Would he know it? Would he hear it? Would he see it? Would he feel it? Would the pile of trash outside of his window that he was now regarding suspiciously be the last thing on earth he would see? Would his last words be what he was saying now into his headset, in response to a soldier's trifling question back on the FOB? "Do you guys have shitters?" That's what he was saying. Is that how it would end? In the midst of a sentence like that?

"Do you guys have shitters?"

"Do you guys have—"

The convoy approached another pile of trash. Maybe one was hidden in there.

The convoy approached a shadowy area in a viaduct. Maybe one was hidden in there.

Eyes sweeping, jammers jamming, the convoy moved along Route Pluto at a very deliberate ten miles per hour, which afforded the chance to see what the surge had accomplished so far. By now, other drivers knew what to do when a convoy of Humvees got near: pull over, wait patiently for it to pass, make no sudden moves, and show no frustration about the inevitable traffic jam that the convoy would leave in its wake. Now the convoy passed a driver with the temerity to bury his head in his hands, and did Kauzlarich and his soldiers happen to notice that?

Did they see the old man sitting in front of a shuttered store watching expressionlessly as he fidgeted with a string of worry beads?

Did they see the boy next to the old man regarding the convoy as if it were something slithering?

Did they see the white car decorated with flowers, and the van behind it filled with a bride and eight other women who were laughing and bouncing up and down in rhythm in their seats?

They moved past some children herding goats. They moved past a man pushing a block of concrete. They moved past a man smoking a cigarette and looking under the raised hood of a stalled car, and maybe the car really was stalled or maybe it was a car bomb that was about to explode. The soldiers slowed to a near stop. The man didn't acknowledge them. No one did. No one smiled at them. No one threw flowers. No one waved.

Now someone did: a young boy dragging a piece of wire. He paused to wave at Kauzlarich, and Kauzlarich saw him and waved back, and what Kauzlarich saw was a waving boy who for all he knew was wired to explode, and what the boy saw was a thick window and a soldier behind it in body armor waving a hand that was encased in a glove.

Suspicion in 360 degrees—this is what four years of war had led to. Before leaving Fort Riley, the soldiers had been given an introduction to Iraq in the form of a laminated booklet called the Culture Smart Card, which told them, for instance, that "Right hand over heart is a sign of respect or thanks," and "Don't make the 'OK' or 'thumbs up' signs; they are considered obscene." It also listed phonetic pronunciations for dozens of commonly used words and phrases, including *arjuke* (please), *shukran* (thank you), *marhaba* (hello), and *ma'a sala'ama* (goodbye).

They were good counterinsurgency terms, but Kauzlarich's gunner had decided he needed only a few phrases to navigate this war, all of which he'd written in English and phonetic Arabic in black marker on his turret:

"Where are we?"

"Insurgent(s)."

"Where is bomb?"

"Show me."

It was the language of IEDs and EFPs. All over eastern Baghdad, their numbers were increasing, and while Cajimat and the four other soldiers in his Humvee had so far been the 2-16's only serious casualties, they hadn't been the only targets. Just the night before, Kauzlarich and Cummings had been in the dining facility, or DFAC, eating dinner when a loud boom rattled the walls and sent dishes, trays, food, and dozens of soldiers crashing to the floor. At first the explosion seemed like a rocket attack on the FOB, the number of which had also been increasing, but it turned out to be an IED a mile or so away that had hit a 2-16 Humvee out on patrol. Somehow none of the soldiers in the Humvee had been injured more seriously than suffering ringing ears and slight concussions, but the Humvee had been destroyed.

That was where Kauzlarich directed the convoy now, to the spot where this had happened, so he could show the neighborhood how the United States of America was capable of responding. "Deny sanctuary to insurgents," it said in the field manual, which was what Kauzlarich intended to do as the convoy eased from Pluto into one of the AO's nicer neighborhoods and rolled to a stop by a fresh hole in the ground, caused by the IED. "Let's go clear," Kauzlarich said to his men, and soon twenty-three heavily armed soldiers were walking the streets and randomly searching houses.

They came to a house with laundry hanging in the courtyard and a neat row of shoes by the front door. Without asking permission, some of the soldiers went inside, through the first floor, up the stairs, through the second floor, into the closets, into the drawers.

They came to another house with a fruit tree out front, and a small metal tank for storing water that struck a soldier as peculiar. In silence, the family that lived in the house watched as the soldier unscrewed the cap of the tank and inhaled to make sure it was in fact water in there, and now watched another soldier reach up into the fruit tree and begin feeling around. He swept along one branch and then another. He stood on his tiptoes and felt among the leaves until he found what he was looking for, and as the family kept watching, he brought a ripe piece of fruit to his mouth and took a bite.

Each search took a few minutes at most and constituted the entire relationship between the Americans and the Iraqis. Unlike the riskier operations that occurred in the middle of the night, in which soldiers broke down doors as they went after specific targets, there was a businesslike feel to these searches: Into the house, search, ask a few questions, out. Next. In, search, out. Not that there wasn't risk—they were here, after all, because someone had tried to kill some of them with an IED. And snipers were a risk as well, which was why soldiers walked with their weapons raised as they approached the next house, outside of which stood a man who invited Kauzlarich inside for some tea.

This had never happened before. In all the searches Kauzlarich had done, people always had passively stepped aside as he and his soldiers entered their houses, but this was the first time someone had invited him in.

So he went in, accompanied by an Iraqi national who worked as his interpreter. Four of his soldiers assigned to guard him also went in, while two other soldiers remained in the front courtyard as the first line of defense in case of an ambush.

The man led Kauzlarich past his surprised-looking family and motioned him toward a chair in a spotlessly clean living room. There was a table with a vase filled with artificial flowers, and a cabinet that was stacked with fragile dishes and teacups. "You have a beautiful house," Kauzlarich said, sitting down, his helmet still on, his body armor still on, his handgun within easy reach, and the man smiled and said thank you even as circles of perspiration began to appear under his arms.

Off in the kitchen, water for tea was heating. Outside, other soldiers continued to clear houses of neighbors who had seen this man ask an American to come inside. Inside, the man explained to Kauzlarich why Iraqis were hesitant to cooperate. "I'm afraid to work with the Americans because the militia threatened me. I have no money. I wish I could," he said in Arabic, pausing so his words could be translated by Kauzlarich's interpreter, and now he switched to English to better describe what his life had become:

"Very difficult."

The two of them continued to talk. The man said he was sixty-eight. Kauzlarich said the man didn't look it. The man said he had been in the Iraqi air force. Kauzlarich nodded again. It wasn't a hot day, but the man's perspiration stains were growing. More than five minutes had gone by now. Surely the neighbors were keeping track.

"If people ask me later on, 'Why Americans are in your house?' I'll just say, 'Searching,'" the man said, more to himself than to Kauzlarich.

Tea was served.

"Hey, Nate," Kauzlarich said to Showman, "walk around. Just have them escort you around the house."

Ten minutes now. The man folded his fingers. He unfolded his fingers. He pulled up his socks. He said, "When I heard the IED go off last night, my heart—my chest . . ." He said he had been sitting in this very room when the IED exploded, eating dinner, and that the walls shook, but nothing had been broken.

Fifteen minutes. The man told Kauzlarich about one of his sons, who he said had been kidnapped two weeks before and repeatedly beaten until the man paid a $10,000 ransom. That's why he had no money.

Twenty minutes. "I like America. When America came, I put flowers out front," the man said. But at this point, "If I put them out, they will kill me." His perspiration stains were huge now. Twenty minutes. House searches didn't take twenty minutes. Everyone knew that. Kauzlarich stood.

"*Shukran,*" he said, taking the man's hand.

"I'm sorry I cannot support you," the man said. "I'm afraid for my life."

He escorted Kauzlarich outside, and as Kauzlarich and his soldiers moved on, the man was immediately surrounded by neighbors.

"He wasn't nervous about us. He was nervous about the people outside wondering what he was telling us while we were in his home," Kauzlarich would say later. "It's a catch-22. They want security. They know we can provide it. They need to tell us where the bad guy is, but they fear for their life, that if we don't do anything about it the bad man will come and kill them. They're damned if they do, damned if they don't."

Where was the bad guy, though? Other than everywhere? Where was the specific one who had set off the IED? Back at the fresh hole now, surrounded by neighborhood children who were shouting, "Mister, mister," and clamoring for soccer balls, Kauzlarich wondered what to do next. Surely someone in the neighborhood knew who had done this, but how could he persuade them that as damned as they thought they would be for dealing with the Americans, they would be more damned if they did not?

Strength was part of counterinsurgency, too. He decided to call in a show of force, which would involve a pair of F-18 jets coming in over the neighborhood, low and without warning. The sound would be ear-splitting and frightening. Houses would vibrate. Walls would shake. Furniture would rattle. Teacups might topple, though Kauzlarich hoped that wouldn't be the case.

He and his soldiers got in the Humvees to leave, and now another thing happened that hadn't happened before—the children applauded and waved goodbye.

Off the soldiers went, feet aligned, hands tucked, eyes sweeping, jammers jamming, creeping back to the FOB.

Here came the jets.

3

MAY 7, 2007

*Our troops are now carrying out a new strategy in Iraq under the leadership of
a new commander, General David Petraeus. He's an expert in counterinsurgency warfare.
The goal of the new strategy he is implementing is to help the Iraqis secure their capital
so they can make progress toward reconciliation and build a free nation that respects
the rights of its people, upholds the rule of law, and fights extremists alongside the
United States in the war on terror. This strategy is still in its early stages . . .*
—GEORGE W. BUSH, *May 5, 2007*

O f all the soldiers in the battalion, none was closer to Kauzlarich than Brent Cummings. Three years younger than Kauzlarich, Cummings had joined the army for the admittedly simple reason that he loved the United States and wanted to defend his admittedly sentimental version of it, which was his family, his front porch, a copy of the Sunday *New York Times*, a microbrewed beer, and a dog. He had been with the battalion since its very first days, and believed, so far, in the 2-16's mission as morally correct. As Kauzlarich's number two, Cummings tried to approach the war with the same level of certainty. But he was more brooding than Kauzlarich, and more introspective than most any soldier in the battalion, which resulted in a deeper need from the war than merely a desire for victory. As he said one day when describing differences between Kauzlarich and himself: "He can see despair, and it doesn't bother him as much as it bothers me."

That ability to be bothered, and the need to ease it by at least trying to act with decency, was why Cummings was on his telephone one day getting increasingly upset.

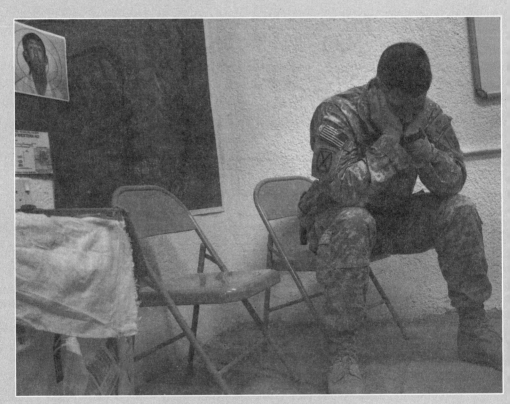

Brent Cummings

"We have to remove the human waste *and* the body. And that's going to cost *money*," he was saying.

He paused to listen.

"Yeah, they'll say, 'Buy the bleach,' but how much bleach do I have to buy? They'll say, 'Buy the lye,' but, Christ, how much will *that* cost?"

He paused again.

"It's *not* water. It's *sewage*. It's *yeccchh*."

He took a breath, trying to calm down.

"No. I haven't seen Bob. Only pictures. But it looks awful."

Sighing, he hung up and picked up one of the pictures. It was an aerial view of Kamaliyah, the most out-of-control area in the AO. Sixty thousand people were said to live there, and they had been largely ignored since the war began. Insurgents were thought to be everywhere. Open trenches of raw sewage lined the streets, and most of the factories on the eastern edge had been abandoned, one of which had a courtyard with a hole in it. That was where soldiers had discovered a cadaver they began calling Bob.

Bob was shorthand for bobbing in the float, Cummings explained.

Float was also shorthand, for several feet of raw sewage.

And what was "bobbing in the float" shorthand for? He shook his head. He was exasperated beyond words. The war was costing the United States $300 million a day, and because of rules governing how it could be spent, he couldn't get enough money to get rid of a cadaver that was obstructing the 2-16's most crucial mission so far, bringing Kamaliyah under control. It needed to be done quickly. Rockets and mortars were being launched from Kamaliyah into the FOB and the Green Zone, and intelligence reports suggested that EFPs and IEDs were being assembled there as well.

The factory, which once produced spaghetti, of all things, was the key to how this was going to be done. An essential part of the surge's counterinsurgency strategy involved moving soldiers off of FOBs and into smaller, less imposing command outposts, or COPs, that would be set up in the middle of neighborhoods. The thinking behind COPs was best summed up by David Kilcullen, a counterinsurgency expert who was an adviser to General David Petraeus and who wrote in a 2006 paper widely circulated in the military: "The first rule of deployment in counterinsurgency is to be there . . . If you are not present when an incident happens, there is usually little you can do about it. So your first order of business is to establish presence . . . This demands a residential approach—living in your sector, in close proximity to the population, rather than raiding into the area from remote, secure bases. Movement on foot, sleeping in local villages, night-patrolling: all these seem more dangerous than they are. They establish links with the locals, who see you as real people they can trust and do business with, not as aliens who descend from an armored box."

So important were COPs to the surge that Petraeus's staff tracked how many there were as one of the indicators of the surge's effectiveness. Every time one was established, battalion would send word of it to brigade, which would send word to division, which would send word to corps, which would send word to Petraeus's staff, which would add it to a tally sheet that was transmitted to Washington. Kauzlarich, so far, had added one to the list—a COP for Alpha Company in the middle of the AO—but wanted to add more. A second COP would soon be installed for Charlie Company, in the southern end of the AO, but, for tactical reasons, the COP needed most of all would be the one for Bravo Company, up north in Kamaliyah. The middle of Kamaliyah was too unstable for one, but the edge seemed safer, and that's where the abandoned spaghetti factory was.

So in went some soldiers, breaching the gate and swarming inside, where they discovered rocket-propelled grenades, hand grenades, mortar shells, the makings of three EFPs, and a square piece of metal covering a hole that they suspected was booby-trapped. Ever so carefully they lifted the cover and found themselves peering down into the factory's septic tank at Bob.

The body, floating, was in a billowing, once-white shirt. The toes were gone. The fingers were gone. The head, separated and floating next to the body, had a gunshot hole in the face.

The soldiers quickly lowered the cover.

By now they had dealt with bodies, including a man they'd hired to help build Charlie Company's COP who had been executed soon after starting work. That death had been especially gruesome; whoever killed him had done so by tightening his head in a vise and leaving him for his wife to discover. But Bob, somehow, seemed even worse. Unless the body were removed, it would be there day and night, afloat in the float during meals and sleep, and how could the 120 soldiers of Bravo Company ever get comfortable with that?

"It's a morale issue. Who wants to live over a dead body?" Cummings said. "And part of it is a moral issue, too. I mean, he was somebody's son, and maybe husband, and for dignity's sake, well, it cheapens us to leave him there. I mean, even calling him Bob is disrespectful. I don't know . . ."

The need for decency: suddenly it was important to Cummings in this country of cadavers to do the proper thing about one of them. But how? No one wanted to descend into the sewage and touch a dead body. Not the soldiers. Not the Iraqis. And not him, either. So Bob floated on as more days passed and soldiers continued to clear other parts of the factory, every so often lifting the cover. One day the skull had sunk from view. Another day it was back. Another day the thought occurred that there might be more bodies in the septic tank, that Bob might simply be the one on top.

Down went the cover.

Finally, Cummings decided to have a look for himself.

The drive from the FOB to the factory was only five miles or so, but that didn't mean it was easy. A combat plan had to be drawn up, just in case of an ambush. A convoy of five Humvees, two dozen soldiers, and an interpreter had to be assembled. On went body armor, earplugs, and eye protection, and off the convoy went, past new trash piles that might be hiding bombs, along a dirt road under which might be buried bombs, and now past an unseen bomb that detonated.

It happened just after the last Humvee had passed by. There were no injuries, just some noise and rising smoke, and so the convoy kept pushing ahead. Now it passed a dead water buffalo, on its back, exceedingly swollen, one more thing in this part of Baghdad on the verge of exploding, and now it came to a stop by a yellowish building topped by a torn tin roof that was banging around in the wind.

"The spaghetti factory," Cummings said, and soon he and Captain Jeff Jager, the commander of Bravo Company, were staring down into the septic tank.

"Well, what I think we do is . . . man," Cummings said, with absolutely no idea what to do now that he was seeing Bob up close.

"I think you gotta clean it out," Jager said. "I think you gotta suck all the shit out of there and you gotta clean it out. I think the first step is sucking the shit out, second step is finding somebody to go down there to get it up. It'll cost some money."

"Yeah," Cummings said, knowing the rules about spending money, none of which covered the removal of a dead Iraqi from a septic tank in an abandoned spaghetti factory.

"I mean, we're gonna have some heartache moving into a building that's got a dead body in a sewage septic tank," Jager said. He picked up a long metal pipe and stirred the float until the skull disappeared.

"I mean, someone has disgraced him as bad as you can possibly disgrace a human being," Cummings said as the skull reappeared. "And there's a not a playbook that we can go to that says when you open it up: 'Here's how you remove a body from a septic tank.'"

Jager gave it another stir. "The one contractor I brought up here, he was willing to do everything here, but he wanted nothing to do with that," he said. "I asked him how much it would take for him to get that out of there, and he said, 'You couldn't pay me enough.'"

"If it were a U.S. soldier, sure. We would be there in a heartbeat," Cummings said.

"We could drop down there and get it out ourselves," Jager said. "But—"

"But what soldier am I going to ask to go in there to do that?" Cummings said, and after Jager put the cover back in place, the two of them went on a tour of the rest of the factory.

It was such a mess, with cracked walls and piles of ruined equipment, that it was hard to see 120 soldiers moving in. But Jager assured Cummings it could be done and had to be done. "We know the militia has used this as a base of operations," he said. "There are reports that they used this for torture and murder." Bob was evidence of that, he said, "and the guys next door will tell you about screams and the sounds of people being beaten."

They stepped out of the front gate, onto the street, and more soldiers joined them as they began walking the perimeter. There was already a solid cement wall surrounding the factory, but for security reasons the height would have to be doubled with blast walls, and the streets would have to be blocked off with coils of razor wire.

Around the first corner now, Cummings noticed a mud-brick hovel that had been built near the factory wall, so close that it would have to be swallowed up inside the blast walls. Then he saw clothing hanging in the yard and realized that someone lived there, so he made his way through a gate that led into the property and walked toward a man who, when he saw the soldiers, began noticeably shaking in fear.

Through an interpreter, Cummings started to explain why he was there, that U.S. soldiers would be moving into the spaghetti factory and that for security reasons they were going to have to build a very high wall that would unfortunately wall him in, but they would include a gate—

I will leave, the man interrupted in Arabic before Cummings could finish.

"No," Cummings said, asking the interpreter to tell the man that he wasn't being told to leave, just that they would be building a wall—

I will leave, the shaking man said again, and he sounded increasingly frantic as he said that he had come to this little bit of land only because his family had been uprooted from their own home by the militia, that he hadn't meant to cause trouble, that he had nowhere else to go, that this borrowed place was all that he had left—and then, at last hearing the interpreter over his own voice, he said, *I don't have to leave?* "No," Cummings said. "I—"

I don't have to leave? the man said again, and it was at that point that the other people who lived in the little shack began pouring out. Out came child after child in raggedy clothes. Out came an old worried woman. Out came more children, who crowded around Cummings and the other soldiers, and finally came a pregnant woman who stood nervously in the doorway, listening to the man saying, *Thank you for saving us, thank you for enclosing us in a wall, thank you for allowing us to stay.*

"You're welcome," Cummings said, taking the man's hand, "and thank you for allowing us in," and the man smiled, and the old woman smiled, and the woman in the doorway smiled, and an hour later, as Cummings headed back to the FOB, it was that disturbing moment of gratitude that he couldn't shake from his mind. There's such goodness in the country, he said, which was why, more than ever, he wanted Bob properly buried.

"I would hope someone would do the same for my body. And for any human being. Otherwise we're not human," he said.

How to be human in this instance, though? He still hadn't figured it out by the following morning, when he received a call from Jager, who had just gotten a tip.

Cummings hung up the phone. He looked stunned. He went in search of Kauzlarich.

"Sir, the spaghetti factory has been destroyed," he said.

The tip was that a dozen masked men, all carrying weapons and some carrying explosives, had gone into the factory after the soldiers left, and that the resulting explosion had been huge.

"Gone," Cummings said of the factory.

Maybe it wasn't. Initial reports were often wrong. Verification was needed.

Even in Iraq, though, some days are more difficult than others. No soldiers were in Kamaliyah this day, and because of high winds and dust, all forms of aerial surveillance had been grounded.

Then, late in the day, the pilot of a fighter jet passing high overhead reported that much of the factory appeared to have been destroyed.

How much was unclear. The pilot didn't say. Cummings didn't know.

What about the house?

"I don't know."

The grateful man?

He shook his head.

The old woman? The pregnant woman? The dozen children?

He shook his head.

What he did know, now that the problem of Bob had been solved:

"I hate this place," he said.

Four days later, First Sergeant William Zappa was standing on a street in Kamaliyah in the middle of the morning when someone shot him in his side.

"At first I thought it was a little nick. I didn't realize I had got shot. I heard a pop and I'm like, 'What the hell was that?' Then I looked down and I felt something, and then I started seeing the blood come out my side, and I'm like, 'Hell, I just got shot,'" Zappa would say after this long day was over.

Most of the battalion had gone to Kamaliyah earlier that morning for the next step in bringing it under control, departing the FOB in a massive convoy early enough to pass the goat peddlers as they were still peeling the skin from the meat they hoped to sell before the sun got too hot. By nine o'clock, as a pair of attack helicopters circled overhead, hundreds of soldiers were fanning out across Kamaliyah and searching homes. By 9:50 a.m., Kauzlarich was looking out the window of his Humvee and saying, "It's all good," and by 10:21 a.m., Zappa had been hit by a single bullet that entered his side and exited through his back, which was starting to leak blood.

"Initially everybody was kind of spazzing, because all they knew was I got shot. 'First Sergeant got shot!'" he would say later, describing it to whoever wanted to hear. "And everybody come running up and pulling out the scissors and getting ready to start cutting stuff, and I was, 'Whoa, whoa, stop. I'm not dead. I can take my own IBA off. I can take it off.' So I took off my own IBA, nobody assisted me.

"Then they sat me down in the backseat, and I was leaning forward so the doc could check the exit wound, and that's when I started getting a little nauseous, and feeling a little light-headed. And I heard one of the soldiers say, 'Hey, First Sergeant's going down,' and then I kind of snapped, 'Give me some water.' I drank some water, I snapped back to, doc put the bandage on, I put my clothes back on, of course I didn't have a T-shirt; he did cut the T-shirt away. My IBA, I just draped it over my left shoulder, and then we took off.

"And I'm in the backseat, and I heard one of the sergeants say, 'I hate all these motherfuckers,' and I was, 'Why? Ain't all of them tried to kill me. It's only a select group out there who's trying to shoot at me. Don't get mad at everybody 'cause one knucklehead shot me.'"

And it was about that same time, on another street in Kamaliyah, that Sergeant Michael Emory was shot in the back of his head.

"Sniper!" Jeff Jager screamed as he saw Emory fall.

They were on the rooftop of a factory with a few other soldiers, overwatching Bravo Company's clearance operation on surrounding streets. The roof was three flights up a narrow enclosed stairwell. It was a big roof spotted with broken glass and dirty puddles from a recent rain, and Emory was near the middle of it when there was a crack and he went down.

"Who's down? Is that Sergeant Emory?" another soldier yelled out. Then, louder, *"Sergeant Emory!"*

Emory was motionless, on his back, in a widening pool of blood.

"We got a sniper. We got a sniper," a soldier said into the radio. "We got a man down."

"Boland! Smoke! Smoke!" Jager yelled to a lieutenant who was on the far end of the roof by the stairwell and had two smoke grenades attached to his body armor.

Alex Boland tossed a grenade. There was a pop, and thick yellow smoke drifted over Emory as a soldier crawled toward him.

"Radio," Jager said to the radio man, motioning for it.

"Sir, can I take my radio off and go help him?" the soldier asked.

"Yeah," Jager said.

"I'm coming," the radio man hollered, and off he went across the roof, running until he was inside the smoke. He knelt by Emory's head and took one of his hands. The smoke dissipated, leaving them exposed.

"More smoke!" Jager yelled. "More smoke!"

Boland tossed his second grenade. Yellow smoke billowed and then thinned. "Drag him over here," Boland hollered.

"More smoke," Jager yelled to him.

"It's all I got," Boland yelled back.

Now a few more soldiers clattered up the stairwell, including a medic, who ran toward Emory, fell, got up, kept running, dropped down into

Emory's blood, and began pushing a pressure bandage into the back of his head.

"You guys stand up and pull him out. Over that way," Jager yelled, pointing toward Boland. "Let's go."

They grabbed Emory under his arms and began pulling, but Emory was dead weight. Now another soldier ran toward Emory, took hold of his body armor, and lifted him. Another soldier grabbed a leg. Another grabbed the other leg.

"I got you covered," Jager called. "Go!"

"Let's go," one of the soldiers said.

"Pull, pull," another urged.

"Go go go go," another said. "Keep going."

They got Emory inside the enclosed stairwell, safe from any more sniper fire, but now they needed to get him down three flights of stairs. It was a big building. There must have been a hundred steps. Emory was placed on a backboard. He was limp. His eyes were opening and closing. Two soldiers hoisted the backboard, but there were no straps to secure him with, and when he began slipping off, another soldier draped him over his back in a fireman's carry.

This was a staff sergeant named Adam Schumann. He was regarded as one of the best soldiers in the battalion. A few months after this moment, having turned into a soldier who was mentally broken, he would say of Emory, "I remember the blood was coming off his head and coming into my mouth. I couldn't get the taste out. That iron taste. I couldn't drink enough Kool-Aid that day."

But on this day, in this moment, Schumann carried Emory down to the second-floor landing, and when Emory was again placed on the backboard, Schumann lifted one end of it onto his shoulders and led the way down to the bottom floor, and when Emory stirred at one point and asked, "Why does my head hurt?" Schumann was one of the soldiers who answered, "You're gonna be all right." He helped get Emory into a Humvee to be evacuated to an aid station, and then he and another soldier went back up to the roof to collect the things Emory had left behind. There were his sunglasses. There was his helmet, wet with blood, and for some reason Schumann and the other soldier decided that no one else needed to see that, so they searched the factory for something to cover it with. They found a sack of flour, ripped it open, emptied it and hid the helmet in there, and while they were doing that, Emory was on the backboard across the rear seat of a Humvee, continuing to talk in a slurred voice.

"Why does my head hurt?" he asked again.

"Because you fell down some steps," said the sergeant who was in the back of the Humvee with him, lying next to him as they headed to the hospital, holding one of his hands.

"Oh," Emory said.

Now Emory raised his other hand and looked at it.

"Why do I have blood on my hand?" he asked.

"You fell down some steps," the sergeant said, holding Emory's hand tighter.

Now Emory looked at the sergeant.

"First Sergeant, I'm fucked up, aren't I?" he said.

And it was about that time, on another street in Kamaliyah, that a staff sergeant named Jared Stevens was shot in his lower lip.

He was moving backward when he was hit. That's what the soldiers were taught: Don't hold still for too long. Keep moving. Don't be a target. So that's what Stevens was doing, and it was his good luck to be moving backward rather than forward, so that when the bullet struck him, instead of going through his mouth, or his jaw, or his chin, it just ever so barely grazed his lip, butterflying it open from one side to the other.

Down he went, into a Humvee, to be evacuated.

"Okay," Kauzlarich said, hearing the report of this third shooting over his radio, and then turned his attention back to his own crisis. He had spent much of the morning clearing houses, trying to track down a suspected insurgent who was considered the brigade's highest-value target, and at least twice taking cover from gunfire, and now he was watching a crowd of several hundred Iraqis massed outside of a mosque. They were chanting and waving Iraqi and Jaish al Mahdi flags, and when the circling helicopters fired flares into the crowd to break it up, the chanting only got louder.

It was a bad situation that was worsening, and Kauzlarich knew it. This wasn't what had been intended. Clearing houses? Yes, they had done that. Rounding up suspected insurgents? Yes, they had done that. But if the goal of the operation, as stated in planning documents, was for the sixty thousand residents of Kamaliyah to realize the Americans had come "to clear your neighborhoods and improve your quality of life," that wasn't happening.

It was time for the operation to end. Kauzlarich radioed his soldiers to begin wrapping things up, and then he directed his convoy around the protesters, first heading north for a few blocks, and then, when gunfire broke out, east, in between the sewage trenches, until he reached a building partly in shreds—the spaghetti factory.

Much of it was caved in. Most of it was still standing, but the walls were lined with deep cracks. It was ruined.

Across the street, however, was another factory, and when Kauzlarich went inside to look it over, he liked what he saw—until he reached the bottom floor and discovered a family of eleven squatters, ranging from young children to an arthritic old man on a mattress over which someone had taped a poster of Muqtada al-Sadr.

"If we pay them, will they leave?" Kauzlarich asked his interpreter. "Tell them I'll give them three hundred dollars."

"It's not enough," the interpreter said, conveying the reply from a man who seemed to be the head of the family.

"Not enough?" Kauzlarich said. "It isn't enough?" He was confused. "They don't even *own* this."

The interpreter shrugged.

"If I pay him a thousand dollars?" Kauzlarich said.

"Give me a little bit more," came the reply. "One thousand five hundred."

Kauzlarich looked around. He needed a COP, and the truth was that this was better than the spaghetti factory even before the spaghetti factory had been bombed.

"Tell them by Tuesday they'll need to be gone," he said, and just like that Bravo Company had a COP, and eleven people with no home had $1,500 to find one.

He headed south now, a very long day nearly done. In the distance, on the far side of the spaghetti factory, was the little house. It was still intact, but there was no one outside, no hanging laundry, no signs of life at all. He kept going, away from Kamaliyah, back to the FOB, back to his office, back to his e-mails, where the initial reports about Emory weren't good. There was a report that he was in surgery and that his condition was extremely critical. There was a report that he went blind at the hospital and began panicking and was now in an induced coma. Now Cummings was telling Kauzlarich that at one point they were erroneously informed that he had died.

"Fucking knuckleheads," Cummings said.

In walked Stevens, Xylocained, stitched up, swollen, and on Percocet, to tell Kauzlarich that he had been taking cover behind walls, moving around, trying to do everything right. "I turned around and pow," he said, all mumbly.

"You *did* do everything right," Kauzlarich said. "Otherwise you wouldn't be here."

In walked Zappa, the two holes in him plugged and stitched, to say that, thanks to God, and Jesus, and a wife who tithes and sings hymns and reads the Bible for two hours a day, sometimes three, he was fine.

"Fucking heroes," Command Sergeant Major McCoy said to the two of them.

Now Stevens excused himself to go outside and call his wife.

"I got shot in the fucking mouth," he said when she answered, his eyes suddenly wet.

Back inside, meanwhile, Kauzlarich reviewed the day as he prepared to write a report about it that would go to brigade first, and then up the line from there.

"Overall, it was a good day," he said.

"We cleared what we wanted to clear.

"We better understand Kamaliyah, a city we have to control.

"We identified our enemy, including the brigade's high-value target number one.

"We found Bravo Company a new COP.

"We had three close calls, and the battalion reacted very well to them.

"The staff fought well from here, and they fought very well out there, which only makes them stronger.

"So today was a very good day."

A week later, the news on Emory wasn't at all encouraging. He had been airlifted to a hospital in Germany and was now in a coma, on life support. There had also been an increase in roadside bombs since the operation, due largely to the high-value target they'd gone after who afterward had been overheard saying angrily over his phone that he was going to put IEDs everywhere.

And perhaps he had, because soon after that conversation a soldier from another battalion who was driving into Kamaliyah with a load of blast walls for the COP lost both of his legs when his truck was hit by an EFP. There were mortar attacks on the COP, too, one of which slightly injured three soldiers from an engineering battalion and one from the 2-16.

Nonetheless, the COP was finished—one more COP by which to gauge the success of the surge—and on May 7, Kauzlarich returned to Kamaliyah to see it.

As usual, before leaving, Nate Showman gathered other soldiers in the convoy to brief them on the latest intelligence reports. He had been awake since before dawn, when an IED had blown up outside the FOB on Route Pluto as soldiers from another battalion rolled by in a tank. Badness circling, closer and closer—that's how 2-16 soldiers were starting to feel. Now they watched Showman trace a road on a map he was holding. "First Street is closed off because of an IED. First Street is black. We're not going that way," he said. Next he pointed to a spot on the edge of the FOB. "Two days ago, on the fifth, this guard tower on the very northernmost section of the FOB was engaged. One round went right through the ballistic glass, impacted on the right side of one of the guards' heads. All it did was hit his Kevlar," his helmet. "He received minor scratches from it, will be all right." Next he pointed to a spot on Route Pluto. "Hey, that thing that woke us up this morning was One-eight hitting an IED just north of Checkpoint Five-fifteen."

"On Pluto?" a soldier said.

"No shit?" another said.

"It hit a tank. The thing blew up, and they just burned right on through. That tank didn't even stop rolling," Showman said. "The bigger thing for us is the fact that in the last three days there have been about six EFPs on Route Predators, right up by Kamaliyah."

"Right where we're heading," another soldier said.

"Yeah," Showman said.

They decided to bypass Predators and take Berm Road, the only other route into Kamaliyah, which was the elevated dirt road that Cummings had been on the day he first went to see Bob. No road felt worse to travel than Berm Road. There were only so many points to climb onto it and drop off of it, and once up there, the feeling was of being utterly exposed and vulnerable, that the places to hide a bomb were limitless, including in the soft dirt underneath. The surrounding landscape didn't help, either: pools of fetid water, dead animals, vast piles of trash being picked through by families and dogs, grotesque pieces of twisted metal that in the dust clouds kicked up by the convoy reminded some soldiers of pictures they'd seen of the wreckage of the World Trade Center after 9/11. On Berm Road, Iraq could seem not only lost, but irredeemable.

But on this day it was the better way. As the convoy inched along, reports were coming in of yet another IED explosion on Predators; on Berm, meanwhile, the worst of it was some kids who paused in their trash-picking to throw rocks at the convoy as it passed by them and coated them in dust.

Kauzlarich, looking out the window, was uncharacteristically quiet. He had slept badly and woken uneasily. Something about the day didn't feel right, he'd said before getting in the Humvee. Once he saw the COP, though, his mood brightened. In a week's time, it had gone from an abandoned building with nothing inside of it other than a family of squatters to a fully functioning outpost for a company of 120 soldiers. Cots stretched from one end to the other. Generators chugged away so there was electricity. There was a working kitchen, a row of new portable toilets, and gun nests on the roof behind camouflage netting. The whole thing was enclosed in a solid perimeter of high blast walls, and even when Jeff Jager mentioned the isolating effect this was having regarding their relationship with the adjacent neighborhood, it was clear that Kauzlarich's confidence about what he was accomplishing in Kamaliyah had returned.

"I'd say about forty percent of the people who live around here are gone," Jager said.

"Forty percent?" Kauzlarich said.

Jager nodded.

"They'll be back," Kauzlarich said.

"Maybe," Jager said.

"Six weeks, they'll be back," Kauzlarich said, and soon after that he was again in his Humvee, now passing the spaghetti factory, now passing the little house that still showed no signs of life, now climbing back up onto Berm Road to leave Kamaliyah—and that's when the EFP exploded.

And was he in the midst of saying something when it happened? Was he looking at something specific? Was he thinking of something in particular? His wife? His children? The COP? The shitters? Was he singing to himself, as he had done earlier, when the convoy was leaving Rustamiyah and he sang, to no recognizable tune, just sang the words he had been thinking, "Oh, we're gonna go to Kamaliyah, to see what kind of trouble we can get in today"?

boom.

It wasn't that loud.

It was the sound of something being ripped, as if the air were made of silk.

It was so sudden that at first it was a series of questions, none of which made any sense: What was that flash? Why is it white out? What is that shudder moving through me? What is that sound? Why is there an echo inside of me? Why is it gray out? Why is it brown out?

And then the answer:

"Fuck," said Kauzlarich.

"Fuck," said the gunner.

"Fuck," said the driver.

"Fuck," said Showman.

The smoke cleared. The dirt finished falling. Thoughts slowed. Breathing returned. Shaking began. Eyes focused on arms: there. Hands: there. Legs: there. Feet: there.

All there.

"We're okay," Kauzlarich said.

"We're good," Showman said.

It had come from the left.

"Stay put," Kauzlarich said.

It had come from the left, where someone had stood watching while holding a trigger.

"Look for secondary," Kauzlarich said.

It had come from the left, where someone had stood watching while holding a trigger and had pressed it a tenth of a second too early or a tenth of a second too late, because the main charge of the EFP passed through the small gap in between Kauzlarich's Humvee and the one in front of it. And though there were flat tires and cracked windows and a few holes here and there from secondary effects of the explosion, all of the soldiers were okay, except for the shaking, and blinking, and headaches, and anger that began to rise in their throats.

"Fucking dirty cocksucker," one soldier said as the convoy moved off of Berm Road and into a place safe enough for the medic to check eyes for signs of concussions and ears for hearing loss.

"When it blew up, everything turned black," another soldier said.

"I just saw a bunch of dust."

"Everything was like fucking crazy."

"I was shaking like a fucking . . ."

"We're alive, guys. That's the name of the fucking game."

". . . like a fucking . . ."

"Trust me. The situation could be a lot fucking worse."

"It's luck. It's fucking luck. That's all it is."

"I can tell you I'll be glad when these days are done for me. Fuck this shit."

"All right. We're going to stay focused. We're in a war," Kauzlarich said, but he was shaken, too, and now, as the convoy limped away from Kamaliyah through a maze of dirt trails and more trash mounds, everything was anger, everything was fucking, everything was fuck.

The fucking dirt.

The fucking wind.

The fucking stink.

They passed a fucking water buffalo.

They passed a fucking goat.

They passed a fucking man on a fucking bicycle and didn't give a fuck when he began coughing from the fucking dust.

This fucking country.

They neared a child who stood by herself waving. She had filthy hair and a filthy face and was wearing a filthy red dress, the only bit of color visible at the moment in this entire place, and as she kept waving at the convoy, and now at Kauzlarich himself, he had a decision to make.

He stared out his window.

He raised his hand slowly.

He waved at the fucking child.

4

JUNE 30, 2007

So America has sent reinforcements to help the Iraqis secure their population,
go after the terrorists, insurgents, and militias that are inciting sectarian violence,
and get the capital under control. The last of these reinforcements arrived in
Iraq earlier this month, and the full surge has begun . . . We're still at the
beginning of this offensive, but we're seeing some hopeful signs.
—GEORGE W. BUSH, *June 30, 2007*

On June 5, at 10:55 at night, a $150,000 Humvee with five sol-
diers inside rolled into a sewage trench, turned upside down,
and sank.

It happened in Kamaliyah, where uncovered, unlined trenches ran
along every street and passed in front of every house. At some point after
the war began, the United States had decided to show its good intentions
by fixing this, appropriating $30 million to bring sewers to Kamaliyah. It
was an ambitious project involving Turkish subcontractors and Iraqi sub-
subcontractors that by the time Kauzlarich arrived had come to a dead
halt because of corruption and incompetence. Kauzlarich was given the
task of resuscitating the project, which, in keeping with his character, he
had taken on enthusiastically. The great leaders of previous wars may not
have had to do sewers, but Kauzlarich did in his version, and in mid-May,
at a meeting with a few of Kamaliyah's leaders, he'd made clear his desire
to succeed. "I know about half the workers working on the sewage project are militants, and they've got a choice. They can either work with me
or against me. If they work against me, I will arrest them. If they sabotage
the sewage project, I will hunt them down and kill them," he'd said.

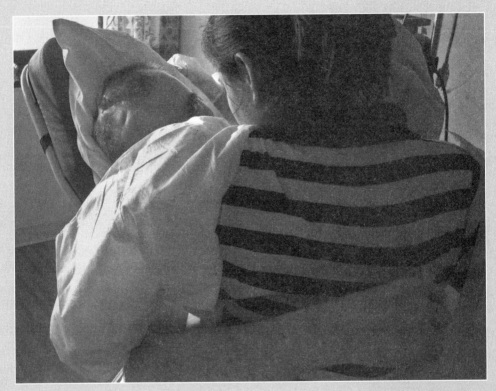

Michael and Maria Emory

Point made, the project resumed. Still, on June 5, Kamaliyah was a long way from having sewers, which meant that the trenches were filled to their rims as a convoy pulled out of the COP on a lights-out mission to rendezvous with an informant.

"Go right! Go right!" one of the soldiers in the last Humvee yelled to the driver, who was fiddling with his night-vision goggles, or NODs, as they rounded a corner, but it was too late.

The Humvee began to slide into the trench. Then it flipped. Then it sank. Then it began filling up.

Four of the soldiers scrambled out a door and got out of the trench relatively dry, but the gunner was trapped inside. "He was yelling," Staff Sergeant Arthur Enriquez would remember afterward, and if there was any hesitation about what to do next, it was only because, "I didn't want to jump in the poo water."

And then?

"I jumped into the damn poo water."

Down he went, into the crew compartment, where the gunner was stuck in his harness straps, his head partly in the sewage water, which continued to seep in. Enriquez got one arm around the gunner and lifted his head higher, and with his other hand began cutting away the straps. Now he and the gunner were nearly submerged as he pushed the straps away and began pulling at the gunner's body armor. Now they were completely submerged as he pulled the gunner's armor away. He squeezed his eyes shut. He wondered how long he could hold his breath. He felt for the gunner's waist and began pulling. Everything was slippery. He tried again. He got the gunner to the door. He kept pulling, and slipping, and pulling, and now they were out the door, out of the Humvee, out of the sewage, and up on the bank, and that's how this month of hopeful signs began for the 2-16, with two soldiers wiping raw Iraqi sewage out of their eyes and ears and spitting it out of their mouths.

On June 6, at 10:49 a.m., Private First Class Shawn Gajdos, twenty-five years old, became the second soldier in the battalion to die when an EFP exploded on Route Pluto as the convoy he was in headed toward the

Kamaliyah COP. Soon after, as Gajdos's body was on its way back home to a grieving mother, who would say, "I'm just very proud of my son, doing what he felt he wanted to do," four other soldiers in the convoy wrote down their recollections of what had happened for a report that would become the official narrative of his death. In his office, Kauzlarich read it carefully as he prepared to write his second memorial ceremony speech.

From the sworn statement of Lieutenant Matthew Cardellino: "Concerning the IED attack on my platoon 061049JUN07, in which PFC Shawn Gajdos was killed and CPL Jeffery Barkdull and PV2 Jordan Brackett were injured; the platoon was traveling in the northbound lane of RTE Pluto enroute to Bushmaster COP to deliver a generator and two mechanics and retrieve a downed vehicle."

From the sworn statement of Sergeant First Class Jay Howell: "We had already passed the site a few minutes prior to the attack, but were told to turn around to pick up the two mechanics back at FOB Rustamiyah. It was the second time we passed the site when the IED went off, hitting the lead truck, in which CPL Barkdull was the TC."

From the sworn statement of Corporal Jeffery Barkdull: "Being the Truck Commander in the attack I don't remember too much of what happened due to the fact that when the EFP hit the truck I was knocked out for a few minutes and plus memory loss of what went on that day. When the truck was hit I remember waking up not knowing what to do so I did what my driver did, if he used the radio so did I when he checked on the gunner, I checked on the gunner. After I checked the gunner I saw the engine of the truck catch fire and I saw my driver exit the truck so I also exit the truck."

From Sergeant Howell's statement: "Cpl Barkdull called across the radio to Lt Cardellino that the gunner had been hit and there were injuries."

From Lieutenant Cardellino's statement: "Over the radio I was told that there were injuries, but it was unclear at first who it was. After I and my driver dismounted from the truck, we ran over to the disabled truck and I began directing immediate security and looked in the truck to see the damage and injuries. I saw that PFC Gajdos was slumped in his gun turret sling unresponsive and bleeding. I do not know offhand whether he was standing or sitting at the time of the blast. I then tasted and smelled an oily smoke and saw that the engine compartment had caught on fire. PV2 Brackett and my driver, PV2 Gomez, grabbed their fire extinguishers and tried to put out the fire. It was at that point that I saw SSG John Jones run up from behind me with his fire extinguisher and helped to put out the fire. I screamed for the medic, SPC Walden."

From the sworn statement of Specialist William Walden: "We were driving down Plutos, I heard a loud explosion. When I look in front of the driver I could see a giant black cloud surrounded by gray smoke. I heard over the radio, 'There is blood everywhere,' and I could hear moaning in the back ground. My truck drove over there to the lead vehicle, I grabbed my Aide Bag and ran over, I saw CPL Barkdull with blood on his face and left arm. He told me not to worry about him he told me to get PFC Gajdos, that Gajdos is unresponsive. I ran over to the lead trucks right rear door, the door was hanging. I got inside I yelled at PFC Gajdos to get out and asking if he was alright. I saw blood coming out of his nose and mouth."

From Sergeant Howell's statement: "Once he was out of the vehicle SPC Walden began treating injuries to PFC Gajdos head while I notice a large area of blood in the groin area. I cut his pants to see if his femoral artery was severed."

From Specialist Walden's statement: "While he was doing that, I removed his IBA to see any chest injuries that could cause the blood coming from the mouth and nose. I saw he had two wounds to the right side of neck, that was not bleeding. I removed his ACH and a piece of brain matter fell on his ACU, I could see his eyes bulging and blood coming from his ears. He had a wound size of a quarter to the right side of head. PFC Gajdos's brain was protruding out of the wound. PFC Gajdos was having agonal breathing with a radial pulse. I sat him up so the blood would not compromise his airway, I started blind finger swipes, all I got was blood clots and more blood. I wrapped the wound to his head and neck with a Kerlix."

From Sergeant Howell's statement: "I asked SPC Walden if he was ready to move him he said yes so we loaded Gajdos into the LT's vehicle which was the nearest . . ."

From Specialist Walden's statement: "I started CPR. I tried two rescue breaths, but the air would not go in . . ."

From Lieutenant Cardellino's statement: ". . . and the three trucks sped northwest to FOB Loyalty, where we dropped him off at the Aid Station. It was shortly after that I was informed he was dead. Nothing follows."

From Sergeant Howell's statement: "Nothing follows."

From Specialist Walden's statement: "Nothing follows."

From Corporal Barkdull's statement: "That is all I can remember of the incedent. Nothing follows."

"On the morning of 6 June, 2007, Ranger Gajdos volunteered to replace one of his previously wounded Brothers to serve as the top gunner in the lead vehicle on a mission that would deliver supplies and a generator to the Bushmaster COP in Kamaliyah," Kauzlarich decided to write in his memorial speech. "Super G, as I called him, always had a kind word and positive attitude each and every time I ran into him. He will be forever missed."

On June 8, an EFP exploded in the area called al-Amin, and even before the smoke finished clearing, Sergeant Frank Gietz, who before leaving Fort Riley had spoken of the "dark place," was running after a man who had come out of a building just after the explosion to stare at the Humvee that had been hit.

"He had run back inside a building and threw himself on the carpet and went down to his knees and started praying," Gietz would remember later, sitting on his cot, his hands folded, his eyes down, his voice low so none of the other soldiers would overhear, his tone troubled. "So maybe out of anger, I don't know, I don't know if he was the triggerman or not, I just ran up to him and tackled him on the ground, and he turned combative on me. He tried to wrestle with me. I remember hitting him in the face, and he kind of started screaming and kind of went limp, and I threw him over on his stomach, and Cooper"—a medic—"ran up and threw his knee in his back and started holding his arms, and I heard Cooper yelling,

'I think you broke his fucking jaw.' And I just said, 'Fuck it,' and ran out to the street."

Out on the street, he would remember next, people on rooftops had begun firing at the soldiers.

"I could hear the crack of the rounds, and for some reason or other I just stood there and brought my weapon up and shot, and I remember seeing one individual's head just, it was weird, like a pink mist come out the back of his head when I shot, and inside my head I was like, 'Great. One down.'"

He would remember looking over at a gunner named Lucas Sassman, who was up in the turret of a Humvee, firing away.

"I saw his head snap back. And the kid stayed in the turret, that's what amazed me, so I didn't really think anything of it, and I came back up and engaged again and when I turned back around to look at the truck, he wasn't in the turret anymore."

He would remember running over to Sassman's Humvee.

"Sassman was laying in the middle of the truck, and I said, 'What happened?' and they said, 'He's been hit, he's been hit.'"

He would remember running through gunfire toward another Humvee, the one that had been struck, and a soldier named Joshua Atchley. Atchley was on his second tour in Iraq. The first time he'd been a cook and had gone home wanting to be in the infantry.

"I went straight to Atchley, because Atchley was just, I mean, covered in blood, and he was quiet, just sitting there, and I walked up to him and said, 'What's up, buddy, are you doing okay?' And he just looked at me and he said, 'They got my fucking eye.' At the time I didn't know his eye had been blown out, so I said, 'You're going to be all right, you're going to be all right.'"

He would remember that next to Atchley was a motionless soldier named Johnson.

"I thought Johnson was dead, I thought he was KIA, so I tried to focus on Atchley, and out of the blue I heard Johnson moan. So I was like, 'Oh *shit*, he's alive,' so I went up to him and he was laying on his side and his hand was tucked in underneath him, so I had no idea that his hand had been blown off, so I called to him, 'Johnson, what's wrong? Talk to me,' and at that time he just pulled his arm out, and I remember his hand was completely gone, I mean it was just pieces of skin and bone, but there was no blood. I remember thinking to myself, 'Wow, there's no blood, a massive amputation and there's no blood,' so I told him he was gonna be all right, and he kept telling me, 'I've lost my fucking hand, Sergeant, I've lost my fucking hand.'"

He would remember turning his attention to another soldier.

"I said, 'Lancaster, what's wrong with you?' and he goes, he goes, he goes, 'I got hit in the arm.' I said, 'How bad?' and he goes, 'I don't know, but it's bleeding a lot,' and he put out his arm and blood just started pouring out."

He would remember yelling for someone to tourniquet Lancaster and turning his attention to another soldier, Campbell.

"I remember Campbell still walking around, just screaming, holding his mouth open because he had shrapnel in his mouth. I remember yelling at him, telling him to get the fuck down."

He would remember that, and more gunfire, and shooting back, and killing a total of four people, and going to the hospital and being officially told that Sassman's head wound was critical, Johnson had lost his right hand, and Atchley had lost his left eye.

"And it's funny," Gietz would say, crying now as he remembered the next thing. "That morning, prior to us rolling out, Johnson had left his NODs inside the vehicle, and I smoked him. I mean I made him do push-ups, crunches, and everything out there in the dirt road for about thirty minutes. I chewed him out. And they let me inside before they medevac'd them out, and I remember Johnson looking up at me and telling me he loved me."

On June 9, in Fedaliyah, Gietz killed another seven. Maybe more. Probably more. "At least seven," he said, but as June deepened and the mission moved away from its beginning clarity and into more maybes and more probablys, it was difficult to keep track. "We're talking about the firefight of our life," Ricky Taylor, the captain who commanded Alpha Company, said. "I mean this was out of control."

Fedaliyah was the spookiest place in the AO, an area of water buffalo farms and squatter hovels, so vaguely defined that even in crystal clear satellite photos it appeared blurry and smudged, as if it existed inside of its very own sandstorm. The soldiers had gone there after dark because of a tip from a source they'd been cultivating, which seemed the best way to penetrate such an unknowable place.

"His nickname was Batman," Taylor said. "He was a seventeen-year-old kid. He was a great guy."

Maybe because he was a source—probably because he was a source—seventeen-year-old Batman wouldn't live to see eighteen, or even July. He would be tortured, presumably by militia members, and then he would be killed. But on June 9, he eagerly directed a convoy of forty-two soldiers and eight vehicles into the heart of Fedaliyah to search for two Jaish al Mahdi leaders he said he might be able to identify.

He couldn't, it turned out. But as the convoy eased along Route To-matoes, intelligence officers picked up chatter that indicated that the two men might be at the local office for Muqtada al-Sadr, the radical cleric who was one of the most powerful Shiites in Iraq, outside of which stood a dozen men. Gietz dismounted to talk to them. So did seven other sol-diers. The dozen men began moving. Gietz told them to stop. The men kept moving. "And then, *pow*, one shot goes off," Taylor said, and a mo-ment later, when gunfire came at the soldiers from every direction, "that's when all hell broke loose."

Gietz and the others chased the dozen men into a mosque. There was a sign inside indicating that the mosque wasn't really a mosque, that it was really the Fedaliyah office for the Jaish al Mahdi, and maybe it was. Probably it was. Or maybe it was a mosque with a sign inside and a bunch of men now running through it and a ladder in the rear courtyard, propped against a wall, that two men began to climb. Gietz fired. He watched the one on top tumble off the ladder and over the wall, dead without a doubt. He fired again. He watched the one midway up the rungs fall. He went over and nudged him with his foot to make sure he was dead and went on from there, back out onto the street and into more gunfire, in the next half hour losing count of how many times he and the other soldiers nearly died. There were grenades. There were mortars. A rocket-propelled grenade whooshed in, hit a Humvee, and set it on fire. The soldiers, each of whom carried at least 240 rounds of ammunition, fired so many rounds there was concern they would run out. They fired at doors, windows, roof lines. They fired at whatever shadows seemed to be firing at them. More soldiers, from other platoons, rushed in, and they began running out of ammunition, too.

"It was an insane night," Taylor said.

The final tally: one soldier slightly injured and thirty-five Iraqis dead, including Gietz's at least seven.

"The men were fired up. They were fired up," Taylor said. "It was an infantryman's dream: close and destroy the enemy."

And maybe so. Maybe it was an infantryman's dream.

But as Gietz said in his troubled voice as he thought of Sassman, Atchley, Johnson, Lancaster, and Campbell, and the fact that he and his soldiers had gone to Fedaliyah to capture two Iraqis and had ended up killing thirty-five: "It's a thin line between what we're calling acceptable and not acceptable. It's a thin line. As a leader, you're supposed to know when not to cross it. But how do you know? Does the army teach us how to control our emotions? Does the army teach us how to deal with a friend bleeding out in front of you?"

Maybe.

Probably.

"No."

On June 11, another soldier died. It was the battalion's worst day yet, when convoys were hit by EFPs or gunfire nine different times. One of the EFPs was hidden in the courtyard of a mosque just off of Inner Berm Road, and whoever pushed the trigger was aiming directly at the gun turret of the second vehicle, behind which sat Private First Class Cameron Payne, who was twenty-two.

"You're gonna have to move your feet so I can close the door," the medic, Charles White, said to Payne as they prepared to evacuate him, and when Payne tried to move his feet, for a brief moment, there was hope.

Number three.

"A devoted family man, Ranger Payne just returned from EML two weeks ago after seeing the birth of his second daughter, Kylie," Kauzlarich wrote in his memorial speech. "Seeing him in the dining facility a couple nights before he died, he shared with me the joy of having a new baby girl."

On June 15, as Lucas Sassman's medical condition was distilled into a daily update for Kauzlarich to read, Sassman was in a hospital bed at the National Naval Medical Center in Bethesda, Maryland. A jagged row of stitches ran from the edge of his right eyebrow to his temple; that was where the bullet had gone in. A long row of staples ran along the top of his head where his scalp had been split open like a hair part, all the way from the front to the back and then curving around toward his right ear. That was where doctors had opened his head to try to extract the bullet, and to help with the swelling of his brain.

Six days after being shot, Sassman was having trouble breathing. It was difficult for him to swallow. He had short-term memory loss. Soon enough, vertigo would set in, and he would develop migraine headaches that rarely went away. But he was conscious, and he could talk a little, and he said to his wife, his mother, and his sister, who were at his bedside, "I've lost my boyish good looks." His words were understandable, if not quite distinct.

"You look good as ever," his mother said.

"You're a liar, Mom," he said, and meanwhile, as they continued to talk, in the next bed over, a woman was leaning close to another soldier who had been shot in the head, stroking his forehead to comfort him.

This was Maria Emory, the wife of Sergeant Michael Emory. It had been seven weeks since Emory had been shot in Kamaliyah, and just as word of Sassman's medical condition was being sent to Kauzlarich, so was Emory's.

He was in Germany, sedated, critical, feverish, and in an induced coma.

He was stable enough to be moved to Bethesda.

His fever was dropping.

His infection was clearing.

He was being brought out of the coma.

He was awake and almost able to breathe on his own.

"That's beautiful," Kauzlarich had said in his office one day in mid-May, reading the latest update on Emory from Bethesda, which had just arrived by e-mail.

"What, sir?" Cummings had said.

"Sergeant Emory opened his eyes today," Kauzlarich had said. "Maria said, 'I want you to move your head,' and he did. She said, 'Look at me,' and he did. She said, 'I love you,' and he started to cry.

"It's all good," Kauzlarich had said.

So went reality in Iraq—but here in Bethesda, on June 15, was another version:

"Give me your hand, baby," Maria Emory said to her husband, who was diapered, who could barely move, who had a ventilator tube inserted into his throat, who was looking in panic at his wife who was armored in a mask and gown and gloves, and when she took his right hand and wrapped it around hers, he emitted a high-pitched whimper.

"Are you cold?" she asked.

He didn't answer. Just looked at her, less panicked now. His head was as misshapen as the moon over Rustamiyah.

"Baby," she said, leaning closer.

"Sweetheart," she said, even closer.

She straightened up.

He whimpered again.

"So, this is what I do now," she explained of what life had been since a phone call at 2:30 p.m. on April 28 in which the Department of Defense informed her that her husband had been shot, and now she added details by reading from a diary she had been keeping since then.

"May the third. I kissed him on his lips. This was in Germany. I told him, 'I'm going to kiss you on the lips, and if you can feel it, move,' and I kissed him twice, and he moved both times.

"May the sixth. We got on the medevac flight and we flew from Germany here to Bethesda.

"May the seventeenth. He opened his eyes for the very first time.

"May the nineteenth. He moved his fingers and his legs and I told him that I loved him and he started crying.

"May the twentieth. He was just sleeping.

"May the twenty-first. He slept most of the time.

"May the twenty-fifth. The president came to see him . . ." and now she put the diary down as she thought about the day that President Bush came to visit. About what he had said to her: "He said, 'Thank you for your husband's service to his country,' and he was sorry for what our family was going through." About what she'd said to him: "Thank you for coming." About what she wished she'd said to him: "That he didn't understand what we are going through because he *doesn't* know how it feels. And that I didn't agree with what was going on with the war." About why she hadn't said it: "Because I felt it would not have made any difference. And my husband of course had his eyes open and I didn't want him getting upset." About what Bush didn't understand: "I mean, when I saw him, I was so angry I started crying, and he saw me and came to me and gave me a hug and said, 'Everything's going to be okay.'"

That was why he came over to her, she said, because he misunderstood the reason for her tears. He'd had no idea they were because of anger, and he'd had no idea they were because of him. And nothing was okay, she said, so he was wrong about that, too. Her husband was ruined. In seven weeks, she had lost so much weight that her dress size had gone from a twelve to a six, her daughter was now living with a relative, she was now living in a hospital, the doctors were saying it could be years before her husband was better, if ever, and hope, if it existed at all, had to be extracted from wherever it could, from the awful day, for instance, in which he lifted his right hand and placed it on her shoulder, and then tried to move it across her breasts, and then started to cry.

So many tears in this place, and now there were more as he closed his eyes and dozed off and she knew he couldn't see her. She stepped out of the room. She removed the gloves, the gown, the mask. She hurried to a vending machine to get something to eat and then came right back so she would be next to him when he woke up. Gown back on. Mask back on. Gloves back on. Waiting. He opened his eyes. For a moment there was alarm, and then he saw her.

There she was, as if she hadn't moved.

"Can you give me a kiss?" she said. "Can you give me a kiss?"

She leaned in until her mask was against his lips.

"I love you, baby," she said, and then drew back, sensing that something was wrong. But what? What could it be?

"Are you cold?" she guessed.

He looked at her.

"Are you cold?"

He moved his lips, ever so slightly. He seemed to be trying to answer. She moved her ear to his mouth.

More hope:

"Yes," he said.

On June 20, Kauzlarich was back on the air on PEACE 106 FM.

"Sir, there is talk that security is bad and getting worse. What is the way ahead to improve security?" Mohammed, whose name was not really Mohammed, asked in Arabic, which was translated into English by an interpreter named Izzy, whose name was not really Izzy and who had replaced Mark, who had been arrested and jailed for extorting money from other Iraqis working on the FOB, all with fake names as well.

"That's a very good question, Mohammed," Kauzlarich said. "Right now, though, I would have to say that I disagree that the security is worse for the Iraqi people in Nine Nissan specifically. I say that because there's been a minimal number of kidnappings and murders.

"Security of the coalition forces, however, *is* becoming an issue. The militia within the Nine Nissan area is biting the hand that is attempting to assist the Iraqi Security Forces and rebuild or build the essential services. As everyone should know by now, militias are illegal in accordance with the Iraqi rule of law and must be dealt with. When was the last time the militia did something positive for you or your neighborhood? Has it provided *you* essential services? Recently the militia has fired mortars, rockets, and IEDs into your neighborhood. And those actions have either killed or injured innocent women and children. Why are Iraqi citizens allowing that to happen? It must stop soon, as time is running out."

"Sir, would you please tell us about some of your recent operations since our last interview?"

"Certainly. Since the last time I was on the air, Mohammed, and that was approximately five to six weeks ago, we've conducted hundreds of combined patrols with our Iraqi Security Forces brothers. The results of those patrols were in excess of fifty militia or criminal detentions. And with each of those detainees we have very strong evidence that they've harmed Iraqi citizens, Iraqi Security Forces, or Coalition Security Forces. And each one of them now will face the Iraqi criminal court system.

"We've also found caches of ammunition that were hidden in Kamaliyah and Fedaliyah.

"With those criminals and caches now gone, Nine Nissan will now become safer for your children and for your children's children."

On June 25, Private First Class Andre Craig, Jr., became the fourth soldier to die when an EFP severed his right arm, fractured his jaw, knocked out his teeth, lacerated his face, and snapped his head against the metal gun turret. He and his platoon were headed from the COP in Kamaliyah to FOB Rustamiyah for a couple of days of rest and relaxation, which had become standard practice once the COPs were built. After a week or so of bad food, hole-in-the-ground toilets, and patrols in 120-degree heat, the soldiers were eager for showers, better food, a chance to sleep, and air-conditioning.

All they had to do for this was get from the COP to the FOB.

"I hate this place," Cummings wrote in a note later that day. "I hate the way it smells, I hate the way it looks, I hate the way these people don't care about freedom, I hate that human beings want to kill one another for nothing."

Kauzlarich wrote some things down, too, for another memorial speech.

"The thought that the bullet has already been fired at each of us and it is only a matter of time when it will hit, brings comfort to some and terror to others," he wrote. His intention was to be symbolic rather than literal, to say that as soon as someone is born he is eventually going to die,

including poor Craig, whose "courage in the face of danger, his commit-
ment to the task at hand, and his loyalty to his comrades was demonstrated daily and ultimately on the morning of last Monday, 25 June 2007,
in the Baghdad suburb of Riassa, when his bullet hit, and took him from
our world into the next."

He was proud of what he wrote, but when he said it out loud at
Craig's memorial service to a chapel filled with soldiers increasingly on
edge, it creeped a lot of them out.

The bullet has already been fired.

Only a matter of time.

On June 27, Kauzlarich was again on PEACE 106 FM.

"Here's something I find personally illogical," he said to Izzy, to Mohammed, to whoever might be listening to their radios instead of out
among the trash piles hiding EFPs.

"On the east side of the river, virtually everyone, the majority of the
people, are Shi'a.

"The Jaish al Mahdi is a Shi'a-based militia.

"The Coalition Forces on this side of the river are helping all Iraqi
people, but most of those are Shi'a.

"So what makes no sense is why is a Shi'a-based militia trying to destroy the Coalition Forces that are trying to aid the Shi'a people?"

On June 28, at 6:50 a.m., another EFP hit another convoy of soldiers
headed from a COP to Rustamiyah for rest and relaxation, and when
reports came over the radio that Private First Class Michael Dunn had
lost an arm, Sergeant William Crow had lost an arm and leg, and Ricky
Taylor was calling into headquarters and saying, "This is bad. I hear them
screaming in the background," Cummings went down to the aid station,
arriving just after Dunn had been medevac'd out by helicopter.

"So I walked in, and the first table to the right is where Dunn was, and
blood was still going into the drain there," Cummings would say afterward. "What I remember is, I remember the blood, and I remember how

many people were there. There's a tape line that you're supposed to stay behind, and everybody was standing behind that line. And at the last table, that's the table that Sergeant Crow was on, and when I came up, they said, 'Okay, CPR again,' and the medics were CPR'ing his chest, and I was trying to look to get status, to see if I could tell how bad off he was, and he was very gray, so I knew it was bad. And I looked over, and I could see that his leg was gone about mid-thigh. You know, you could see the bone, and you could see the flesh, just ripped out, hanging there. I saw he had a tourniquet on him, couldn't really see his arm. I knew his arm was messed up. It was kind of covered by the docs, and then I saw Doc Brock was there; Doc De La Garza, Al, was there; one of our medics was doing the bag; one of our medics was doing CPR.

"It was just an ugly scene," he continued. "It was hard to watch. You know how you have those moments where you remember where you were? I remember where I was in ninth grade when the *Challenger* blew up. I was walking between fifth and sixth period, and they made the announcement. I remember where I was when President Reagan was shot. I was by Glenn Norwicki's house, walking up the street. And it'll be one of those things. I'll know where I was when Sergeant Crow, at the moment— because Doc De La Garza had a machine; I'm assuming it was an EKG machine, and I'm sure he had leads onto his body—he said, 'Stop,' and he looked at it, and he said, 'Continue,' and then he pumped, pumped, pumped, pumped, and he said, 'Stop,' and he looked, and he said, 'I'm still not getting anything,' and he looked at Doc Walters, and he looked over at Doc Brock, and he said, 'Okay, it's time to call it,' and that's when I was, 'Oh shit.' And I remember the look on Al's face. It was just one of those looks of pain, and sadness, frustration, and professionalism, if that makes any sense. 'Okay. It's time.'

"They stopped doing CPR, and I walked out. I didn't stay. I didn't go up to the body. I just stayed back, and I went outside and went through those doors, and Sergeant King was there. He was in the far corner. I walked by Sergeant Kitchen, and Sergeant King looked at me, and I shook my head, and he was like, 'What?' And I said, 'No. He didn't make it. Sorry.' And then Sergeant Kitchen ran up and grabbed me and turned me and said, *'What? What?'* And I said, 'Sergeant, he didn't make it. I'm sorry.'

I said, 'I'm sorry.' I said, 'You guys did everything you could do.' I said, 'You guys did a good job.' And he just kept saying, *'Fuck. Fuck. Fuck.'* And then the platoon was down at the end of the ramp, around the corner, and Sergeant Kitchen went out and told them, and there was just rage and tears. They were in a rage at this bullshit. They wanted to hit something. They were just mad. I said, 'Hey man, I'm sorry,' to a couple of them standing there. And a bunch of them, I noticed, their boots were stained with blood. That's what I remember, too. So many guys had blood on their boots.

"And then I walked back and told Colonel Kauzlarich, 'Sir, Sergeant Crow didn't survive.'"

"This past Monday night," Kauzlarich said in his memorial speech, "at Ranger Craig's memorial ceremony I made mention that the bullet had already been fired at each of us, and it was only a matter of time when it would hit. I also said that knowing the bullet had already been fired brings comfort to some and terror to others. I sincerely believe that Sergeant Crow was the kind of soldier and noncommissioned officer that found comfort knowing that his fate was predetermined by a force much greater than himself. I can say that confidently by Will Crow's reputation and the way he lived his life."

On June 30, in the final minutes of a month in which four soldiers died, one lost a hand, one lost an arm, one lost an eye, one was shot in the head, one was shot in the throat, eight were injured by shrapnel, eighty IEDs or EFPs detonated on passing convoys, soldiers were targeted by gunfire or rocket-propelled grenades fifty-two times, and Rustamiyah and the COPs were hit with rockets or mortars thirty-six times, Kauzlarich had a dream.

He was in a hunting lodge of some sort. He went into the bathroom, shut the door, locked it, and was alone at the urinal when he realized someone had come in and was standing by the sink.

"How'd you get in here?" he said.

"I just came in," was the reply.

"Yes, but are you a ghost or something?" he asked. "Am I dead?"

"No," was the reply. "Not yet."

Kauzlarich had never had a dream like this. "Never," he would say. "Never, never."

It woke him up. He couldn't get back to sleep. Eventually he checked the time. It was after midnight.

The hopeful signs of June were over, and now it was July.

JULY 12, 2007

We're helping enhance the size, capabilities, and effectiveness of the Iraqi
security forces so the Iraqis can take over the defense of their own country.
We're helping the Iraqis take back their neighborhoods from the extremists.
—GEORGE W. BUSH, *July 12, 2007*

W hat's happened that has turned everything into a fight?"
Kauzlarich had wondered in June. "What the hell is going
on?" Now, in July, as the daily explosions continued, he had
his answer.

"We're winning," he explained. "They wouldn't be fighting if we weren't
winning. They wouldn't have a reason to. It's a measure of *effectiveness.*"

Cummings believed it, too, although he said it differently.

"Good thing we're winning," he'd begun reciting on the five-minute
walk from his desk to the DFAC as he continuously scanned for the closest place to run to for cover in case of a rocket attack. "Because if we
were losing . . ."

Meanwhile, at Alpha Company's COP, which had been renamed COP
Cajimat, someone put up a handmade morale meter with seven different
settings.

"Embracing the suck," was one.

"Fuck this shit, I quit," was another.

"Bend over. Here it comes again," was another.

But it wasn't as if they had a choice. They were soldiers whose choices
had ended when they had signed contracts and taken their oaths. Whether
they had joined for reasons of patriotism, of romantic notions, to escape

Al-Amin, Baghdad, Iraq

a broken home of some sort, or out of economic need, their job now was to follow the orders of other soldiers who were following orders, too. Somewhere, far from Iraq, was where the orders began, but by the time they reached Rustamiyah, the only choice left for a soldier was to choose which lucky charm to tuck behind his body armor, or which foot to line up in front of the other, as he went out to follow the order of the day. Order: "enhance the size, capabilities, and effectiveness of the Iraqi security forces so the Iraqis can take over the defense of their own country." So out they went to do that, day after day, even though the fact was that the Iraqi Security Forces were a joke.

Every one of the soldiers knew it. How could they not? Just about every time an EFP exploded, it seemed to be within sight of an Iraqi Security Forces checkpoint, and did the Iraqis manning those checkpoints not see someone who was two hundred feet away digging in the dirt, emplacing an EFP, and unspooling some wire? Did they know the EFP was there and not say anything because they were in partnership? Were they merely incompetent? Was there another explanation that would make them worthy of an American soldier's respect? Did they ever come running to help? No. Even once? No.

And yet in the strategy of the surge, Americans and Iraqis were supposed to work together, so Kauzlarich began building a relationship with a man named Qasim Ibrahim Alwan, who was in charge of a 550-member National Police battalion whose AO overlapped the 2-16's. It was Colonel Qasim's men who were often the ones suspiciously nearby when the EFPs went off. Qasim himself, however, seemed to be sincerely trying to work with Kauzlarich and his soldiers, even though he was in constant jeopardy for doing so. He received frequent text messages on his cell phone telling him that he was going to be killed. He was a Sunni, and most of his soldiers were Shiite, and for all he knew they were the ones sending the text messages.

As a result, Qasim led a wary, uneasy life. But instead of running away from Baghdad and becoming one of Iraq's three million internally displaced people, or running away from Iraq entirely and becoming one of the war's two million refugees, he continued to align himself with the Americans, even showing up to pay his respects at Cajimat's memorial service. As he took his seat, some soldiers openly seethed that an Iraqi was in their midst. But he seemed genuinely moved by the display of a dead soldier's empty boots and the mournful tone of eulogies, and when the Americans bowed their heads in silent prayer and he raised his palms and lifted his eyes skyward, the splendor of the moment was not lost on Kauzlarich. "If I lose Qasim, I'm fucked," he told his soldiers one day. "We're fucked." That's how deeply Kauzlarich was coming to trust Qasim.

But Qasim was the only one. The rest were to be suspicious of, starting with the very first Iraqi some of them had met back at Fort Riley, just before they deployed, a visiting general who couldn't have seemed less interested as soldiers performed an exercise for him in which they showed how they had been trained to enter a building. Flawlessly, they did it once for the general, and then again, and what the general did for them was to stuff his hands in his overcoat, look down at some melting snow, kick at it with his polished maroon shoes, and make some perfunctory comments about how he was "very hopeful" that the Iraqi and American soldiers would be able to work well together.

Five months later, that hadn't yet happened. It was now the Americans' turn to watch Iraqi soldiers in training, and what they were seeing was a sorry collection of thirty Iraqi Army soldiers and twenty National Police officers who didn't even have the rudimentary skills that were taught to American soldiers in basic training. Their uniforms didn't quite fit. Their hair was shaggy. Their helmets were on cockeyed. They were at a weedy, rundown Iraqi military academy adjacent to Rustamiyah, doing an exercise in which they were supposed to learn the American way of patrolling, and one soldier who was walking backward swiveled around just in time to walk face first into a tree trunk. Now they were supposed to rest by kneeling down on one knee—"Take a knee" was the instruction— and one who was clearly too old to be a soldier, and too overweight to be a soldier, instead sprawled on the ground and began plucking at some weeds.

"Pretty good," a major named Rob Ramirez, who was observing the training for Kauzlarich, called out, and when the soldier on the ground smiled and waved at Ramirez, Ramirez smiled and waved back, while saying under his breath, "When we leave, they're going to get whacked."

It was a hot day, above 110 degrees. Everyone was sweat-soaked, the old, overweight soldier most of all. He had been a tank driver in the days of Saddam's army, but now, with unemployment rates in this part of Iraq said to be over 50 percent, he was just trying to hang in there with the others, all of whom were trying to hang in, too. In spite of the heat, they were glad to have been selected for this training course. Their rooms were air-conditioned. The toilets and showers worked. They would be here a total of four weeks before having to go back to their regular, post-invasion lives in Baghdad, and they wondered sometimes if the Americans understood what life for them had become. The lack of electricity. The lack of equipment and money. The lack of everything, really, other than threats. "We are afraid," an Iraqi Army lieutenant colonel named Abdul Haitham confided, and did the Americans understand that?

Break over, the Iraqis stood and moved down a dirt road with their mismatched guns as Haitham stayed back to ask Ramirez a question.

"If anything happens to us, what will happen to our families?" he asked, and then explained that when word circulated that he worked with the Americans, his name was read aloud in a mosque, a death threat was issued, and, as he and his family fled to the safety of a relative's house, his house was destroyed. "Even my kids' photos," he said of what he saw when he was able to return briefly. "They used a knife. They cut the neck. They burned the eyes. They cut the ears." Then they set the house on fire, he said, and three months later his family was still with relatives and he was living in a room at the academy. "I am waiting for a visa to America," Haitham said. "Because I hate this country."

He looked at Ramirez anxiously, the question of help implicit, and Ramirez looked back at him, at his worried face, at his sweat-stained uniform, at his thick chest, at his big hands, at his fat fingers, and finally at a shiny ring on one of those fingers, a ring with a large stone. It was a stone favored by members of Jaish al Mahdi, and, in particular, Jaish al Mahdi triggermen.

Who is this man? Ramirez wondered, and so he changed the subject. "On a good note, training is going good, I think," he said.

Haitham sighed. "For thirty-five years I built that house step by step. I buy it with my own money, and then I built it, and then I lose it," he said, and then excused himself so he could catch up with his men.

On they went, through a series of tests that were supposed to prepare them for leading patrols in Baghdad. The first involved the discovery of a suspicious box. They noticed it hidden in some weeds and cordoned it off. The second involved celebratory gunfire at a wedding. They guessed what it was and didn't shoot the bride or the groom. The third involved an assault by rock throwers, which turned out to be a couple of guys halfheartedly lobbing a few small stones that the Iraqis picked up and laughingly threw back. Then came a fourth scenario that hadn't been planned, an actual rocket attack. The Iraqis heard the warning horn drifting over from Rustamiyah, where radar had picked up the approaching rockets, and as several came down in the distance and exploded, some of the Iraqis used the occasion to grab a leisurely smoke until the all-clear.

A few hours later, the exercises done for the day, the temperature even higher, everyone gathered on some bleachers next to a sun-beaten field to review how had they done. Suddenly one of them collapsed.

It was the old, overweight tanker. He was quickly surrounded by other Iraqis, but there wasn't much they could do. Not only were they a collection of mismatched uniforms and weapons, but they had no supplies on hand other than useless bottles of hot drinking water, which they dumped onto the man, and the man's sweat-soaked shirt, which they removed and used to wipe down his face.

It was the ready-for-anything Americans who came to the rescue. Ramirez's medic had cool water and a portable IV kit. He uncoiled the plastic tubing and prepared the IV bag as the collapsed Iraqi watched through half-open eyes. Next the medic began readying the needle, and now the Iraqi was trying to sit up.

"I'm okay," he said weakly.

"You look sick," Abdul Haitham said.

"Believe me, I'm good," the man insisted.

"Are you scared?" Haitham said. He started laughing.

Then everyone, except for the man, started laughing and drifted away until only the American medic was left. *"Shukran,"* the man said gratefully after drinking the cool water, and with whatever dignity a too-old, too-heavy soldier could muster, he rose to his feet, wobbled his way from the bleachers to a parked pickup truck, climbed in, shut the door, closed his eyes, and slumped forward onto the dashboard.

He appeared to be passed out.

"Oh shit," the medic said, spying this, and while the others went off with Haitham and his shiny ring that may have meant something or may have meant nothing, the American ran over to further help and enhance.

Kauzlarich's strategy for helping, in addition to befriending Qasim, was to go to meeting after meeting with Iraqi officials and to treat each one as if the outcome of the entire war hung in the balance. If the Iraqis served a platter of sheep's brain, he reached toward the skull and ate a handful of sheep's brain. If they wanted to talk about trash, he would talk about trash until even they were exhausted by his enthusiasm.

"In America, we do not put trash out in the street," he said at one meeting with a man named Esam Al-Timimi, who was the civil manager of Kauzlarich's part of Baghdad. "We have garbage *cans*, and the garbage *man* drives up to the garbage cans, and throws the garbage in the garbage *truck*, and takes it away." He paused for translation. Timimi sat behind an ornate desk decorated with fake red flowers and vines. On the wall was a broken cuckoo clock. "Do we want to do that here?" Kauzlarich asked.

Timimi leaned forward. "We cannot compare to America," he said.

Kauzlarich started to reply, but Timimi cut him off. "Let me give you an example," he said and launched into a story about a time years before, during the time of Saddam Hussein, when Spain decided to clean up the garbage of Sadr City. Contractors were hired with the promise that they could sell anything valuable that they found in the trash and keep the money. And it might have worked, Timimi said, except that the scavenging children of Sadr City got to the garbage first. "I saw children with black arms. I thought they were wearing clothing. Actually it was dirt.

They recycled everything, even the plastic inside medical bags," he said. "This is an example. Our life is very hard."

"So, Mr. Timimi," Kauzlarich said, pressing on. "Do we want to buy big trash cans for people to put garbage in?"

And so Timimi told another story about a time when there *were* big trash cans for people to put garbage in, but the problem, he said, was that in their culture, children take out the trash, and the children were often too short to reach the big trash cans. "So they dumped it in the street next to the containers."

"Let's do this," Kauzlarich tried. "Let's buy the right-size plastic containers."

And so Timimi told another story about a time when plastic containers for water were distributed, and people used them sometimes to store water, and other times to store petrol, and ended up getting sick. "Educated people—they understand. But it's very difficult to teach the citizens of Nine Nissan," he said.

And so Kauzlarich suggested putting the big trash cans not in homes but in schools. "So we can teach kids to put garbage in the garbage cans," he said.

And Timimi thought about this, and ignoring the fact that so many schools had been ransacked and were closed, he said: "Good!"

That was an outstanding meeting.

But more often, the meetings were like the one Kauzlarich had with a sheik who began by saying, "I wanted to have a meeting with you to thank you. I want to be the leader who brings peace to our area."

And then he said that to do this he would need money and a car.

Also, "I need a new pistol."

And bullets, too.

"Everybody wants something in this country," Kauzlarich had said before the meeting, predicting what would happen. "Where is my telephone? Where is this? Where is that? When is America going to bring in paint? Walls? Electricity? Where's the TV? Where, where, where?

"It's a gimme gimme gimme society," he continued, and then backed down a bit. He wasn't blind to how bad things had become because of the war's ruinous beginnings, and unlike many soldiers, he had read enough about Iraq, and about Islam, to have at least a fundamental awareness of the people he was among. "The whole religion of Islam is supposed to be a peaceful religion, in which the jihad is supposed to be that internal fight to be the best person you can be," he said. "I mean the Iraqi people, they're not terrorists. They're good people."

Where things got blurry for Kauzlarich, though, was in the meaning of *good*, especially in the subset of Iraqis whom Kauzlarich found himself dealing with. The sheik, for instance: at one point Kauzlarich threatened him with jail for possibly being involved in an IED cell, but then let him go after he promised to provide information about what was going on inside Kamaliyah and to help keep things under control. So was the sheik good or bad? Was he an insurgent, or was he an informant? All Kauzlarich knew for sure was that he was making uncertain bargains with someone who wore a heavy gold watch and a pinky ring with a turquoise stone, smoked Miami-brand cigarettes, lit those cigarettes with a lighter that had flashing red-and-blue lights, blew smoke from those cigarettes into Kauzlarich's face while asking for money, for guns, for bullets, for a new cell phone, for a car, and referred to Kauzlarich as "my dear Colonel K."

He also called Kauzlarich "Muqaddam K" at times, and in this he had plenty of company. *Muqaddam* was the Arabic equivalent of lieutenant colonel. It was what people began calling Kauzlarich soon after his arrival in February, which so pleased him that in response, to show his respect, he had been trying to use Arabic, too.

He learned to say *habibi*, which was "dear friend."

He learned to say *shaku maku* ("what's up?"), *shukran la su'alek* ("thank you for asking"), and *saffya daffya* ("sunny and warm").

He learned to say *anee wahid kelba* ("I am one sexy bitch"), which made people laugh every time he said it.

The months went by. The meetings grew repetitive. The same complaints. The same selfish requests. The same nothing done.

He learned to say *marfood* ("disapproved") and *qadenee lel jenoon* ("it drives me crazy").

June came.

He learned to say *cooloh khara* ("it's all bullshit") and *shadi ghabee* ("stupid monkey").

July now.

Allah ye sheelack, he found himself saying. I hope you die. "May God take your soul."

On July 12, Kauzlarich ate a Pop-Tart at 4:55 a.m., guzzled a can of Rip It Energy Fuel, belched loudly, and announced to his soldiers, "All right, boys. It's time to get some." On a day when in Washington, D.C., President Bush would be talking about "helping the Iraqis take back their neighborhoods from the extremists," Kauzlarich was about to do exactly that.

The neighborhood was Al-Amin, where a group of insurgents had been setting off a lot of IEDs, most recently targeting Alpha Company soldiers as they tried to get from their COP to Rustamiyah for Crow's memorial service a few days before. Two IEDs exploded on the soldiers that day, leaving several of them on their hands and knees, alive but stunned with concussions, and now Kauzlarich was about to swarm into that area with 240 soldiers, 65 Humvees, several Bradley Fighting Vehicles, and, on loan to them for a few hours from another battalion, two AH-64 Apache helicopter gunships.

All together, it made for a massive and intimidating convoy that at 5:00 a.m. was lining up to leave Rustamiyah when the radar system picked up something flying through the still-dark sky. "Incoming! Incoming!" came the recorded warning as the alert horn sounded. It was a sound that, by now, after so many such warnings, seemed less scary than melancholy, and the soldiers reacted to it with shrugs. Some standing in the open reflexively hit the dirt. The gunners who were standing up in their turrets dropped down into their slings. But most did nothing, because the bullet had been fired, it was only a matter of time, and if they knew anything by now, it was that whatever happened in the next few seconds was the province of God, or luck, or whatever they believed in, rather than of them.

Really, how else to explain Stevens's split lip? Or what happened to a captain named Al Walsh when a mortar hit outside of his door early one morning as he slept? In came a piece of shrapnel, moving so swiftly that before he could wake up and take cover, it had sliced through his wooden door, sliced through the metal frame of his bed, sliced through a 280-page book called *Learning to Eat Soup with a Knife*, sliced through a 272-page book called *Buddhism Is Not What You Think*, sliced through a 128-page book called *On Guerrilla Warfare*, sliced through a 360-page book called *Tactics of the Crescent Moon*, sliced through a 176-page *Calvin and Hobbes* collection, sliced through the rear of a metal cabinet holding those books, and finally was stopped by a concrete wall. And the only reason that Walsh wasn't sliced was that he happened in that moment to be sleeping on his side rather than on his stomach or back, as he usually did, which meant that the shrapnel passed cleanly through the spot where his head usually rested, missing him by an inch. Dazed, ears ringing, unsure of what had just happened, and spotted with a little blood from being nicked by the exploding metal fragments of the ruined bed frame, he stumbled out to the smoking courtyard and said to another soldier, "Is anything sticking out of my head?" And the answer, thank whatever, was no.

Another example: How else to explain what had happened just the day before, in another mortar attack, when one of the mortars dropped down out of the sky and directly into the open turret of a parked Humvee? After the attack was over, soldiers gathered around the ruined Humvee to marvel—not at the destruction a mortar could cause, but at the odds. How much sky was up there? And how many landing spots were down here? So many possible paths for a mortar to follow, and never mind the fact that every one of them comes down in a particular place—the fact that this one followed the one path that brought it straight down through a turret without even touching the edges, a perfect swish, the impossible shot, made the soldiers realize how foolish they were to think that a mortar couldn't come straight down on them.

Resigned to the next few seconds, then, here they were, lined up at the gate, listening to the horn and the incessant, "Incoming! Incoming!" and waiting for whatever was up there to drop.

One second.

Two seconds.

A boom over there.

One second.

Two seconds.

Another boom, also over there.

And nothing here, not even close, no swish this time, so the gunners stood back up, the soldiers in the dirt dusted themselves off, and the massive convoy headed toward Al-Amin to begin a day that would turn out to feature four distinct versions of war.

Arriving just after sunrise, Charlie Company broke off from the convoy and headed to the west side of Al-Amin. It was a *saffya daffya* day, and the soldiers found no resistance as they began clearing streets and houses. Birds chirped. A few people smiled. One family was so welcoming that Tyler Andersen, the commander of Charlie Company, ended up standing under a shade tree with a man and his elderly father having a leisurely discussion about the war. The Iraqis asked why the Americans' original invasion force had been only one hundred thousand soldiers. They talked about the difficulties of life with only a few hours of electricity a day, and how much they mistrusted the Iraqi government because of the rampant corruption. The conversation, which lasted half an hour and ended in handshakes, was the longest, most civil one Andersen would have with an Iraqi in the entire war, and it filled him with an unexpected sense of optimism about what he and his company of soldiers were doing. That was the first version of war.

The second occurred in the center of Al-Amin, where Kauzlarich went with Alpha Company.

Here, sporadic gunfire could be heard, and the soldiers clung to walls as they moved toward a small neighborhood mosque. They had been tipped that it might be a hideout for weapons, and they wanted to get inside. The doors were chained shut, however, and even if they hadn't been, American soldiers weren't allowed in mosques without special permission. National Police could go in, but the three dozen NPs who were supposed to be part of this operation had yet to show up. Kauzlarich radioed Qasim. Qasim said they were coming. Nothing to do but wait and wonder about snipers. Some soldiers took refuge in a courtyard where a family's wash was hanging out to dry. Others stayed bobbing and weaving on the street, which was eerily empty except for a woman in black pulling along a small girl, who saw the soldiers and their weapons and burst into tears as she passed by.

Here, finally, came the NPs.

"There are weapons inside," Kauzlarich told the officer in charge, a brigadier general.

"No!" the general exclaimed in shock, and then laughed and led his men toward a house next door to the mosque. Without knocking, they pushed through the front door, went past a wide-eyed man holding a baby sucking his thumb, climbed the steps to the roof, took cover for a few minutes when they heard gunfire, jumped from that roof down onto the slightly lower roof of the mosque, went inside, and emerged a few minutes later with a rocket-propelled grenade launcher, an AK-47, ammunition, and, placed carefully into a bag, a partially assembled IED.

"Wow," Kauzlarich said after all this had been brought down to the street, and for a few moments, defying his own order to always keep moving, he stared at the haul, disgusted.

Weapons in a mosque. As a commander, he needed to understand why an *imam* might allow this, or even sanction it, because as it said in the field manual on Cummings's desk, which was getting dustier by the day, "Counterinsurgents must understand the environment." Good soldiers understood things. So did good Christians, and Kauzlarich desired to be one of those, too. "For he who avenges murder cares for the helpless," he had read the night before in the *One Year Bible*. "He does not ignore the cries of those who suffer."

Were these people suffering? Yes. Were they helpless? Yes. Was this their version of crying, then? Was the explanation somewhere in the words of Psalms?

But what about a statement released a few days before by an Iraqi religious leader, which said, in part: "Yes, O Bush, we are the ones who kidnap your soldiers and kill them and burn them. We will continue, God willing, so long as you only know the language of blood and the scattering of remains. Our soldiers love the blood of your soldiers. They compete to chop off their heads. They like the game of burning down their vehicles."

What a freak show this place was. And maybe that was the explanation for the pile of weapons Kauzlarich was looking at, that it deserved no understanding whatsoever.

Weapons in a mosque, including an IED to burn vehicles and kill soldiers.

Unbelievable.

Shadi ghabees. Cooloh khara. Allah ye sheelack.

"*Shukran,*" Kauzlarich said out loud to the general, keeping his other thoughts to himself. He made his way to his Humvee to figure out where to go next and was just settling into his seat when he was startled by a loud burst of gunfire.

"Machine gun fire," he said, wondering who was shooting.

But it wasn't machine gun fire. It was bigger. More thundering. It was coming from above, just to the east, where the AH-64 Apache helicopters were circling, and it was so loud the entire sky seemed to jerk.

Now came a second burst.

"Yeah! We killed more motherfuckers," Kauzlarich said.

Now came more bursts.

"Holy shit," Kauzlarich said.

It was the morning's third version of war.

One minute and fifty-five seconds before the first burst, the two crew members in one of the circling Apaches had noticed some men on a street on Al-Amin's eastern edge.

"See all those people standing down there?" one asked.

"Confirmed," said the other crew member. "That open courtyard?"

"Roger," said the first.

Everything the crew members in both Apaches were saying was being recorded. So were their communications with the 2-16. To avoid confusion, anyone talking identified himself with a code word. The crew members in the lead Apache, for example, were Crazy Horse 1-8. The 2-16 person they were communicating with most frequently was Hotel 2-6.

There was a visual recording of what they were seeing as well, and what they were seeing now—one minute and forty seconds before they fired their first burst—were some men walking along the middle of a street, several of whom appeared to be carrying weapons.

All morning long, this part of Al-Amin had been the most hostile. While Tyler Andersen had been under a shade tree in west Al-Amin, and Kauzlarich had dealt with occasional gunfire in the center part, east Al-Amin had been filled with gunfire and some explosions. There had been reports of sniper fire, rooftop chases, and rocket-propelled grenades being fired at Bravo Company, and as the fighting continued, it attracted the attention of Namir Noor-Eldeen, a twenty-two-year-old photographer for the Reuters news agency who lived in Baghdad, and Saeed Chmagh, forty, his driver and assistant.

Some journalists covering the war did so by embedding with the U.S. military. Others worked independently. Noor-Eldeen and Chmagh were among those who worked independently, which meant that the military didn't know they were in Al-Amin. The 2-16 didn't know, and neither did the crews of the Apaches, which were flying high above Al-Amin in a slow, counter-clockwise circle. From that height, the crews could see all of east Al-Amin, but the optics in the lead Apache were now focused tightly on Noor-Eldeen, who had a camera strung over his right shoulder and was centered in the crosshairs of the Apache's thirty-millimeter automatic cannon.

"Oh yeah," one of the crew members said to the other as he looked at the hanging camera. "That's a weapon."

"Hotel Two-six, this is Crazy Horse One-eight," the other crew member radioed in to the 2-16. "Have individuals with weapons."

They continued to keep the crosshairs on Noor-Eldeen as he walked along the street next to another man, who seemed to be leading him. On the right side of the street were some trash piles. On the left side were buildings. Now the man with Noor-Eldeen guided him by the elbow toward one of the buildings and motioned for him to get down. Chmagh followed, carrying a camera with a long telephoto lens. Behind Chmagh were four other men, one of whom appeared to be holding an AK-47 and one of whom appeared to be holding a rocket-propelled grenade launcher. The crosshairs swung now away from Noor-Eldeen and toward one of those men.

"Yup, he's got one, too," the crew member said. "Hotel Two-six, Crazy Horse One-eight. Have five to six individuals with AK-47s. Request permission to engage."

It was now one minute and four seconds before the first burst.

"Roger that," Hotel 2-6 replied. "We have no personnel east of our position, so you are free to engage. Over."

"All right, we'll be engaging," the other crew member said.

They couldn't engage yet, however, because the Apache's circling had brought it to a point where some buildings now obstructed the view of the men.

"I can't get them now," a crew member said.

Several seconds passed as the lead Apache continued its slow curve around. Now it was almost directly behind the building that Noor-Eldeen had been guided toward, and the crew members could see someone peering around the corner, looking in their direction and lifting something long and dark. This was Noor-Eldeen, raising a camera with a telephoto lens to his eyes.

"He's got an RPG."

"Okay, I got a guy with an RPG."

"I'm gonna fire."

But the building was still in the way.

"Goddamnit."

The Apache needed to circle all the way around, back to an unobstructed view of the street, before the gunner would have a clean shot.

Ten seconds passed as the helicopter continued to curve.

"Once you get on it, just open—"

Almost around now, the crew could see three of the men. Just a little more to go.

Now they could see five of them.

"You're clear."

Not quite. One last tree was in the way.

"All right."

There. Now all of the men could be seen. There were nine of them, including Noor-Eldeen. He was in the middle, and the others were clustered around him, except for Chmagh, who was on his cell phone a few steps away.

"Light 'em all up."

One second before the first burst, Noor-Eldeen glanced up at the Apache.

"Come on—fire."

The others followed his gaze and looked up, too.

The gunner fired.

It was a twenty-round burst that lasted for two seconds.

"Machine gun fire," Kauzlarich said quizzically, a half mile away, as the sky seemed to jerk, and meanwhile, here in east Al-Amin, nine men were suddenly grabbing their bodies as the street blew up around them, seven were now falling to the ground, dead or nearly dead, and two were running away—Chmagh and Noor-Eldeen.

The gunner saw Noor-Eldeen, tracked him in the crosshairs, and fired a second twenty-round burst, and after running perhaps twelve steps, Noor-Eldeen dove into a pile of trash.

"Keep shooting," the other crew member said.

There was a two-second pause, and then came the third burst. The trash all around where Noor-Eldeen lay facedown erupted. A cloud of dirt and dust rose into the air.

"Keep shooting."

There was a one-second pause, and then came the fourth burst. In the cloud, Noor-Eldeen could be seen trying to stand, and then he simply seemed to explode.

All of this took twelve seconds. A total of eighty rounds had been fired. The thirty-millimeter cannon was now silent. The pilot was silent. The gunner was silent. The scene they looked down on was one of swirling and rising dirt, and now, barely visible as some of the swirling dirt began to thin, they saw a person who was taking cover by crouching against a wall.

It was Chmagh.

He stood and began to run. "I got him," someone said, and now he disappeared inside a fresh explosion of dirt, which rose and mingled with what was already in the air as the Apaches continued circling and the crew members continued to talk.

"All right, you're clear," one said.

"All right, I'm just trying to find targets again," another said.

"We have a bunch of bodies laying there."

"All right, we got about eight individuals."

"Yeah, we definitely got some."

"Yeah, look at those dead bastards."

"Good shooting."

"Thank you."

The smoke was gone now and they could see everything clearly: the main pile of bodies, some prone, one on haunches, one folded into impossible angles; Noor-Eldeen on top of the trash; Chmagh lying motionless on his left side.

"Bushmaster Seven, Crazy Horse One-eight," they radioed to Bravo Company, whose soldiers were on their way to the site. "Location of bodies Mike Bravo Five-four-five-eight-eight-six-one-seven. They're on a street in front of an open courtyard with a bunch of blue trucks, a bunch of vehicles in a courtyard."

"There's one guy moving down there, but he's wounded," someone now said, looking down, scanning the bodies, focusing on Chmagh.

"This is One-eight," the crew member continued on the radio. "We also have one individual who appears to be wounded. Trying to crawl away."

"Roger. We're gonna move down there," Bravo Company replied.

"Roger. We'll cease fire," the Apache crew responded and continued to watch Chmagh, still alive somehow, who in slow motion seemed to be trying to push himself up. He got partway and collapsed. He tried again, raising himself slightly, but again he went down. He rolled onto his stomach and tried to get up on his knees, but his left leg stayed extended behind him, and when he tried to lift his head, he could get it only a few inches off the ground.

"Do you see a shot?" one of the crew members said.

"Does he have a weapon in his hands?" the other said, aware of the rules governing an engagement.

"No, I haven't seen one yet."

They continued to watch and to circle as Chmagh sank back to the ground.

"Come on, buddy," one of them urged.

"All you gotta do is pick up a weapon," another said.

Now, as had happened earlier, their circling brought them behind some buildings that obstructed their view of the street, and when they were next able to see Chmagh, someone they had glimpsed running up the street was crouching over him, a second man was running toward them, and a Kia passenger van was approaching.

"Bushmaster, Crazy Horse," they radioed in urgently. "We have individuals going to the scene. Looks like possibly picking up bodies and weapons. Break—"

The van stopped next to Chmagh. The driver got out, ran around to the passenger side, and slid open the cargo door.

"Crazy Horse One-eight. Request permission to engage."

Ready to fire, they waited for the required response from Bravo Company as two of the passersby tried to pick up Chmagh, who was facedown on the sidewalk. One man had Chmagh by the legs. The second man was trying to turn him over onto his back. Were they insurgents? Were they people only trying to help?

"Come *on!* Let us *shoot.*"

Now the second man had hold of Chmagh under his arms.

"Bushmaster, Crazy Horse One-eight," the Apache said again.

But there was still no response as the driver got back in his seat and the two men lifted Chmagh and carried him around the front of the van toward the open door.

"They're taking him."

"Bushmaster, Crazy Horse One-eight."

They had Chmagh at the door now.

"This is Bushmaster Seven. Go ahead."

They were pulling Chmagh to his feet.

"Roger, we have a black bongo truck picking up the bodies. Request permission to engage."

They were pushing Chmagh into the van.

"This is Bushmaster Seven. Roger. Engage."

He was in the van now, the two men were closing the door, and the van was beginning to move forward.

"One-eight, clear."

"Come on!"

A first burst.

"Clear."

A second burst.

"Clear."

A third burst.

"Clear."

Ten seconds. Sixty rounds. The two men outside of the van ran, dove, and rolled against a wall as some of the rounds exploded around them. The van continued forward a few yards, abruptly jerked backward, crashed into the wall near the men, and was now enveloped in smoke.

"I think the van's disabled," a crew member said, but to be sure, now came a fourth burst, a fifth, and a sixth—ten more seconds, sixty more rounds—and that, at last, was the end of the shooting.

Now it was a matter of waiting for Bravo Company's soldiers to arrive on the scene, and here they came, in Humvees and on foot, swarming across a thoroughly ruined landscape. The battlefield was theirs now, from the main pile of bodies, to the trash pile with Noor-Eldeen, to the shot-up houses and buildings, to the van—inside of which, among the bodies, they discovered someone alive.

"Bushmaster Six, Bravo Seven," a Bravo Company soldier called over the radio. "I've got eleven Iraqi KIAs, one small child wounded. Over."

The Apache crews were listening.

"Ah, damn," one of them said.

"We need to evac this child," Bravo Seven continued. "She's got a wound to the belly. Doc can't do anything here. She needs to get evac'd. Over."

"Well, it's their fault for bringing their kids to a battle," a crew member said.

"That's right," the other said, and for a few more minutes they continued to circle and watch.

They saw more Humvees arriving, one of which drove up onto the trash pile, right over the part containing what was left of Noor-Eldeen's body.

"That guy just drove over a body."

"Did he?"

"Yeah."

"Well, they're dead, so——"

They watched a soldier emerge from the van cradling the wounded girl and run with her in his arms to the army vehicle that was going to evacuate her to a hospital.

They watched another soldier emerge from the van a few minutes later cradling a second wounded child, this one a little boy who had been discovered under a body presumed to be his father's, which was draped over the boy, either protectively or because that was how a dead man happened to fall.

And then they flew on to another part of Al-Amin as more and more Bravo Company soldiers arrived, one of whom was Jay March, the soldier who on the battalion's very first day in Iraq had climbed a guard tower, peeked out at all of the trash, and said quietly and nervously, "We ain't ever gonna be able to find an IED in all this shit."

Since then, March had learned how prophetic he was, especially on June 25, when an EFP killed his friend Andre Craig, Jr. Craig's memorial service had been on July 7, and now, five days later, as March saw all of the bodies scattered around, blown open, insides exposed, so gruesome, so grotesque, he felt—as he would later explain—"happy. It was weird. I was just really very happy. I remember feeling so happy. When I heard they were engaging, when I heard there's thirteen KIA, I was just *so* happy, because Craig had just died, and it felt like, you know, we got 'em."

As the Apaches peeled off, he and another soldier went through a gate in the wall that the van had crashed into and against which Chmagh had tried to take cover.

There, in the courtyard of a house, hidden from street view, they found two more injured Iraqis, one on top of the other. As March looked closer at the two, who might have been the two who had been lifting

Chmagh into the van, who as far as March knew had spent the morning trying to kill American soldiers, he realized that the one on the bottom was dead. But the one on top was still alive, and as March locked eyes with him, the man raised his hands and rubbed his two forefingers together, which March had learned was what Iraqis did when they wanted to signal the word *friends*.

So March looked at the man and rubbed his two forefingers together, too.

And then dropped his left hand and extended the middle finger of his right hand.

And then said to the other soldier, "Craig's probably just sitting up there drinking beer, going, 'Hah! That's all I needed.'"

And that was the day's third version of war.

As for the fourth version, it occurred late in the day, back on the FOB, after Kauzlarich and the soldiers had finished their work in Al-Amin.

They knew by now about Chmagh and Noor-Eldeen.

They had brought back Noor-Eldeen's cameras and examined the images to see if he was a journalist or an insurgent.

They had gotten the video and audio recordings from the Apaches and had reviewed them several times.

They had looked at photographs taken by soldiers that showed AK-47s and a rocket-propelled grenade launcher next to the dead Iraqis.

They had reviewed everything they could about what had prefaced the killings in east Al-Amin, in other words—that soldiers were being shot at, that they didn't know journalists were there, that the journalists were in a group of men carrying weapons, that the Apache crew had followed the rules of engagement when it fired at the men with weapons, at the journalists, and at the van with the children inside—and had concluded that everyone had acted appropriately.

Had the journalists?

That would be for others to decide.

As for the men who had tried to help Chmagh, were they insurgents or just people trying to help a wounded man?

They would probably never know.

What they did know: the good soldiers were still the good soldiers, and the time had come for dinner.

"Crow. Payne. Craig. Gajdos. Cajimat," Kauzlarich said on the walk to the DFAC. "Right now? Our guys? They're thinking, 'Those guys didn't die in vain. Not after what we did today.'"

Inside the DFAC, the TVs were tuned to Bush's press conference, which had begun in Washington just a few minutes before.

"Our top priority is to help the Iraqis protect their population," Bush was saying, "so we've launched an offensive in and around Baghdad to go after extremists, to buy more time for Iraqi forces to develop, and to help normal life and civil society take root in communities and neighborhoods throughout the country.

"We're helping enhance the size, capabilities, and effectiveness of the Iraqi security forces so the Iraqis can take over the defense of their own country," he continued. "We're helping the Iraqis take back their neighborhoods from the extremists . . ."

This was the fourth version of war.

Kauzlarich watched as he ate. "I like this president," he said.

6

JULY 23, 2007

I'm optimistic. We'll succeed unless we lose our nerve.

—GEORGE W. BUSH, *July 19, 2007*

Eleven days later, just after midnight, Jay March was gang-tackled by a half dozen other soldiers.

For a moment, it seemed he would get away. He was sitting in a dreary, smoke-filled hookah bar called Joe's that was located on a quiet part of the FOB. Two soldiers grabbed him, but he shook them off and tried to run. Then all six jumped on him and down he went, banging against a table and landing on his back. The table tipped. Chairs fell. A hookah pipe that a few soldiers had been smoking toppled as did several cans of the drink of choice in this alcohol-free place, a high-energy drink called Boom Boom. March tried to protect himself, but he was quickly overwhelmed. The other soldiers, all members of his platoon, lifted his shirt and began slapping his stomach, hard enough for the slaps to sound like ricocheting gunshots. He squirmed and yelled and tried to use his elbows, but they pinned his arms. Open-handed, they hit him harder and harder on his stomach until he was scraped raw and bleeding in a few places and his entire midsection was a bright pink. Only then, laughing, did they stop and let him go.

"Happy birthday," one of them said.

"Happy birthday," said another.

"Assholes," March said, getting up, gasping, looking at his stomach, wiping at the blood, but he was laughing as well.

The death of James Harrelson

Twenty-one years old and pink-bellied in Iraq. Jay March couldn't have seemed happier. The other soldiers, too, who now took turns congratulating him.

But their eyes gave them away, every one of them. Even as they laughed, it was clear that something was off. They looked frantic. They looked exhausted. To hear them laugh was to hear that everything was all right, but to see them laugh was to see otherwise.

There had been signs of cracks starting to appear, not just in March's platoon but across the battalion. As bad as June had been, July had brought the worst weeklong stretch yet—forty-two incidents of IEDs, small-arms fire, and rocket attacks—and even though there were no serious injuries, the relentlessness of it was having a measurable effect. The battalion chaplain was seeing an increasing number of soldiers who would knock on his door late at night for discreet counseling, including two who were talking about suicide. The FOB's mental health counselors were writing an increasing number of prescriptions for sleep aids and antidepressants—not in alarming numbers, they assured Kauzlarich, but worth tracking. Rumors of rule-breaking were on the increase, too, and so a "health-and-welfare" inspection was held that turned up all kinds of things that good soldiers weren't allowed to have: packages of steroids manufactured in Iran, a stack of Iraqi currency that might have been taken during a search of an Iraqi's house, a couple of Iraqi cell phones, a "Vibrating Showgirl Slut" inflatable sex doll, and a boxful of hardcore porn, including a magazine that had been disguised with a glued-on cover of a *Martha Stewart Living* magazine and a DVD that a soldier had helpfully entitled in black marker: PORN.

"We got some stupid fuckers," Kauzlarich said after the inflatable doll had been tossed into a burn barrel and set on fire, which created a thick column of oily black smoke that rose over the center of the FOB.

"We got what we got," Cummings said—and what he and Kauzlarich were wondering was whether these first cracks were just the effects of war, or also the effects of an army forced to take more and more stupid fuckers.

It was something they had been dealing with since they began forming the battalion. For several years, in order to meet recruiting goals, the army had been accepting an ever-increasing number of recruits who needed some kind of waiver in order to become soldiers. Without the waivers, those recruits would not have been allowed into the army. Some of the waivers were for medical problems and others were for low scores on aptitude tests, but the greatest percentage were for criminal offenses ranging from misdemeanor drug use to felonies such as burglary, theft, aggravated assault, and even a few cases of involuntary manslaughter. In 2006, the year the 2-16 was getting most of its soldiers, 15 percent of the army's recruits were given criminal waivers. Most were for misdemeanors, but nearly a thousand were for some type of felony conviction, which was more than double the number granted just three years before.

This was the "we got what we got" army that Kauzlarich got. The result, for the army, was enough soldiers to fight a war, but for Kauzlarich it meant that he spent a lot of time that year weeding out soldiers, such as the one who was arrested for aiming a handgun at a man who turned out to be an undercover police officer. And one who drank too much and couldn't stop crying and talked all the time about all the ways he wished to hurt himself, a level of sadness too destructive for even the army.

Most of the soldiers he got weren't that way. A lot of them were great, some were brilliant, and almost all were unquestionably courageous: Sergeant Gietz, who was being nominated for a Bronze Star Medal with Valor for what he had done in June. Adam Schumann, who had carried Sergeant Emory on his back. The list went on and on. Every company. Every platoon. Every soldier, really, because now, in July, as the explosions kept coming, and coming, the daily act of them jumping into Humvees to go out of the wire and straight into what they knew was waiting for them began to seem the very definition of bravery. "Stupid fuckers," someone watching them might think, but it was in a prayerful, lump-in-the-throat way. "Here we go," Kauzlarich, who had now been in three near-misses with EFPs, would say, and there they would go, without hesitation, protecting their hands, lining up their feet, and keeping private their fears, sometimes by listening in silence to the soothing clangs that came from deep inside the frames of the Humvees that sounded like drowsy cow bells, and other times by playing a game of what they wanted their last words to be.

"Kill 'em all."

"Fuck Nine-eleven."

"Tell my wife I really didn't love her."

They were vulgar. They were macho. ("At no time did he scream. Strong kid." was the compliment given a soldier who was severely hurt by an EFP.) They were funny. (A conversation between two sergeants: "No matter where you are, kids are kids." "Kids are the future." "But I saw a video this morning on the news of a kid, thirteen or fourteen years old, maybe here or in Afghanistan, about to cut off a guy's head with a knife. What was that kid thinking?" "Probably thinking about cutting that guy's head off.") With only a few exceptions, Kauzlarich was enormously proud of the battalion they had become, but what had been essential was his getting rid of roughly 10 percent of them before they deployed. They were the 10 percent he never should have gotten in the first place, a percentage that could have been higher except for his penchant for second chances. The knucklehead who got in a fistfight at Fort Riley because he kept eating the French fries of someone who kept warning him, "Don't eat my French fries"? He got a second chance and turned out to be a good soldier. The goofball who spilled gasoline on his boots and decided the best way to clean them was to light the gasoline on fire and ended up with leg burns because he didn't think to take the boots off? He got a second chance, too, as did a soldier who was arrested for driving under the influence as he tried to drive onto Fort Riley, and then insisted to his sergeant that someone else had been at the wheel and the guards at the gate were lying. "Hey, Craig, you know there's a video camera there, right?" his sergeant had said, and so Andre Craig, Jr., backed down and took responsibility and got to go to Iraq, where on June 25 he was killed by an EFP.

Another second-chancer: a soldier they called Private Teflon because he was always in the vicinity of bad things, from fights to a rumored drive-by shooting, but was never implicated. So he got to go to Iraq, too, and when his friend Cameron Payne was killed, he delivered a eulogy so overflowing with hurt it was like listening to the exact moment of someone being transformed by heartbreak. Which of course is what wars did, in every way imaginable, bad and good. Kauzlarich knew this from having been around soldiers for twenty years, and now that he was in charge, he wanted to make sure that his soldiers, even the few stupid ones, especially those stupid ones, maintained control. He could imagine what some of them were saying: "We're in battle everyday, and they're doing a health-and-welfare? It's bullshit." And he agreed. "But we gotta do it right," he said. So when word came one day that some soldiers had ransacked a house during a clearance operation, he did two things. He launched a formal investigation, because as he told his command staff, livid, "There's no reason to ratfuck anybody's house in a search. We've got to show respect to the Iraqi people." And he called a meeting with his company commanders and first sergeants to remind them of the God-given moment they and their soldiers were lucky enough to be in.

"You guys are living the dream right now. You truly are living the dream," he said in the slow, precise diction he used when he was all about persuasion. "Talk to your people about that. Make sure they understand why we do what we do."

It was classic Kauzlarich, full of belief, the Fort Riley speech all over again. But more and more of them weren't understanding.

"Sometimes I wonder what type of world the chain of command is living in. To think we're winning?" Gietz said one day.

"None of the kids believe in this anymore," he went on. "The kids are hurting. The kids are scared. They don't need the bravado. They need understanding. They need someone to tell them, 'I'm scared, too.'"

The Lost Kauz. That was what soldiers in one platoon had begun to call Kauzlarich, in need most of all of a target for their growing anger.

President Bush. That was what soldiers in another platoon, this one in Bravo Company, were calling him because of his ability to see what they couldn't, and to not see what they could.

The platoon had been Andre Craig's platoon. Now, on September 17, it was headed south along the baking dirt of Outer Berm Road, moving from Kamaliyah to the FOB, when the second Humvee in the convoy passed over three buried 130-millimeter projectiles that were wired to a handheld trigger. This time the explosion was thunderous. The Humvee shot straight up in the air—it must have been ten feet, soldiers would say later—and when it came down, it bounced and then exploded into flames.

Immediately, Jay March and other soldiers ran toward the Humvee and began dragging injured soldiers away.

Now they watched helplessly as the driver, nineteen-year-old James Harrelson, burned to death in front of their eyes.

Now they were in the tall, green grass on the side of the berm, tending to the snapped bones and hemorrhaging wounds of the four soldiers they had been able to get to.

Now, at the Rustamiyah aid station, medics ran toward the first arriving Humvee and the howls of a soldier in pain.

Now, inside the aid station, a soldier who had been unconscious was screaming, and a second soldier was moaning, and a third soldier was swearing and apologizing as a doctor filled him with morphine.

Now the fourth soldier was asking, "What happened to Harrelson?" and waiting with begging eyes for the answer.

And now the remnants of the platoon were gulping down sleeping pills with their Boom Booms. Nearly a week after James Harrelson's death, they were not yet under control.

At Joe's, soldiers drank Boom Booms and Mountain Dews, rented hookahs, smoked cigarettes, dipped tobacco, and played cards. There was another, nicer place to go to on the FOB that was run by Army Morale, Welfare, and Recreation, but it could feel a little too clean, like a supervised rec room, and for a soldier who was feeling poorly, nothing was more suitable than Joe's. On the night before Jay March's birthday, most of Harrelson's platoon was here.

This was their fifth day straight as they waited for Harrelson's memorial service. They never came during daylight, only after dark, dinner done, the long night just beginning. As bleak as it was, with its bare-bulb lighting and dirty Christmas wreath hanging cockeyed on a wall, Joe's did have the benefit of a big-screen TV whose volume was always cranked up. There had been so many rocket attacks lately that some soldiers were getting jumpy as they moved around the FOB, always listening for the high-pitched, cartoonish whistle of a rocket on its descent. Inside Joe's, though, you couldn't hear whistles, warning horns, or even impacts unless they were close enough to shake the walls, so you were spared that particular anxiety. All you could hear were soldiers talking loudly over whatever was on TV, which at the moment, as the soldiers arrived and settled in, was a country music video for a song called "What Hurts the Most." "Do you ever think about the future?" a young woman in the video, beautiful and wholesome and about the right age to be a soldier's girlfriend, was asking a young man. "What do you see?" she asked, and meanwhile Jay March, who could see James Harrelson on fire, shuffled a deck of cards and dealt a hand of spades.

Harrelson had been in the second Humvee and March had been right behind him in the third. All of the other soldiers had been in the convoy, too, except for Phillip Mays, Jr., a thirty-year-old platoon sergeant, who had stayed back that day because of a broken hand and was here at Joe's at a separate table, trying to read a book. The soldiers loved Mays, who was all jaw and muscles and newly formed circles under his eyes. They were absolutely loyal to him, and in return, he was so devoted to them that for weeks he'd fought alongside them without mentioning that he'd hurt his hand during a middle-of-the-night raid when he'd chased two suspicious Iraqis into a stable. Describing it now, he said he should have known something was going to go wrong when he went through the doors and straight into the rear ends of two camels, but the fact was that such things were always happening here. It was like what Kauzlarich had said after another platoon had chased someone into a house at 4:00 a.m. and found an entire family not only awake but sitting in a circle around a little cow: "Expect the unexpected." Or after another platoon had chased someone into the courtyard of a house and discovered a mentally retarded child tethered to a pole. "The normal abnormal," Brent Cummings called it. So Mays pushed the unexpected camels out of the way by their unexpected rear ends and grabbed one of the Iraqis by his shirt, and when he went after Mays's M-4 and got hold of it, Mays started hitting him with his left hand. "I knew it was hard, because I had blood on me," he said. "He still wouldn't let go of the weapon. That's when I transitioned to my right hand and knocked him out, breaking my hand in the process." He didn't expect that, either, and when he realized what the crunching sound was, he told no one, because it would have meant a cast and he'd be out of the fight and there was no way he was going to let that happen, not after waiting so long to get here. "I wanted this my whole life, since I was a little boy," he explained. "Not to be a warmonger, necessarily, but to be in the army, serving my country." So he took aspirin and stayed in the fight, and that's how tough and devoted Mays was—and how uncharacteristic it was that he had spent much of this day in his room, behind a closed door with a sign on it saying that he didn't want to be disturbed.

What he wanted was to sleep. Since Harrelson, however, he'd hardly slept at all. "Too much in my head," he had said earlier, sitting on his bed, behind that closed door, before coming to Joe's. He'd been given a sleep aid called Ambien, with instructions to try one and take it from there, and when one didn't work he'd tried two, and when two didn't work he'd tried four. But four wasn't enough, either, and meanwhile, on the other side of the room, his roommate was rearranging his furniture yet again, which he had been doing somewhat obsessively for several days.

This was the officer in charge of the platoon, Lieutenant Ryan Hamel, twenty-four, for whom all of the decisions yet to come in his life would be shaded by the decision he made to travel down Outer Berm Road. "I made the call" is how he put it in his sworn statement. He was in the Humvee directly behind Harrelson's. He saw it rise, saw it fall, saw the flames, saw Harrelson inside of them, might have heard a scream, might not have, and now was wondering if he'd be able to sleep better if his bed were over here rather than over there, and his shelves were over there rather than over here.

"Truck went up. Smoke and fire," he said, shaking his head, neatly summing up a day.

"Nineteen years old," Mays said, summing up a life, and meanwhile, in another room just down the hall, the platoon's medic, twenty-three-year-old Michael Bailey, who couldn't save Harrelson, and couldn't save Craig, was saying that instead of sleeping, he now spent his nights looping aimlessly through the dark parts of the FOB. He said of Craig, "I basically held on to him as he died." He said of Harrelson's reaction to Craig, "He saw it, and he was scared. It scared the shit out of him." He said of the platoon's reaction, "It scared the shit out of everyone. And this"—meaning Harrelson's death—"has scared everyone, too. Me, every time I go out on patrol, I feel sick. It's like, I'm gonna get hit, I'm gonna get hit, I'm gonna get hit . . ."

And meanwhile, in another room, Jay March was listening to another soldier, Staff Sergeant Jack Wheeler, describe what the two of them had done after they had seen Harrelson die and Wheeler had noticed a thin wire coming off the top of the berm.

The wire was red, and of all the colors to remember from that day, Wheeler would easily remember that, because of the obscene way it suddenly stood out against the brown of the dirt and the tree trunks, and the green of the grass and the leaves. In what had been a two-color world at that point, before it was joined by the orange of the fire, how could he not have spotted a red wire? How could no one have seen something that now, as Wheeler followed it with his eyes, seemed so conspicuous? It emerged from under the dirt on top of the berm and led toward a grove of palm trees, passing in the air like a tightrope above where the bleeding soldiers lay. "I got the wire!" he shouted, taking off with some soldiers to track it, and when March saw them, he took off, too. They followed it to a tree that stood slightly apart from the others, probably the aiming point, around whose trunk it had been wrapped. From there, it stretched tautly to another tree, and then ran for a while along the ground to a house amid a cluster of houses beyond the palm grove, far enough from the Humvee that the exploding ammunition sounded like nothing more than distant firecrackers.

Now, out of the house that the wire led to, came three men who saw the approaching soldiers and broke into a run, going in different directions. Wheeler, March, and two other soldiers ran after two of the men, who had cut across a street toward a row of four houses. Wheeler kicked open the door of the first house and found himself face-to-face with an elderly, terrified man who motioned down a hallway. Weapons shouldered, the soldiers moved toward the first room, where, in a corner, they found six women and children huddled together and crying. The normal abnormal. They moved down the hallway to a second room, in which they found a man who was on his knees, as if praying. Expect the unexpected. He was perhaps five feet away. He swiveled toward them with an AK-47 in his hands. "I shot him three times," Wheeler said, as March listened in silence, looking away for a moment. The man toppled forward, dead, with two holes in his stomach and one in his head, Wheeler continued, and from there they moved to the house next door, and then to the next house, and then to the next house, where Wheeler found and killed the second man, and now, almost a week later, after shooting two people within spattering distance and seeing a friend die, he wasn't sleeping well, either.

"I start thinking about what happened, and then I start thinking about why I'm here," he said. "It's pointless. They say on TV that the soldiers want to be here? I can't speak for every soldier, but I think if people went around and made a list of names of who fucking thinks we should actually be here and who wants to be here, ain't nobody that wants to be here. There ain't probably one soldier in this fucking country, unless you are higher up and you're trying to get your star or you're trying to make some rank or a name for yourself—but there ain't nobody that wants to be here, because there's no point. What are we getting out of fucking being here? Nothing." He paused for a moment, and then said, "Man, if I could just do it all over again. If I had taken a different route. What if we had left earlier? What if we had left later?"

And Jay March continued to listen.

Now, at Joe's, Sergeant Mays put down his book and watched some of his soldiers play spades. "Solid guy," he said of one of them. "Lazy," he said of another. "Tough," he said of another. He looked at March, a favorite of his. "March is from a fragile background," he said, without elaborating. "They're angry. Very angry," he said of the platoon, which of course included himself. "How can anybody kill and function normally afterward? Or see someone get killed and function normally afterward? It's not the human response."

Eleven o'clock now. Bailey, the medic, was talking about holding Craig. "Every time he exhaled, there'd be blood all over the back of the driver's seat," he was saying.

Midnight. March got his vicious pink belly. It was the first one the platoon had given since a month before, when James Harrelson had turned nineteen.

One a.m. and beyond. The horn went off. A rocket whistled overhead. Wheeler dealt. March looked at his cards. Everyone was wide awake. The video came back on the TV. "What do you see?" the girl said to the boy. "What do *you* see?" the boy said back to the girl.

The following morning, after going to sleep at sunrise and waking up two hours later, March was sitting outside bleary-eyed when the crack of gunfire came from the direction of the chapel. *Bang* . . . pause . . . *bang* . . . pause . . . *bang*. By now, everyone on the FOB knew the sobering rhythm of a rifle squad practicing for a memorial service, and when the echoes of the first volley slapped off the buildings and blast walls surrounding him, March barely reacted. Maybe it was because of exhaustion, or maybe he was too lost in thought. He had been the first to reach Harrelson and realize there was nothing to be done, and six days later his eyes were as red as the raw parts of his stomach. He lit a cigarette. "In Alabama, you gotta be nineteen to buy cigarettes," he said, repeating what Harrelson, who was from rural Alabama, had once told him.

This was one of the hottest days yet. Midmorning, it was already well above one hundred degrees, but March was outside because he wanted to talk about what had happened when he and Wheeler were in that first house, and he wanted to do it in a place where Wheeler and the others couldn't hear. There was no doubt in anyone's mind about the guilt or innocence of the man who'd been killed. There'd been a wire. The wire had led to the man. The man had been turning toward them with an AK-47. Still, on his twenty-first birthday, March sat under a tree, from which hung a sweet-smelling sack of poison filled with dead flies, and sighed. "I also engaged the guy," he said. "Sergeant Wheeler shot him in the stomach, twice, and as he was falling, I shot him in the head."

That was what really happened, he said, and the reason he hadn't said anything the day before was that afterward, when he had run back to the rest of the platoon and another soldier said, "You all right?" and he said, "I got one," and the soldier said, "Good job, drink this water," and he drank the water thinking over and over, *'You've just killed someone, You've just killed someone,'* he'd realized he didn't want any soldiers asking him how it felt to kill another human being. So he'd asked Wheeler and the others who'd been in the house not to spread it around, and Wheeler especially understood because he'd been to Iraq before and had gotten the question and knew what it was like, and that was why Wheeler had done all the talking, out of kindness. For five days, March just hadn't wanted to talk about it, he said, not to anyone. He wasn't sure why, just as he wasn't sure why now, on the sixth day, he did want to talk about it. But he did want to, he said, and after months of EFPs, IEDs, RPGs, snipers, rockets, mortars, watching Craig dying, watching the Iraqi rubbing his fingers together, and watching Harrelson's Humvee flying into the air, there was no swagger in his voice whatsoever.

He described seeing Harrelson: "All you could see, you could see his Kevlar and his body figure and his head against the radio mount, and his whole body was engulfed in flames. I just remember seeing the outline of the Kevlar and his face on fire."

He described running through the palm groves and seeing the men coming out of the house and firing at them: "I was firing on the run. You could see my rounds hitting by them, but they weren't hitting them. It was just so weird. I was thinking to myself as I ran up to the house, *'How did I not hit them?'*"

He described going into the house: "We hit the door, and we entered the room, and there's a bunch of females and little kids in a corner, all holding each other, and I looked at them, and Sergeant Wheeler said in plain English, 'Where the fuck is he?' And the guy pointed to a back room. You could see the door, and it looked like it was open, like somebody had run in, and we went down the hallway, and it was like an open space, and the only thing in there was a fridge, a big fridge in a corner. And we came in, and the guy hopped up, and he had an AK."

He described the three shots: "Sergeant Wheeler shot him in the stomach, and he went like this"—he stood and sagged—"and he was coming down, and as his head went like this"—he tucked his chin into his chest—"I shot him. It went in the top. As soon as I pulled the trigger, I immediately saw the hole, and he went from a slow fall to an immediate limp body."

Finally, he described what happened next: "And I heard a scream. And I was thinking, 'Is the other guy behind the fridge?' Because I thought I saw something move. And I turned, and behind the fridge there's this eight-year-old girl and her mother, just sitting. She's hugging the daughter, behind the fridge. And I looked at her, and the guy's head is bleeding, and I stepped in his blood to see—it was the only way—I stepped and I looked, and I seen the little girl, and the little girl immediately saw me, and she just started bawling. And her mom grabbed her, you know, like *please don't kill us*. And it hit me, like, wow, an eight-year-old girl just saw me shoot this guy. And they don't even know him. It's their house, they're just sitting here one day, and an IED blew up, and somebody got killed in their house, and the fright on their face, like I was gonna murder them, was just so shocking to me. Because they're supposed to *want* us there." Another sigh. "And it was like an eight-year-old girl and her mom."

He fell silent. *Bang*, pause, *bang*, pause, *bang*. The memorial service was supposed to start in eight hours. March had a lot to do before then. He needed to clean his weapon. He needed to straighten his room. He needed to sleep. But he continued to sit.

Here's something about Harrelson, he said now: he had so much confidence in himself he didn't need to be drunk to get out on a dance floor. He didn't drink at all. He was happy to be the designated driver. Something else: he'd come back from leave talking seriously about a girl who'd been a friend in high school. And something else: so far, for whatever reason, he himself hadn't cried about Harrelson, as he'd done with Craig. With Craig, he said, as soon as Lieutenant Hamel told him, he'd started crying right away. The platoon had been out fighting for several days. His body armor was soaked in sweat and dotted with bits of Craig's blood, and he cried as he walked away from Hamel and took off his armor and lay down against it and woke up a few hours later with the sinking feeling a person gets when he realizes that nothing changed while he was asleep, that all of it is still true.

"It's just, I was twenty years old and I'd never seen anything like that," he said. "I saw him fall from the turret. I seen his eyes roll back in his head. And it sounds weird, and I don't like telling people this, but the reason I joined the army is because I've always looked up to soldiers."

The soldier he might have looked up to most of all, he said, was one named Phillip Cantu, who had recruited him into the army. He was nineteen at that point and at the tail end of a terrible childhood in a dysfunctional family. This was not an uncommon story in the battalion; one soldier, whose entire family was in prison, said that his brother told him in all sincerity just before he deployed, "I hope you get killed." In March's case, he was out of options after high school and wandered one day into the recruiting office in Sandusky, Ohio, where he talked to a recruiter who seemed so old and so sour that March got up and left. A few months later, still out of options, he went in again, and the sour recruiter had been replaced by Cantu, who was twenty-three and recently back from Iraq. They talked that day about all of the options the Army offered, and as March for the first time saw possibilities in his life, he began stopping in several times a week. Each visit left him more inspired, and over time he and Cantu grew increasingly closer. "You're not supposed to be friends with your recruiter," he said, "but we were friends." They started grabbing meals together and hanging out a bit, and once, when he dropped by Cantu's apartment, Cantu showed him photographs of the day he was outside the spider hole where Special Ops soldiers had just captured Saddam Hussein. It turned out that Cantu had been there, not in the hole, but close to its edge, as Saddam was pulled out, and it had been documented in a hometown newspaper article headlined SANDUSKIAN HELPED BAG SADDAM, in which Cantu's wife said, "Our great-grandkids are going to get to hear about how he captured Saddam," and his mother said she had telephoned so many people that "my ear was starting to hurt," and his sister said, "I am just so proud; I am a really proud sister." "He told me there's nothing like the brotherhood when you deploy," March said, and that was it. For a nineteen-year-old from a family of dysfunction, his decision was made. He enlisted in the army brotherhood, got through basic training, was assigned to Fort Riley and the 2-16, and had just arrived when his mother called in tears to say that Phillip Cantu was dead. And it was true. He was. The part of the war he hadn't told March about had caught up with him, and once again, he was in the newspaper: "A local man whose military unit in Iraq helped capture Saddam Hussein in December 2003 died Saturday morning. Sgt. Phillip Cantu,

24, killed himself," is how the article began, and thirteen months later, here was March, in Iraq, red-eyed and pink-bellied and unable to sleep because of what he was seeing, day and night, whether his eyes were open or closed. What did *he* see?

"It's photographs," he said.

"Like a picture of Harrelson burning, in flames. I can't get that out of my head right now.

"I see myself shooting the guy. I see a still frame of the guy halfway hitting the ground with the hole in his head.

"I can see the little girl, the face of the little girl. And as much as people say that they don't care about these people and all that, *I* don't care about these people—but I do, at the same time, if that makes any sense. They don't want to help themselves, they're blowing us up, yeah, that hurts, but it also hurts to know that I've seen a girl that's as old as my little brother watch me shoot somebody in the head. And I don't care if she's Iraqi, Korean, African, white—she's still a little girl. And she watched me shoot somebody.

"I see me walking to the truck, just having my head down and my weapon in one hand, not looking around, not pulling security, not think-ing nothing. Just walking to the truck.

"It's like a slide show in my head," he said. "Does that make sense?"

A few days before all of this, at just about the time President Bush was speaking in Nashville at the Gaylord Opryland Resort about his optimism concerning the war, Kauzlarich was interviewed in his office by an army historian who was traveling around Iraq asking commanders about the surge.

"Share with me some things that aren't going well," the historian had said at one point.

"You know we have not been given a problem that we have not been able to come up with a solution for," Kauzlarich had said, and then had tried to make a joke. "The only thing I can bitch about right now is that at times we run out of certain flavors of ice cream."

Now, a few nights later, he and the soldiers he got were crowded into the chapel for the memorial service, which ended with something called the Final Roll Call.

"Sergeant Jubinville," a sergeant called out.

"Here, First Sergeant," Jubinville called back.

"PFC Devine," the sergeant called out.

"Here, First Sergeant," Devine called back.

"PFC Harrelson," the sergeant called out.

The chapel was silent.

"PFC James Harrelson," he called out.

The chapel remained silent.

"PFC James Jacob Harrelson," he called out.

And the silence continued, unbearably, until it was interrupted by the sharp slap of gunfire.

Bang, pause, *bang*, pause, *bang*.

At the Opryland Resort, President Bush had said, "I'm optimistic. We'll succeed unless we lose our nerve."

Here, six versions of what nerve can mean filed out of the chapel.

Mays went back to his Ambien.

Hamel went back to his furniture.

Bailey went back to his loops around the FOB.

Wheeler went back to his what-ifs.

March went back to his slide show.

And Kauzlarich, red-eyed too now, went back to his office.

7

SEPTEMBER 22, 2007

We're kicking ass.

—GEORGE W. BUSH, *September 4, 2007*

On September 22, General David Petraeus, who was a four-star general, the commander of all U.S. forces in Iraq, and the architect of the surge, came to Rustamiyah to visit the 2-16.

"Ooh, that's nice!" Kauzlarich said just before Petraeus's arrival, checking out the second floor of the operations center, which soldiers had spent the morning attempting to clean up. This was where Kauzlarich would brief Petraeus on everything the 2-16 had accomplished. He had never briefed a four-star general before, and he was feeling a little nervous.

There were muffins, cookies, and fresh fruit, all arranged on a table covered with a green hospital bedsheet. "It's brand new," a soldier assured Kauzlarich. "We got it from Supply this morning."

There was an urn of fresh coffee and a bowl of iced drinks, which Kauzlarich noticed didn't contain Diet Coke. "That's all he drinks," he said, always the master of detail, and a soldier hustled off to find Diet Coke.

The long, three-section conference table where Kauzlarich held staff meetings had been broken down and reconfigured into a *U*, and marking Petraeus's spot at the center of it were a new nameplate, a new pen, a new notebook, a jug of water, a jug of juice, and a coffee mug filled with ceremonial American flags.

General David Petraeus and Ralph Kauzlarich

Everything was ready. "There's only so many ways to polish a turd," Cummings said, and with that Kauzlarich went off to meet Petraeus and bring him back to the operations center.

Every once in a while a day in Iraq would feel good. As Kauzlarich approached with Petraeus, this seemed one of those days. The temperature was under one hundred degrees. The sky was a wonderful, dustless blue. The air stank neither of sewage nor of burning trash. The only odor, in fact, was the comparatively pleasant chemical bouquet wafting from some portable latrines near where Petraeus paused to shake hands with a few soldiers who had been selected to meet him and were lined up at attention.

Petraeus and Kauzlarich entered the operations center, which, thanks to the work of a bomb-sniffing dog that had been brought by earlier, had been certified as booby-trap free.

They climbed steps that had been swept clean of the dust that came in through cracks every time there was a close explosion.

They entered the conference room, and Petraeus sat in a high-backed chair that had been wiped down to a shine. Kauzlarich took the chair next to his. Cummings took a chair nearby. Various junior officers filled chairs behind them. All eyes were on Petraeus as he ignored the muffins, cookies, coffee, Diet Cokes, pen, notebook, and flags, and simply reached for a grape.

He popped it into his mouth.

"Okay," he said, swallowing. "Fire away, Ralph."

David Petraeus at that moment was one of the most famous people in the world. He had just returned to Baghdad from a trip to the United States where he had testified before Congress about the surge. All summer long, the anticipation of his testimony had grown to the point of frenzy, and by the time he showed up on Capitol Hill, he had been so written about, analyzed, profiled, and politicized that he was no longer just a general. He had become the very face of the Iraq War, its celebrity and star.

It would be difficult to overstate his fame, just as it would be difficult to overstate how in need Kauzlarich was of this good day. Eighteen days before, on September 4, another perfectly aimed EFP had torn into the

first Humvee of a five-truck convoy on Route Predators, and three soldiers had died—Sergeant Joel Murray, twenty-six; Specialist David Lane,
twenty; and Private Randol Shelton, twenty-two. The other two soldiers
in the Humvee had survived but were in terrible shape, with burns and
multiple amputations, and Kauzlarich, who was in a convoy nearby, had
been seeing images of dying soldiers and body parts since. It was something he didn't talk about openly, because subordinates didn't need to
know such things about their commander. But other commanders would
have understood if he had said it to them, including General Petraeus
himself, who once, in a moment of reflection on a day when the death
count of American troops was nearing 3,800, had said, "The truth is you
never get used to losses. If anything, I almost think sometimes there's
sort of a bad-news vessel, and it's got holes in the bottom, and then it
drains. In other words, you know, it's really your emotions, but I mean
there's so much bad news you can take. And it fills up. But if you have
some good days, it sort of drains away."

So Kauzlarich was in need of some draining away.

Did anyone else understand that, though, other than those in the war?
Because while the news in Rustamiyah on September 4 was all about
three dead soldiers and a fourth who had lost both legs, and a fifth who
had lost both legs and an arm and most of his other arm and been severely
burned over what remained of him, that wasn't the news in the United
States. In the United States, the news was all macro rather than micro. It
was about President Bush arriving in Australia that morning, where the
deputy prime minister asked him how the war was going and he answered, "We're kicking ass." It was about a government report released in
the afternoon that noted the Iraqi government's lack of progress toward
self-sustainability, which Democrats seized on as one more reason to get
out of Iraq pronto, which Republicans seized on as one more reason why
Democrats were unpatriotic, which various pundits seized on as a chance
to go on television and do some screaming.

Sometimes, in the DFAC, the soldiers would listen to the screaming
and wonder how the people on those shows knew so much. Clearly, most
of them had never been to Iraq, and even if they had, it was probably for
what the soldiers dismissively referred to as the windshield tour: cork-

screw in, hear from a general or two, get in a Humvee, see a market surrounded by new blast walls, get a commemorative coin, corkscrew out.
And yet to listen to them was to listen to people who knew everything.
They knew why the surge was working. They knew why the surge wasn't
working. They not only screamed, they screamed with certainty. "They
should come to Rustamiyah," more than one soldier said, certain of only
one thing: that none of them would. No one came to Rustamiyah. But if
they did, they could get in the lead Humvee. They could go out on Route
Predators. They could go out on Berm Road. They could experience the
full pucker. They could experience it the next day, too, and the day after
that—and then maybe they could go back on TV and scream about how
bewildering all of this really was. At least then they would be screaming
the truth.

The soldiers would laugh about this, but after more than half a year
here, one thing they had lost sight of was how different the Iraq War was
in Iraq as opposed to in the United States. To them, it was about specific
acts of bravery and tragedy. The firefight in Fedaliyah—that was the war.
Three dead inside a fireball on Predators—what else could a war be?

But in the United States, where three dead on Predators might be
mentioned briefly somewhere inside the daily paper under a heading
such as FALLEN HEROES or IN OTHER NEWS, and the firefight in Fedaliyah wouldn't be mentioned at all, it was about things more strategic,
more political, more policy-driven, more useful in broad ways. Three dead?
Yes, damn, how sad, and God bless the troops, and God bless the families,
too, and this is exactly why we need to get out of Iraq, to honor the sac-
rifice, and this is precisely why we need to stay in Iraq, to honor the sacri-
fice, but you know what? Have you seen the numbers? Have you seen the
metrics? Have you seen the trend lines?

"We're kicking ass," said President Bush.

". . . it is unclear whether violence has been reduced," said the GAO
report.

A third assessment: "One boom and an entire fire team was gone"
was what Kauzlarich said that very same day, but six days later, as Petraeus made his first appearance on Capitol Hill, Kauzlarich's was the one
that mattered least of all to what was about to happen. It was footnote

material. Soldiers such as Kauzlarich might be able to talk about the war as it was playing out in Iraq, but after crossing the Atlantic Ocean from one version of the war to the other, Petraeus had gone to Washington to testify about the war as it was playing out in Washington.

It was a distinction that Petraeus was well aware of. A West Pointer with a doctorate in international relations from Princeton University, he had ascended to the top ranks of the army on the strength of his intellect, and on his political skills as well. He knew how to analyze and prepare for just about any situation, and if he had any illusions about the political nature of this one, they were taken care of when he awakened on the morning of his first day of testimony to a full-page ad in *The New York Times* headlined GENERAL PETRAEUS OR GENERAL BETRAY US? The ad was taken out by a left-leaning political organization called MoveOn.org. It accused Petraeus of "cooking the books for the White House," and went on to assert that "Every independent report on the ground situation in Iraq shows that the surge strategy has failed."

And that was just the beginning. A few hours later, when Petraeus entered a U.S. House of Representatives hearing room, the scene was of Washington at its most starstruck. Could there have been more photographers surrounding someone walking into a congressional hearing? And when in this war had so many members of Congress shown up for a hearing? Typically a handful might make a brief appearance; for this—a joint hearing involving two committees—there were 112, each of whom would get five minutes to question Petraeus and Ryan C. Crocker, the U.S. ambassador to Iraq. If everyone took his full five minutes, that was nine hours right there, and it didn't include bathroom breaks and delays for protests, the first of which came right away, from several women who had waited in line since dawn for some of the twenty-three seats allotted to the public, all so they could immediately stand up and yell, "War criminal," and get hauled off by the police.

"Out they go!" the Missouri Democrat who was running the hearing, Representative Ike Skelton, bellowed. "No disturbances will be tolerated." And it went on from there, into opening statements, in which the chairman said to Petraeus, and live TV cameras, and that night's newscasts, and the next morning's newspapers: "In a poll of Iraqis released this

morning, sponsored by ABC News, the BBC, and the Japanese broad-
caster NHK, we learned that at least 65 percent of Iraqis say the surge is
not working and 72 percent say the U.S. presence is making Iraqi security worse. This is troublesome . . . I hope, General Petraeus, and I hope,
Ambassador Crocker, that you can persuade us that there is a substantial
reason to believe that Iraq will turn around in the near future."

He talked for a while, and then another Democrat talked for a while
("We need to get out of Iraq, for that country's sake and for our own. It
is time to go—and to go now"), and then a Republican talked for a while
(". . . and the idea that this Congress is going to arbitrarily overlay a requirement for a reduction in America's forces when we are moving
toward a maturing of the Iraqi forces and a successful hand-off, which
will be a victory for the United States, I think should not be supported by
this body"), and then another Republican talked for a while ("I am dis-
tressed by the accusations leveled by some in the media and by some
members of Congress during hearings like these, calling into question
the integrity of our military, accusing the military of cherry-picking positive numbers to reflect a dramatic decline in sectarian violence"), and
forty-five minutes into the hearing, Petraeus still hadn't said a word.

Not that his testimony was going to be a surprise. There'd been hints
and leaks for weeks that he would say the early signs were good, but that
more time, and money, were needed. As he had written in a letter to the
troops that had been leaked three days before, "We are, in short, a long
way from the goal line, but we do have the ball and we are driving down
the field." He was going to be specific. He was going to be pragmatic. He
was going to use graphs and charts about attack trends, and none of them
would be depicting his bad-news vessel, not on this day. Washington
wasn't that kind of crowd.

Still, when the committee chairman announced, "General David Petraeus, the floor is yours," there was so much anticipation in the room
that even the remaining protesters in their GENERALS LIE, SOLDIERS DIE
T-shirts were absolutely silent in their seats.

Petraeus began speaking. But there was a problem. His mouth was
moving, but no one could hear what he was saying.

"We will have to ask you to stand a bit closer to the microphone, because the acoustics in here are not—well, not good at all," the committee chairman said.

Petraeus moved closer to the microphone and began again.

Again, nothing.

"Would somebody please fix the microphone?" the chairman said.

Hours later, the microphone fixed, the sun setting, the last of the protesters hauled away, the questioners pretty much repeating questions and Petraeus wearily repeating answers and gobbling down Motrins on breaks, because sitting still and straight for so long had become painful, the hearing came to an end.

The next day, though, on September 11, after a moment of silence for the victims of the attacks on the World Trade Center and the Pentagon, Petraeus was at it again, this time before the Senate. There were two hearings that day, and the buzz was about how the various senators who had announced they were running for president would do when their turn came to question Petraeus. Would Hillary Clinton use the occasion to explain why she had initially been in favor of the war? Would Barack Obama use it to remind people he'd been adamantly against it? What about Joe Biden, what would he say? And what about John McCain?

Such were the interests in Washington this day about the war. They were political interests. And yet every so often the war as the 2-16 saw it would make an appearance.

"Let's just put on the table as honestly as we can what lies ahead for the American people and U.S. military if we continue to stay in Iraq," Lindsey Graham, a Republican senator from South Carolina who had been one of the most consistent supporters of the surge, said to Petraeus at one point. "Now, I know you're not—you can't predict with certainty the numbers we're going to have, but can you agree with this statement, General Petraeus, 'It's highly likely that a year from now we're going to have at least 100,000 troops in Iraq'?"

"That is probably the case, yes, sir," Petraeus said.

"Okay," Graham said. "How many people have we been losing a month, on average, since the surge began, in terms of killed in action?"

"Killed in action is probably in the neighborhood of sixty to ninety,"

Petraeus said. "Probably on average, eighty to ninety, average, killed in action. That does not include the nineteen soldiers, for example, tragically killed last month in that helicopter crash."

"But here's what lies ahead for the American military," Graham said. "If we stay in Iraq and continue to support the surge through July, we're going to lose somewhere in the neighborhood of sixty military members, most likely hundreds more."

"Yes, sir," Petraeus said.

"We're spending $9 billion a month to stay in Iraq, of U.S. dollars," Graham continued. "My question for you: Is it worth it to us?"

"Well, the national interests that we have in Iraq are substantial," Petraeus said. "An Iraq that is stable and secure, that is not an al Qaeda sanctuary, is not in the grip of Iranian-supported Shi'a militia, that is not a bigger humanitarian disaster, that is connected to the global economy, all of these are very important national interests."

"Would that be a 'yes'?" Graham said.

"Yes, sir. Sorry," Petraeus said.

"So you're saying to the Congress that you know that at least sixty soldiers, airmen, and Marines are likely to be killed every month from now to July, that we're going to spend $9 billion a month of American taxpayer dollars, and when it's all said and done we'll still have 100,000 people there, and you believe it's worth it in terms of our national security interests to pay that price?"

"Sir, I wouldn't be here, and I wouldn't have made the recommendations that I have made, if I did not believe that," Petraeus said.

"Don't you think most soldiers who are there understand what lies ahead for them, too?" Graham asked.

"Sir, I believe that's the case," Petraeus replied.

In Iraq, those soldiers had been watching as much of the testimony as they could, especially in the beginning. It was evening in Rustamiyah when the first hearing began, and so they watched for a while on the TVs scattered around the DFAC, and then continued to watch in the operations center, where there were two mounted TVs. One showed video feeds from surveillance cameras around eastern Baghdad. That was the one they had begun calling "Kill TV." The other showed news feeds from various American news networks, and that was the one they watched until well past midnight.

It was a standing-room-only crowd with a typical chattering-crowd dynamic, especially a crowd of young male soldiers. They marveled that protesters had gotten into the hearing room, which led to some back-and-forth about the limits of free speech. They paid particular attention whenever a woman was shown, which led to discussions about whether she was someone with whom they would consent to have sex. The consensus in most cases was that of course they would. The consensus about the MoveOn.org ad—"General Petraeus or General Betray Us"—was that it was "catchy." They thought that Petraeus spoke well and had prepared well, and they listened intently, at least at first, to what he was saying.

Would he say "winning"? Would he say "done"? Would he say "over"? Would he mention "East Baghdad" or "New Baghdad" or "Kamaliyah" or "Fedaliyah," or that anyone who doubts the greatness of American soldiers should know about a battalion called the 2-16 Rangers?

But of course he wouldn't say that because, like everyone in the hearing room, he had never been to Rustamiyah. No one came here. No member of Congress had ever come. Only a couple of journalists had come, which was a couple more than the number of Washington think-tank scholars who in some cases were already declaring the surge a success after quick windshield tours through other parts of Iraq. Even the USO celebrities who were always coming in and out of Baghdad tended to avoid the place. One time three professional golfers showed up whom no one had heard of. Another time, in came some cheerleaders from a professional football team, who later wrote on their website: "Today we stopped at two bases that really don't get to see anyone, Falcon and Rustamiyah. We went to Falcon first for a meet and greet and after that we had a really fun and crazy helicopter ride to Rustamiyah. Rustamiyah has a high threat level, we were a little scared but we were very safe and nothing happened." Another time it was a country music singer who went by the name "The Singing Cowboy." "Would you like to meet The Singing Cowboy?" a Public Affairs officer asked a group of soldiers who were outside watching a reenlistment ceremony, and when they looked at him in confusion, he pointed to a lone figure standing at a distance, coated in Rustamiyah dust.

The dust, the fear, the high threat level, the isolation—all of that was the surge the soldiers knew, and the more they took in of the hearing, the more surreal it became to them. "Those people have no idea how bad it is here," Cummings thought to himself at one point. There, the war was a point of discussion. Here, the war was the war. There, the sound of a gavel echoed off high walls, a vaulted ceiling, Corinthian pilasters, four chandeliers, and a full entablature. Here, Cummings had another thought: "This place is a complete shithole."

Maybe it was natural, then, that as the discussion continued in Washington, the soldiers paid less and less attention. On the second day of Petraeus's testimony, when Lindsey Graham was saying, "Don't you think most soldiers who are there understand what lies ahead for them," Kill TV was back in action, and by the end of the week they were getting their news in snippets from the TVs in the DFAC, where Kauzlarich and Cummings watched images of thousands of people gathering in Washington for an antiwar protest.

"A lot of people there," they agreed, and then dug into their food as the protesters continued to gather in a seven-acre park directly across from the White House. The protesters' plan was for a rally, followed by a march along Pennsylvania Avenue from the White House to the Capitol, followed by a culminating event at the Capitol called a "die-in." "Whatever," some of the soldiers said about that, but the protesters were taking it far more seriously.

On a website promoting the protest, for instance, the die-in was described as "a civil disobedience action that will involve at least 4,000 people who are able to risk arrest." It also said, "Please read this important note. If you are participating in the Die-In/Funeral and feel compelled to select the name of one of the almost 4,000 soldiers who have been killed in Iraq, you are encouraged to do so. You can select a family member, friend or someone from your city, town or state. Please bring a photograph of that person and a sign with his/her name on September 15 . . . Click here for a list of U.S. soldiers."

Those who clicked were taken to a list of the dead, which included Joel Murray, David Lane, and Randol Shelton, who, on the day before the protest, had been memorialized in the Rustamiyah chapel. "May they rest in peace as their memories shall live on forever," Kauzlarich had said in his eulogy, just before the *bang*, pause, *bang*, pause, *bang*. "This is who I will lie down for," was the next option on the website, and that was followed by a box in which to type someone's name and reserve that person for the die-in.

Hundreds of people did this, and tens of thousands more showed up for the rally. With public opinion polls saying that 65 percent of Americans thought Bush was mishandling the war, 62 percent thought the war was not worth fighting, and 58 percent thought the surge had made no difference, organizers were hoping for a turnout on the scale of the very biggest protests of the Vietnam War.

This wasn't that, but there were enough people to fill much of a seven-acre park on a perfect late-summer day. Butterflies were out. So were late-summer honeybees. Ralph Nader—he was one of the featured speakers, talking and talking away as usual, but into a microphone so dead that people in the crowd were yelling politely, "We can't hear you, Mr. Nader." Ramsey Clark, the former U.S. attorney general who'd been one of Saddam's defense lawyers, was there, as were representatives of organizations such as Iraq Veterans Against the War, Hip Hop Caucus, and Code Pink, as was the ubiquitous, eternally sad, always sleepless Cindy Sheehan, who talked about her dead son, Casey. "It's time for us to stand up and lay down," she exhorted. "It's time for us to lay down for peace, but it's also time for us to lay down for accountability." Many in the crowd held signs that read, IMPEACH BUSH, and many held signs that read, END THE WAR NOW, and most seemed to realize that wasn't going to happen anytime soon, but here they were anyway, trying to make it happen by cheering for Cindy Sheehan, who stood in front of a perfectly positioned American flag that was being displayed upside down and who paused now to look out into the sloppy, sprawling sea of what the American peace movement had become.

The drummers were out there.

The guy with the American flag headband tied across his mouth was out there.

The guy in the "Save Darfur" cap was out there.

The guy in the Gandhi T-shirt was out there.

The guy handing out a newsletter called "Proletarian Revolution" was out there, talking to a young woman with the word PEACE painted across her forehead like a rainbow, assuring her that this wasn't a waste of time, that people everywhere were "going to see this demonstration and know not everybody agrees with Bush."

"They'll see it?" the woman said.

"They *will* see it," the man promised. "On TV. On the Internet. All over the world, people will see it."

At Rustamiyah, though, dinner was over, and so the soldiers got up and emptied their trays and went on their way, missing the Iraq War veteran who at some point had been just like them and now stood at a microphone in Washington, D.C.

"March with us. Honor the dead with us," he implored, trying to get enough people to represent every one of the 3,800 dead, including Cajimat, Gajdos, Payne, Craig, Crow, Harrelson, Murray, Lane, and Shelton, and then he gave instructions on what to do at the Capitol: "Die when you hear the air raid siren."

In Rustamiyah, the evening patrols were headed out now. In Washington, the time to die was almost at hand. The protesters lined up shoulder to shoulder across Pennsylvania Avenue, between the park and the White House, for the march to the Capitol. Some people sang. Some people chanted. Most people carried signs. Some carried American flags. The drummers kept drumming. The chants got louder. Then came a sudden wind gust, and all of the loose dirt and fallen leaves in the park swirled into the air. For a moment, there was so much dust that it could have been a Rustamiyah dust storm that would coat a singing cowboy from head to toe in a matter of seconds. But of course it wasn't that. The dust quickly settled and the leaves that had been kicked up floated back down, and one of the protesters who was about to die in order to honor the dead turned her face up to the sun.

"Isn't it gorgeous?" she said.

Maybe clear skies travel unbroken sometimes, ever eastward, even across oceans and war zones, because a week later that same gorgeous sky had become the sky over Rustamiyah. It was September 22, a week after the protest and two days past the halfway point of the 2-16's deployment, and that was when David Petraeus arrived, on the very best day in a while. His schedule to visit soldiers whenever he could had finally brought him to the place no one came to. The visit hadn't become official until the night before, but it was like a guest arriving at a house where the table had been set for years.

"Fire away, Ralph," he said, and after taking a breath, that's what Kauzlarich did. The general who had mesmerized Washington was now sitting shoulder to shoulder, inches away, and Kauzlarich had a lot he wanted to say—not about the bad days, but about all of the battalion's accomplishments. One leadership lesson he'd absorbed well was the importance of knowing what to leave out of a conversation. There was no point, for instance, in describing the three dying faces of September 4, the way Shelton kept asking, "Am I gonna be okay?" or the weird search on the roadway for the correct number of severed limbs. Petraeus knew the details, in his own way, through his own bad-news vessel experiences. Every soldier who went out of the wire knew the details, and so it was better to just move along. It was like an interview Kauzlarich had done a few nights before on PEACE 106 FM, when Mohammed had begun the show by asking him, "Sir, would you please tell us a little bit about your current operations?" "Absolutely," Kauzlarich had said enthusiastically, as if three soldiers of his hadn't just been killed and he hadn't been surreptitiously visited by one of the FOB's mental health counselors the next day to see if he was okay. "Over the course of this last week, for the first time since early March, it's the first time in my area of operation in which there was not a single enemy action taken," he'd continued. "So I would like to congratulate right now the people of Kamaliyah, Fedaliyah, Mashtal, and Al-Amin on a job well done as far as security goes."

And that was how he started things off with Petraeus, by telling him about the place he'd congratulated for not trying to kill him and his soldiers for seven entire days in a row.

He talked about how a cease-fire that had been announced at the end of August by the radical cleric Muqtada al-Sadr hadn't meant much in his area because of all the renegade JAM members who lived in Kamaliyah and Fedaliyah and who were being supported by Iran. He explained how his soldiers were using covert information-gathering technologies to track those insurgents down, and how the battalion had created its own "fusion cell" to distill the intelligence, something normally done at the brigade level. Without seeming to brag, he showed how, after a shaky start, the battalion's success rate in rounding up suspected insurgents had become the highest in the brigade, and that he knew from seeing some of them that they were some of the meanest human beings ever born.

"So you're going into Fedaliyah," Petraeus said.

"Yes," Kauzlarich said.

As for counterinsurgency strategy, he mentioned his growing relationship with members of the District Area Council (the *habibis* and *shadi ghabees*), and with Colonel Qasim of the Iraqi National Police (who continued to get daily death threats, but who so far had not run away). He said he hoped to soon finish the $30 million sewer project in Kamaliyah (still stalled because of corruption issues), and that he had begun an adult literacy program in local schools to do something about New Baghdad's 50 percent illiteracy rate (an $82,500 project the soldiers couldn't monitor in person because participants said they feared being killed if Americans were present).

"Great. That's super," Petraeus said, fully engaged, and now one of Kauzlarich's officers began detailing the battalion's greatest counterinsurgency success so far, a program called Operation Banzeen.

There were two gas stations in the area, the Rustamiyah station on Route Pluto, directly across from the FOB, and the Mashtal station up on Route Predators. Both had been a mess when the 2-16 arrived, because insurgents had taken over day-to-day control of them as a way to fund their operations, including their EFP cells. Each day, the insurgents would either show up in large trucks, take all of the fuel that had been delivered by the government, and sell it on the black market, or they would shake people down in order to move up in lines that stretched for more than a mile. For those who didn't pay, their wait could last a couple of days. They would sit unmoving in 120-degree heat, getting angrier and angrier at what their country had become since the American invasion.

Kauzlarich's beautifully simple solution was to put a platoon of soldiers in each of the stations. That was Operation Banzeen. The platoons remained there all day, and the results were immediate. The insurgents disappeared. Two-day waits became waits of a few minutes. Fuel was available. Prices stabilized. Early on, the insurgents had fought back—three soldiers had been wounded by sniper fire at the Mashtal station—but the platoons draped the perimeter of the station in camouflage netting and continued to show up every day, and there hadn't been an attack in a month.

"A great success for us," the soldier concluded, and Petraeus, who'd heard of the operation, turned to Kauzlarich and said, "Actually, all of Baghdad has learned from that."

And you could just about hear Kauzlarich's bad-news vessel becoming a good-news vessel.

At the end of the briefing, Kauzlarich showed one last slide. "Sir, our fight as I define it," he said. It was a circle-and-spoke diagram. The circles had labels such as "JAM" and "COP" and "ISF," and lines from those circles led to more circles, and those circles led to even more circles, which led to even more: "Militia," "Sheiks," "Trash Removal," "Small Kill Teams," "Chow." There were 109 circles in all, and all of them were connected either directly or indirectly to the circle in the middle that was Kauzlarich and the 2-16. "Our Fight," the diagram was called, and as brilliant as it might be, at first glance it appeared to be the most complicated diagram ever designed. Kauzlarich had put it together late one night when he was unable to sleep, and when he showed it to his command staff, they looked at it in stunned silence. Even the chaplain, who always had something to say, didn't know what to say. "Fuck," one company commander mouthed as they continued to stare, and now Petraeus was staring at it in silence, too.

"It's very simple," Petraeus finally said, and everyone in the room, except for Kauzlarich, began to laugh.

"Just the fact that you can construct this shows how far our army has progressed," Petraeus continued, and the laughter got louder.

"No, I mean it," Petraeus said, and when it became clear that he did mean it and the laughter died out, only then, for the first time since the briefing began, did Kauzlarich smile.

"Well, you guys keep up the terrific work," Petraeus said, and a few minutes later, when everyone stood outside posing for photographs and one of the world's most famous people put his left arm around Kauzlarich's shoulder, Kauzlarich looked the happiest he'd looked in a long time.

Away went Petraeus, to his helicopter, and Kauzlarich went back inside to welcome eight soldiers who had just arrived on the FOB as mid-tour replacements. All were brand-new soldiers who had joined the army after the 2-16 had deployed, which was one way to think of how long the 2-16 had been here. Four of them were medics and were sent to the aid station for training, and the other four stood at attention as Command Sergeant Major McCoy introduced himself. .

"Well," McCoy said, "you're in the shit now."

He continued to look them over. There was no need to explain to them why the battalion needed new soldiers. One was two days shy of turning nineteen. McCoy assigned him to Charlie Company, which had been the company of Murray, Lane, and Shelton. "What'd you do before you came here?" he asked the next one. "Not a whole lot, Sergeant Major." He was sent to Delta Company, which had been the company of Gajdos and Payne. So was the third one, who said nothing at all. The fourth one was named Patrick Miller. He was twenty-two and from Florida. He said he'd been in college, premed, had good grades, was close to graduating, but had run out of money, and so here he was, and McCoy decided a smart guy like him would be useful in the operations center. Miller smiled. He had a great smile. It lit up the room. Kauzlarich noticed it, too, as he shook hands with each of the new soldiers. The army may have been getting more waiver cases than ever, but it was also getting its Patrick Millers.

"Welcome to the team," Kauzlarich said, and he went outside to exult a little bit more in this day.

All of Baghdad has learned from that.

That was what Petraeus had said.

Keep up the terrific work.

He had said that, too. And on the way out, one of Petraeus's aides had said that of all the battalion briefings Petraeus had gotten, this had been one of the best.

The good day. "It's all good," Kauzlarich said, just so happy. It was late afternoon now, and he was starting to say something else when he was interrupted by the sound of an explosion.

He swiveled his head, unsure of what it was.

It had been close by, near the main gate. He listened for a moment. It had sounded like an EFP. He looked at the sky. It was still gorgeous and blue. He kept looking. Here it came now, a coil of rising black smoke, and he immediately knew that it was spiraling up from near the Rustamiyah fuel station, where the platoon that had spent the day there as part of Operation Banzeen had just radioed in that they were heading back to the FOB.

Now the radio crackled again.

"Two casualties," a soldier was yelling. "One not breathing. Life-threatening."

Kauzlarich took off for the aid station.

He got there just after the arrival of two Humvees, one of which had six holes in it, a ruined engine, and a shredded tire, and had been chain-dragged from the fuel station to the FOB by the other. He passed two of his soldiers, who were crying. He passed another soldier, who was kicking a Humvee as hard as he could, over and over.

"Fucking war," Kauzlarich said, nearing the doors.

There was a trail of bright red blood drops leading from the damaged Humvee to the aid station, and he followed it inside.

Inside:

A soldier was howling. He'd been the driver. Part of the EFP had gone under the Humvee and sent shrapnel up through the floorboards, breaking the bones in one of his feet and slicing off the heel of the other. As Kauzlarich made his way through the aid station, Brent Cummings, who'd also come, went to the soldier, took hold of his hand, and told him he would be all right. "How's Reeves?" the soldier said, and when Cummings didn't answer, he asked again. "Tell me how he's doing."

"Just worry about yourself right now," Cummings said.

Joshua Reeves, a twenty-six-year-old specialist, was the one at the end of the blood trail, and he was who Kauzlarich went to. He'd been in the right front seat when the EFP exploded, much of which had gone through his door. He had arrived at the aid station unconscious and without a pulse, and doctors were just beginning to work on him. He wasn't breathing, his eyes weren't moving, his left foot was gone, his back side was ripped open, his face had turned gray, his stomach was filling with blood, and he was naked, with the exception of one bloodied sock—and as if all that weren't enough with which to consider Joshua Reeves in these failing moments of his life, now came word from some of the soldiers gathered in the lobby that he'd begun this day with a message from his wife that she had just given birth to their first child.

"Jesus," Kauzlarich said upon hearing this, his eyes filling with tears as he watched another soldier dying in front of him.

"Let me know when it's three minutes," the doctor overseeing everything that was going on called out loudly, so her voice could be heard over the rumble of some machinery. The room smelled dizzily of blood and ammonia. There must have been ten people around Reeves. Someone was holding an oxygen mask over his face. Someone was stabbing him with a dose of Adrenalin called epinephrine. Someone, maybe a medic, was pushing up and down on his chest so violently it seemed every one of his ribs must be breaking. "You need to go harder and faster," the doctor in charge told him. The medic began pushing so hard that pieces of Reeves's shredded leg began dropping to the floor, and Kauzlarich continued to watch in silence, as did Cummings and Michael McCoy and the chaplain, all of them in a row.

"It's been two minutes," someone called out.

"Okay, check for a pulse, please."

The CPR stopped.

"No pulse."

The CPR resumed.

More of Reeves dropped to the floor.

In went a second dose of epinephrine.

"Someone feel for a pulse in his neck."

"Three minutes."

"Continue CPR, please."

In went a third dose of epinephrine as someone who was trying to clean up what had been falling accidentally kicked something small and hard, which skidded across the floor until it came to a stop next to McCoy.

"That's a toe," he said quietly.

He was fighting back tears now. So was Cummings. So was Kauzlarich. Behind them, open-mouthed, not moving, were the four medics they had just welcomed to the FOB, and out in the lobby, waiting for news, were some of the soldiers and the interpreter who had done their best to save Reeves in the first moments after the explosion.

"We said we couldn't trust these fuckers . . ." one of them was saying.

Another was saying nothing, just walking in circles, hearing in his head what Reeves had said right after the explosion: "Oh my God." And then: "I can't feel anything." And then had passed out.

Another, the interpreter, a twenty-five-year-old Iraqi national whose name was Rachel and who was covered in blood, was also saying nothing. In the days ahead, she would explain that she had been in the second Humvee when the EFP went off, had run to the first Humvee, had crawled inside until she was wedged next to Reeves, and had seen him pass out and go white. "I started slapping him in the face. Hard. He was bleeding a lot. His blood was in my boots," she would say, but for now she stood in those boots, the blood thickening in her socks and drying against her skin, waiting like the rest of the platoon.

It was 5:25 p.m. now, thirty minutes since the explosion, sixteen minutes since doctors had begun their work, and 9:25 a.m. in an American hospital where a new mother was expecting a phone call.

"Has anybody packed that wound on his left buttock?" one of the doctors was saying.

"Left *and* right," another doctor corrected.

"Check for a pulse, please," the doctor in charge said.

"No pulse," another doctor called out.

"Continue CPR."

"Okay, your fifth dose of EPI just went in now."

"We're at twenty minutes."

There was so much commotion, so many people doing so many things, that a discreet nod from one of the physician assistants who was standing near Reeves might not have been noticed. But the chaplain, who was waiting for it, did notice, and he now made his way to Reeves, placed a hand on his forehead just above his open, unmoving eyes, and began to pray.

The doctor in charge gave it a few more minutes to be sure.

"Feel for a pulse, please," she said for a final time, and the room became still. The oxygen machine that had been breathing for Reeves was switched off. The violent chest compressions that had been pushing blood through him came to an end. Everything stopped so a doctor could touch his fingers to Reeves's neck in perfect silence and make the death of another soldier official.

"Wait," he said after a moment. "Wait wait wait wait." He adjusted his fingers slightly. "I have a pulse," he said. "I have a pulse!"

Another doctor placed his fingers on Reeves to be sure. "Yes!" he said, and as Kauzlarich and everyone else looked on in astonishment, a room that had been so quiet switched back into motion as Reeves's heart fought to beat on its own.

There was a medevac helicopter on its way that would be landing in a few minutes, and the doctors and nurses worked frantically to prepare Reeves to be placed on it with the other soldier. They finished packing the wounds across his lower back and shattered pelvis. They wiped some of the blood away and wrapped him tightly in twenty rolls of gauze, so much that they emptied an entire supply cabinet.

"How much time do we have?" the lead doctor called out.

"Four minutes," came the answer.

"Can I get a blanket, please?" the lead doctor said.

She swaddled him in a blanket.

Time to move.

They lifted him onto a stretcher and carried him out of the treatment room and past the soldiers in the lobby, who had no idea of what had just occurred. What they saw was that he was alive. Outside now, the helicopter was in sight on the horizon. It swooped in fast, kicking up dust and creating a terrible racket, and even with that and the jostling as Reeves was loaded on board, his eyes remained unmoving. But his heart continued to beat.

"A great save," Kauzlarich shouted to one of the doctors who had worked on Reeves.

"I'm hoping. I'm hoping," the doctor replied.

Up the helicopter went, into the sky, away from all of this, and Kauzlarich watched until it disappeared. It was still a blue sky, and a gorgeous sky, and he walked beneath it back to the office where a few hours before he had stood with David Petraeus, and where he would now wait for an update. Eight months before, he had wondered what it would be like to see a soldier die. Now he had seen a soldier brought back to life.

The phone rang sooner than he had expected.

"Yes," he said. "Yes. Okay. Okay."

He hung up. Reeves was at the hospital and was headed into surgery. There'd be another update once he was out.

Then the phone rang again, too soon.

He had died.

Outside, Brent Cummings was examining Reeves's Humvee, trying to figure out the path that the EFP had taken and feeling a little sickened by the faint smell of burnt hair, when he got the news from one of the medics. "Any word?" he asked. "We lost him, sir," the medic said. "Okay, thanks," Cummings said and then walked in sudden tears over to a nearby building and began hitting it and kicking it for a while.

And inside, Kauzlarich stayed in his office, by himself, reading an e-mail that had just arrived and wondering what to write back. "Ranger 6," it began. "I appreciate you hosting me today and laying out what is going on in New Baghdad. Your many initiatives, such as securing the gas stations, creating your own fusion cell, and optimizing the DAC all seem to be developing significant traction. You guys are making big progress, and I am very proud of the 2-16 IN Team."

And so, late that night, as another platoon of soldiers moved into sleeplessness and a new mother in the United States still waited for a phone call, Kauzlarich wrote back to General Petraeus.

"It was our pleasure," was how he began, describing Petraeus's visit as "an absolute highlight of our deployment thus far," and then he paused to consider what to say next.

There were just so many ways to describe this war, that was the thing.

Congress had needed two days of hearings.

Protesters had needed a die-in.

George W. Bush had needed just three words: "We're kicking ass."

Now Kauzlarich managed to do it in one. "Unfortunately," he typed as he started the next sentence, and in the truth of that word, a bad day came to an end.

8

OCTOBER 28, 2007

*In Iraq, our campaign to provide security for the Iraqi people has been difficult
and dangerous, but it is achieving results . . . In Baghdad, the number of Iraqi civilians
murdered by terrorists and death squads is down sharply. Throughout Iraq, the number
of American service members killed in September was the lowest since July 2006.*
—GEORGE W. BUSH, *October 22, 2007*

The number of American KIAs for September was forty-three.
The number of deaths for the month was sixty-six, or slightly
more than two a day, but once the White House subtracted what
the Pentagon in press releases called the "non-combat related vehicle
rollover" deaths, the "non-combat related accident" deaths, the "non-
combat related injury" deaths, the "non-combat related illness" deaths,
and the "non-combat related incident" deaths, the number left over was
indeed the lowest since July 2006.

Forty-three in all of Iraq—and five of those forty-three were soldiers
of the 2-16.

Reeves had been the fourth, and then, a week later, almost to the
minute, an EFP blew into a Humvee in which sat thirty-seven-year-old
Sergeant First Class James Doster. "He ain't gonna make it. He's as
fucked-up as Reeves," Kauzlarich said after seeing him in the aid station,
barely alive. Like Reeves, Doster had been in the right front seat; like
Reeves, his lower left leg was gone and his pelvis was ruined; like Reeves,
he was airlifted to the hospital, where he bled out and died. "Fucking the
same. Everything the same," Kauzlarich said as he waited for confirma-
tion, and when it came, he simply said, "Fuck."

Izzy

Eleven dead now. Another forty-four injured. Gunshots. Burns. Shrapnel. Missing hands, arms, legs, an eye. Ruptured eardrums, a mangled groin, gouged-out muscles, severed nerves. One guy took it in the stomach as he waited to use a pay phone on the FOB and a rocket landed nearby. Rockets, mortars, RPGs, sniper fire, EFPs. "The thing is, they can't kill all of us," Kauzlarich said as he prepared to telephone the war's newest widow, who lived with two young daughters in a house in Kansas on a street called Liberty Circle, and when he was done with the call, he hung his head and said, "That's probably the saddest woman I've talked to yet."

Sometimes Kauzlarich and Cummings would wonder what exactly the Iraqis hated about them. What were they doing, other than trying to secure some Iraqi neighborhoods? What made people want to kill them for handing out candy and soccer balls, and delivering tankers of drinking water to them, and building a sewer system for them, and fixing their gas stations, and never being aggressive except for rounding up the killers among them?

"I'm offering peace and a shit-free life, and you want to fight me? Fine. Live in shit," Cummings said one day in the midst of an exasperated conversation with Kauzlarich as they tried to figure it out.

"The bottom line is these guys are the most ungrateful fucks I've ever met in my life," Kauzlarich said, and then, as he had been doing for eight months now, five or six times a week, he got in his Humvee and headed to another meeting with their local political leaders.

He was just turning off Route Pluto when he was once again nearly hit by an EFP. This time it exploded as the first Humvee in the convoy passed by. Two soldiers were lacerated by flying shrapnel. But the main charge missed, and though Kauzlarich didn't make it to that day's meeting, at the next one his patience was just about gone.

There they were, waiting for him—the same cast of characters he had been dealing with for nearly eight months, who promised anything, and delivered nothing, and wanted everything, and always had another complaint.

Around the room it went, one more time.

The schools aren't fixed.

The generators you promised haven't arrived.

The fence you're building on Route Pluto is ugly.

The fence is a security fence, and the reason we're building it is because Route Pluto is where you keep trying to kill us, Kauzlarich thought but didn't say.

The electricity is still out most of the time.

The sewer project is not done and winter is coming and Kamaliyah is a mess.

We need you to paint the mosque.

Why can't *you* paint the mosque? Kauzlarich thought.

We get nothing from the Americans.

Fuck off, he thought to himself, and this time he did say it out loud.

"Fuck 'em," he said, but only to Colonel Qasim, who nodded enthusiastically, as if he understood.

Did Qasim understand? Maybe. In this place, maybe *fuck* was one of English's universally understood words. Or maybe he had sensed the declining mood of the man who had become his favorite American of all. He called Kauzlarich "Muqaddam K." The two had spent hours and hours together, and even though their conversations required an interpreter, Kauzlarich talked to him not only about the war, but sometimes about personal things: His wife. His kids. Things such as holidays and birthdays and family pizza night. After the meeting, lingering a bit, they found themselves talking again, and when Kauzlarich mentioned that he would be turning forty-two in a few weeks, Qasim said he would have a party for him.

"A party?" Kauzlarich said.

A party, Qasim said. A party for Muqaddam K's birthday. A party with a cake.

Kauzlarich was touched. Another promise to be broken, he thought, but at least this was a nice one.

If Kauzlarich were to pick a favorite among the Iraqis he had met, Qasim would be up there, and so would Mr. Timimi, the civil manager, who day after day did whatever he did in his office with the big desk and the broken cuckoo clock.

But Izzy, his interpreter, was the one Kauzlarich had grown closest to and who had come to represent all the reasons Kauzlarich continued to find faith in the goodness of Iraqis, even after eleven deaths. Six years older than Kauzlarich, Izzy was a thin man with a melancholy face, the face of someone who understood life as something to be resigned to. At one point, he had lived for a few years in New York City, as part of Iraq's delegation to the United Nations, which was when he became fluent in English. Now his job was to interpret everything said in Arabic to Kauzlarich, as well as what Kauzlarich wanted to say to Iraqis, no matter what it was. When rumors of a cholera outbreak were sweeping through Baghdad and Kauzlarich announced on PEACE 106 FM, "If you have explosive diarrhea, go to your nearest clinic or hospital," Izzy interpreted that. If he had been close enough to hear when Kauzlarich had muttered, "Fuck 'em," to Qasim, he would have interpreted that.

There were times when Iraqis would look at Izzy in obvious disgust, as if he were nothing more than a tool of the Americans. But he did his job enthusiastically, partly because of his affection for the United States— his older daughter, now seventeen, was born in New York City—and partly because of something that had happened over the summer when he had gone home to spend a few days with his family in central Baghdad.

Late one afternoon, a bomb had exploded just outside of his apartment building. Even by Baghdad standards it was a monstrous explosion. Twenty-five people died and more than one hundred others were injured, but seven miles away, no one on the FOB knew anything about it until Brent Cummings's cell phone rang and Izzy was on the other end, in a panic.

There had been an explosion, he said. His apartment was in ruins, his building was on fire, and one of his daughters had been badly injured by something that had pierced her head. He had taken her to a hospital, but there were so many other injured people that doctors had said there was nothing they could do, that she needed more help than they could give, and so he was standing on a street with his bleeding daughter at his side, afraid that she was going to die.

"The only hope you have is to get her to an American hospital?" Cummings asked, repeating what Izzy had just said. Izzy started to answer. The cell phone went dead. "Izzy?" Cummings said. "Izzy?"

How did moments of decency occur in this war?

"Izzy," Cummings said, calling him back. "Bring your daughter here."

That was how.

"Oh thank you, sir. Thank you, sir," Izzy said.

And that's when things got complicated. Even this war had its rules, and one of them covered who could be treated at an American aid facility. Americans could, of course, but Iraqis could not, unless they were injured by the American military, and only if the injury was life-threatening. Since the car bomb had been an Iraqi bomb, none of the injured was entitled to American care, including, it seemed, Izzy's daughter.

But Cummings had in mind Izzy's previous life, before he was an interpreter. If the daughter who was injured had been born in New York City, did that make her eligible? Could an American-born Iraqi who was injured by a non-American bomb receive medical care in an American military medical facility?

Cummings didn't know the answer. He phoned some doctors at the aid station, but they didn't know, either. He tried the FOB legal representative, but couldn't get through. He wasn't even sure which of the daughters had been injured—the one born in New York, or the eight-year-old who was born in Baghdad. He called Izzy back. The connection was terrible. He dialed again and again.

"Izzy . . . okay . . . where is your daughter that is from the United States?"

Again the phone went dead.

He called again. The connection kept breaking up. "Is your daughter from the United States with you right now? . . . Is she hurt? . . . Which daughter is hurt? . . . Is she on the street with you? . . . You can't what? . . . What?"

Again the phone went dead, and at that point Cummings made a decision not to ask any more questions, just to assume what the answer would be. He was making a guess. He understood that. But with Kauzlarich away for a few hours on another FOB to attend a memorial ceremony, there was no one else to ask what to do.

He telephoned an officer in another battalion who controlled access to the FOB and whose approval would be needed for someone not in the military to get through the gate without being turned away, detained, or shot. "Yes," he said. "I'm sure we can produce a birth certificate." He wondered whether such a certificate, if it even existed, had burned up in the fire. He checked the time. The sun was going down. A curfew would be in effect soon, at which point Izzy and his daughter wouldn't be allowed outside until sunrise. The officer kept asking questions. "We'll figure that piece out," Cummings said impatiently. "Right now, I just want to help the guy."

Next he called the battalion's physician and told him to be ready to treat one female, age unknown, in a matter of minutes. "A U.S. citizen," he added, and then to that added, "maybe."

Next he tried Izzy again, to see how close he was to the FOB, and Izzy, his voice more panicked than before, said he wasn't close at all, that he was still on the street, still next to his daughter, trying to find a taxi. "Thank you, sir," he kept saying. "Thank you, sir. Thank you, sir."

There was nothing to do but wait. It wasn't as if a convoy could go pick up Izzy. He would have to get here on his own. The sun was almost down now. A call came from an officer in another battalion who said he'd heard that the 2-16 had lost some soldiers somewhere. "No," Cummings said. Then another officer called saying he'd heard some soldiers had been injured in an apartment bombing. Then another: the rumor was that some 2-16 soldiers had died in an EFP attack.

"No, there are no injured Coalition Forces," Cummings kept saying. "It is an Iraqi—an Iraqi American—who was hurt. It is the interpreter's daughter."

He phoned Izzy again.

Still trying to find a taxi.

Another call, from the doctor: "I don't know the extent of the injuries . . . I don't know if he's even in a cab yet . . . I don't know if they're going to make it here before curfew."

Another call. It was Izzy. They were in a taxi. They were on the bridge, two minutes from the base.

Cummings hurried to the gate. It was dark now. The FOB's ambulance pulled up to receive the girl. Five minutes had gone by. Where was the taxi? Now the guards said they had stopped it in the distance and that there was no way it would be allowed any closer than it had gotten, which was somewhere out of sight. "Get a litter," Cummings yelled to the ambulance crew. Sprinting, he went out the gate, passing coils of razor wire and blast walls, and then stopping when he saw Izzy walking toward him, illuminated by the headlights of the ambulance.

Izzy's clothing was filthy.

Next to him was his wife, who was crying.

On his other side was one of his daughters, the one born in New York, who appeared to be uninjured.

And in front of them all, wobbly but walking, was a young girl with shiny purple sandals, blood all over her blue jeans, and a bandage covering the left side of her face.

It was the eight-year-old, the daughter born in Baghdad, the one who according to the rules had no standing whatsoever to be treated on the FOB. "Izzy," Cummings called out, knowing right then that he had guessed wrong. He ran toward the family as other soldiers reached the girl. They lifted her up. She began crying. They carried her through the gate without stopping. They ran with her into the aid station, and as the doors swung shut she cried out in Arabic for her father, who'd been told to remain in the lobby.

Izzy took a seat in a corner. Cummings stood nearby. "Was it a car bomb?" he asked after a while.

"No, sir," Izzy said. "It was two car bombs."

And then he said nothing more, not until one of the doctors came into the lobby to tell him that his daughter was going to be all right.

"Thank you, sir," he managed to say, and when he was unable to say anything else, he bowed his head, and then wiped his eyes, and then followed the doctor into the treatment area, where he saw his Iraqi daughter surrounded by American doctors and medics.

What do the rules say?

At that moment, anyway, no one seemed concerned one way or another: not the doctors, not the family, and not Cummings, who stood at the very same spot he'd stood at as he watched Crow die, watching once again.

The injuries to the girl were serious. There was a deep cut across her cheek, and worse, something had gone into the left side of her forehead, near her temple, and was deeply embedded in bone. Izzy held her hand as the doctors wrapped her in a sheet, making sure to secure her arms tightly. Her mother closed her eyes. The doctors leaned in. It took a while, and at the worst of it the little girl couldn't remain quiet, but then the doctors were showing her what they had pulled out—a thick piece of glass nearly two inches long.

The glass had been part of an apartment that no longer existed, in a section of Baghdad where the sounds that night were of mourning.

But here on the FOB, the sounds were of a mother whose home was ruined kissing her daughter's face, and a father whose home was ruined kissing his daughter's hand, and a little girl whose home was ruined saying something in Arabic that caused her family to smile, and Cummings saying quietly in English, "Man, I haven't felt this good since I got to this hellhole."

Because of the curfew, they stayed on the FOB that night in a vacant trailer that Cummings found for them. He offered to take them to the DFAC, but Izzy insisted that they weren't hungry, even though they hadn't eaten for hours. "We'll get you some ice cream. We'll get you some food," Cummings said, but Izzy politely declined. He did accept sheets, which they used with embarrassment in the middle of the night to clean up the trailer when their daughter got sick and vomited, but that was all they accepted before closing their door, and when Cummings knocked just after sunrise they were already gone.

They wanted to get home to see what they had lost, which turned out to be almost everything. Their clothing. Their furniture. Their prayer rugs. Their generator. Their plastic tanks that held the drinking water they got from a pump on the roof. What was left was the shell of an apartment with blown-out windows and soot-covered walls, but they had nowhere else to go, and so they continued to live in a building that was abandoned and ghostly now, where six of the twenty-five dead had been their neighbors. One of them was a boy who'd been the age of Izzy's injured daughter and liked to hang out with Izzy, talking about soccer. "Marvin," Izzy said one day after he had returned to the FOB, thinking back. "His mother was a Christian. He was a lovely child." He had been on the roof of the four-story building when the bombs had exploded, probably to get water, or perhaps in search of a breeze on a hot summer day, and the shaking had thrown him over the edge. He landed in front of the doorway, and when people saw his body, no one wanted to go past, even though much of the building was on fire. "'Please, someone move Marvin,'" Izzy recalled his wife crying out, "but no one would, because everyone liked Marvin very much." Finally an uncle rushed forward to cover the body with a blanket, at which point people eased past and hurried out to the street.

An Iraqi's life: the soldiers simply had no idea. Every so often, on a clearing operation, they would see something such as a cross on a wall or a pair of high heels shoved under a teenage girl's dresser and feel a brief sense of commonality, but for the most part, Iraq continued to be men with prayer beads and women in black drapes and calves in living rooms and goats on roofs. This place wasn't just strange after eight months, it was ever stranger. Like the guy being tracked one night in October on a night-vision surveillance camera as he walked alone through a field, holding something suspicious-looking in his hand. "What's that?" a soldier monitoring the feed said with concern, and as calls went out with the man's coordinates and snipers trained on him to take him out, a man who thought he was obscured by darkness looked around, bent over, dug a shallow hole, lifted his robe, squatted, went to the bathroom, and used whatever was in his hand to scoop some dirt and cover up what he'd done. Was the man all right? Was he without a home? What conditions of a life would lead him into a field as curfew approached? Had his building been destroyed, like Izzy's? Every act in Iraq came freighted with so many questions—but to the soldiers, once they stopped laughing, and groaning, and covering their eyes, and peeking through their fingers, the question was simply: *Why the fuck would some dude shit in the middle of a field?*

So the interpreters were around to broker behavioral mysteries as well as languages. There were several dozen of them on the FOB. A few were Iraqi Americans who lived in the United States, had a security clearance, and earned more than $100,000 a year. Most, though, like Izzy, were out-of-work Iraqis from nearby neighborhoods who happened to speak some English. They were paid between $1,050 and $1,200 a month, and in exchange for that they took on a soldier's risks of EFPs, snipers, rockets, and mortars, and the additional risk of being seen by their fellow Iraqis as pariahs.

"You're a spy," they would say in Arabic to Izzy when he climbed out of an American Humvee wearing the same camouflage as the soldiers.

"You're a traitor," they would say as he stood by during clearance operations, disguised behind large, dark sunglasses and a name tag identifying him as Izzy.

"You're one of us. You should explain," they would say as soldiers searched through cabinets and dressers, sometimes roughly, sometimes breaking things.

"No, no, no, no," Izzy said quietly one time to a soldier who was piling a family's clothing in the middle of a floor. "Why are you doing this?"

"This man's lying to us," the soldier said, and as he stepped on some of the clothing in his dirty boots, Izzy felt ashamed, even though he suspected the soldier was right.

It was that sense of shame, always nearby, that made being an interpreter feel dishonorable at times, not only for Izzy, but for all of them.

"Hey, Mike, please tell him I'm going to take off his pants, but I'm going to leave his underwear on," a soldier said one day to another of the interpreters for the 2-16 as they began a medical screening for a new detainee. A few hours before, five Iraqis had been rounded up for possible involvement with an EFP cell after being pursued through the sewage trenches of Fedaliyah, and now they were standing blindfolded and flex-cuffed, and were being examined one at a time by a soldier wearing protective gloves. This one was the second of the five. He was filthy and wore a knockoff athletic shirt that read *abibas*. He stood absolutely still as the soldier undid his pants, and when they dropped to his ankles, he continued to stand still in underwear that had a large wet area across the front.

"Ask him if he peed himself," the soldier said, by now knowing that the innocent ones often lost control of their bladders, or defecated, or trembled uncontrollably, while the guilty ones tended to smirk.

"Peed?" Mike said, confused by the term.

"Ask him if he wet himself," the soldier said. "Urinated."

"No," Mike said, relaying the answer, after asking and seeming embarrassed to have done so. "It happened when he tried to wash his face."

"Does he drink?" the soldier asked now, continuing down a checklist.

"No drink."

"Does he smoke?"

"No."

"Is he on any illegal drugs?"

"No."

"Ask him if he's cold," the soldier said. "Ask him why he's shaking." Then, directly to the detainee, who couldn't see him, and couldn't understand him, he said, "We won't hurt you," and waited for Mike to say the Arabic words for that.

Mike, of course, wasn't really Mike, just as Izzy wasn't Izzy and Rachel wasn't Rachel. They were given American names, army uniforms, a room to sleep in, a cot to sleep on, and free meals at the DFAC, although, unlike soldiers, they were patted down and wanded before they were allowed inside.

Rachel, who had tried to save Reeves, pushing on his chest as his blood leaked into her boots, was one of the few females who did this work. Twenty-five years old, she had been an interpreter since 2003, when the war seemed as if it would be brief rather than everlasting. "When I began this, it was safe. Everybody loved the Americans. Everybody wanted to work with them," she said one day, explaining how she had become who she had become, which on this day was one more person in Iraq in tears kept out of sight of the Americans. She was trying to hide her face. She didn't want the soldiers to see. "I speak English. I love America. I was so excited for them to be here. I wanted to work with them, just to feel victory."

Since then, by her own count, she had been in forty explosions, from car bombs to EFPs, including the one that killed Reeves. She had been burned, knocked out, could no longer hear clearly out of her right ear, and was having trouble seeing out of her left eye. "You go through a lot of stress, and then you're okay," she said of what each of the explosions had done to her. "You figure out a way to handle it. For me, it's a lot of crying, and thinking the good is coming. Nothing good has come yet. But I'm staying positive."

It was hard, though. Her family was in Syria now, mixed in with the million other Iraqi refugees there and dependent on the money she sent them. They were there and she was here, living a life that offered $1,200 a month and little else. "Nobody," she said of whom she was close to anymore, "just the unit I am working with," and so her life now was largely imagined. "I am from Syria," she would tell Iraqis when she was out with the Americans. Or, "I am from Lebanon." Usually she was married, "with kids," although sometimes she was just engaged. "Just to make up a story for my safety, because if they know I'm Iraqi, they'll be mean to me," she said. But the fact was that she never could be who she actually was, not when she was among Iraqis, or with the soldiers, either, a lesson she had learned when she was working with another battalion and an IED exploded and soldiers who had seemed her friends stopped calling her Rachel after that and began calling her "you bitch." So far, she said, that was the thing that hurt most of all, and it was why, after Reeves died, she had stood before the platoon with his blood on her and said, "I'm sorry," and then had said, "I'm not bad like my people," and then had gone on her own to her room, which she had decorated with twelve photographs of her departed family, an Iraqi flag, an American flag, and a stuffed animal that, if she pressed on its foot, which she did again and again that day, would say, "Oh, you're a little wild thing, aren't you?"

This was an Iraqi life. The soldiers couldn't understand it, and they didn't understand Izzy's, either. But he had a sense of theirs. He had lived in the United States from 1989 to 1992. He knew America, and even though he hadn't been there in fifteen years, he knew what its soldiers liked because of what one of them had written on the door of a metal locker that was in the room he'd been given to live in. "Sex, potato soup, and Johnny Cash," it said. It had been written in black marker, just above where, in smaller letters, someone had written, "No Iraqi man, woman, or child is worth one drop of an American soldier's blood."

Izzy remembered the day he got the room. He didn't get many visitors, but that day a 2-16 soldier stopped by and saw the locker. "No, that's not right," the soldier had said apologetically, and had used a wet cloth to wipe away the second set of words until they were smudged enough to be mostly unreadable.

So that was another thing that Izzy knew, how kind an American soldier could be.

Though not always.

"Old man," one of them said one morning, as Izzy, sleepy-eyed, tooth-brush in hand, stepped outside, on his way to the latrines.

"Faggot," another said, picking up a rock and tossing it at Izzy.

"Fuck you," another said to him, also tossing a rock.

Izzy laughed, even as one of the rocks skipped off the ground and hit him in the leg. "Bastards," he said back to them, kidding as much as they were.

It was a Friday toward the end of October. Two days before his birth-day, Kauzlarich was staying in the wire, and Izzy had the day to do what-ever he wanted. Not that there were a lot of options. He wouldn't get time off to go see his family for another week, and he couldn't contact them, because whenever he entered the FOB his cell phone was confis-cated until he left. He wasn't allowed to have a phone, a camera, a com-puter, an MP3 player, or anything electronic except for a Chinese TV he had bought on the FOB for thirty dollars. It had been luck, or Iraqi luck, anyway, that he happened to be home when his daughter was injured and his apartment was ruined, because otherwise he wouldn't have known. No one could contact him when he was on the FOB. No one knew where he worked or what he did for a living except for his wife, two brothers, and a few friends, and they knew only a little. His wife, for instance, didn't know about the half-dozen times EFPs had hit his convoy, or the constant rocket attacks on the FOB. She knew only that he had a job as an interpreter, that for their safety no one could know what he did, and that every few weeks he would show up at home, unannounced.

"Please, can we live in Jordan?" she had been asking him on his recent visits, usually on his last night, as the daughter who had been injured slept between them, which she had been doing since the apartment bombing. "Can we live in Syria? Can we run away? Can we escape?"

"We don't have enough money," he would tell her.

"I cannot handle this life," she would say. "What kind of life is this?"

"Just be patient," he would say. "You see me working hard."

And then he would disappear until the next time he got the chance to go home, bringing with him the money he had been paid that month, minus what he had spent on gifts. He liked bringing his family things, though it was never very much. Whatever he brought had to fit neatly in a backpack, so that Iraqis who saw him walking along Route Pluto, or getting into a taxi once he was a mile or so away from the FOB, or getting out and tying his shoes until the taxi disappeared and then getting into a second taxi, or into a third taxi, or standing on a street near his home for a while smoking cigarettes as he decided whether he had been followed, would have no reason to be suspicious.

"I swear, every night I spend home, I can't sleep, because I expect a knock on the door. 'Come, sir.' But anyway, this is our life, so we have to deal with it," he said. He was walking to the PX now, to see what he could buy for his next trip home. He paused at the entrance so he could be patted down, and then, for $25.11, he bought three bottles of shampoo, a tube of cocoa butter lotion, two bags of Cheetos, a bag of Lifesavers Gummis, two packages of Starbursts, two bags of Hershey's Kisses, one bag of Skittles, one Twix bar, and one bag of M&Ms.

He took it all back to his room and put it in his locker, next to what he had bought previously: pencils, hair bands, and some lotion for his daughter's scars. There was a file folder in the locker as well, which contained recommendation letters that he hoped would get him and his family back to the United States, this time as refugees. It was the one promised benefit of being an interpreter, that if you lasted at least a year and had the right recommendation letters, you would be considered for refugee status. The requirement was for five recommendation letters. Izzy had collected nine so far, attesting to how, in one example, his "patriotism landed him in the hospital as he was beaten almost to death for trying to gather information about our area of operations." The nine were all like that, but he wanted more. He wanted a dozen, if that would help. He wanted two dozen. The notion of escape to his wife might have meant Jordan or Syria, but he wanted the United States, even if it meant the bare-bones existence of a being a refugee. It didn't matter. This, here, in Baghdad, was a bare-bones existence, and that, there, was the place he had lived for three years as a low-level diplomat and had kept in mind ever since.

His daughters had American names.

He had visited thirty-five states.

He still possessed his Pan American World Airways frequent-flier membership card.

He'd wanted to stay longer, but in 1992 the government brought him back to Baghdad for what they'd said would be a two-week review of the Iraqi mission, revoked his passport, called him, as he remembered it, "a fucking failure," and told him that if his family asked for political asylum in the United States he would be killed. "Please pack up your things and come back," he said on the phone to his wife, still in the United States, without elaborating, and of course she understood the meaning of that sentence and came back.

Seven years passed.

Now it was 1999, the daughter who would be injured in the car bombing had just been born, and Izzy was scooped off the street one day by government agents who wanted to know about his feelings toward the United States. They took his shoes, removed his belt, bound his hands, taped his eyes, beat him with electrical cables, kicked him when he fell to the ground, and left him tied-up, blindfolded, bleeding, and alone in a room without food or water. They continued to beat him for several more days, and then they moved him to a jail cell, where he remained for eight months, until his family was able to bribe a judge with money they got by selling their house, their car, and a little boat they would use sometimes on the Tigris River. Freed, unable to sleep, waiting for the middle-of-the-night visitors who would say, "Come, sir," Izzy made his way to Syria and into Lebanon. His family tried to follow, but they were rounded up at the Syrian border and sent back to Baghdad.

Four years passed.

Now it was 2003. The war had begun. The Americans were in Baghdad, and Izzy, watching from Lebanon, realized he could go back. He took a train into Iraq, then a bus into Baghdad, and then began walking, searching for the right apartment building. There was no electricity.

Buildings were on fire. There was shooting in the streets. He found the building and knocked on the door, and when it opened, there was his wife, lit by a few candles, peering into the dark hallway, trying to make out who was there, and then seeing him. Thanks to the American invasion, he was home.

Another four years passed.

Now it was October 26, 2007, and Izzy was thinking back to those first moments after the door opened. "I could not say any words," he said as he sat in his room on the FOB. "Just kiss her. Hug her." His older daughter, the one born in New York, ran to him. The younger one, whom he hadn't seen since she was a newborn, remained in the room's shadows. "Who's this girl?" he said, moving toward her, reaching for her, but she had no idea who he was and didn't yet know the tenderness of a father's voice. She shrank from him, frightened. It took her a while to become the girl who would trust him so thoroughly that when she was being worked on in the FOB's aid station, his hand would be the one she held, and now that he had that trust, the least he could do when he went home was to take her some candy and hair bands and American-made lotion.

He wondered every so often: What would American soldiers think if they came to his apartment in the middle of the night on a clearance operation? They would see very little furniture. They would see recently painted walls bruised with soot stains. They would see a refrigerator with a deep dent in it, and not know that it came from the flying glass produced by a bomb blast. They would see a young girl with a scar on the side of her head sleeping in the middle of her parents' mattress. They would see that among the clothing they had piled in the middle of the floor was a pair of purple sandals, and for a fleeting moment a soldier might be reminded of home. Five minutes in, five minutes out. One more Iraqi family. That's what they would probably think. And they would be right.

"I hate being alone," Izzy said now, looking around his little room. "Believe me, this place is killing me."

He turned on the TV and fiddled with a piece of wire he'd fashioned into an antenna until a picture appeared. He was hoping for soccer, but all he could get was a snowy image of four men in long beards wearing robes called *dishdashas* and talking to one another. They seemed angry. They were raising their voices. Jihadists, an American in need of an interpreter might think, but Izzy said they were just four Iraqi men reciting poetry.

"My life is like a bag of flour, thrown through wind and into thorn bushes," he said, interpreting what one of them was saying.

"No, no. Like dust in the wind. My life is like dust in the wind," he said, correcting himself.

"It's like a hopeless man," he explained.

"You know," Kauzlarich said of Izzy, "if you put a monocle and a top hat on him, he'd look like Mr. Peanut."

October 28 now. Kauzlarich's birthday had arrived, and he, Izzy, and Brent Cummings were about to leave to see Colonel Qasim, who had continued to promise a big party.

"You boys ready?" Kauzlarich asked the soldiers in his security detail.

"Let's do the damn thing," one of the soldiers said.

"Not many getting hit lately," said Staff Sergeant Barry Kitchen, who by his own count had been in twenty-five IED explosions and firefights in two deployments, the most recent explosion leaving him with a wrenched back and some minor burns.

"Shut up, man," another soldier said.

Everyone had their doubts about this trip.

"I don't think it's gonna be much of a birthday, sir," a soldier said. "I think it's gonna be a bunch of complaining."

Cummings, meanwhile, worried that they were being set up. A specific time, a specific place, a specific route—were they going to a party or an ambush? "That Qasim, he's a great guy—I think," he had said the night before, wondering.

And Izzy had his doubts, too, if only because while children had birthday parties in Iraq, adults did not. At least not the adults he knew.

"To be honest, we don't even remember our birthdays," he'd said one day when he was talking to another interpreter about Qasim's promise to give Kauzlarich a party.

"When you pass twenty, no one cares about you," the other interpreter had agreed.

"For our children, we do things," Izzy had said. "But even wedding anniversaries, anything, no." He had no idea even when he was born, he said. His documents gave a date of July 1, 1959, but for the men of his generation, birth dates were nothing more than a way for the government to divide the population for military service. Half of the men had birth dates of January 1, and the other half had birth dates of July 1, and the fact that his was July 1 meant only that he'd been born in the first half of the year. His mother had once told him that he'd been born during the spring harvest, while she was working in the fields, so he supposed he could isolate the date a little further, but what would be the point?

It was the same attitude he had about death: "We believe that God created us in one day, and God will take our life in one day. No matter if we are staying home, or doing work, by heart attack, by disease, by bullet, by IED—that's it. One day you're born, one day you're going to die. No matter what you do, it's destiny. That's it. Nobody can go beyond his age or his destiny."

And about the dangers of being an interpreter: "Yeah, I know. You can die any minute. You see, I'll feel happy when I just get killed by a bullet in my head—because I expect worse than that. I expect they will put me in the back of a truck with two cats, hungry cats, to maybe scratch my face, eat pieces of my flesh, and then they will hang me on the walls, nails, like what happened to Jesus Christ, they will put a drill in my head, cut pieces, and then shoot me, torch me, and then throw me to the garbage to be eaten by dogs. It has happened before. So if I get killed, it would be very easy to die from one bullet."

"So what day is his birthday?" the other interpreter asked Izzy of Kauzlarich.

"Actually, I don't know," Izzy said.

"So how are you going to celebrate it?" the other interpreter said.

How? When? Why? Izzy had no idea. But he did think Kauzlarich deserved some sort of tribute. "Cross my mother's grave, I have never seen an American officer understand what he is doing like Colonel K," he said. Colonel K was the rare one trying to learn some Arabic, he said. Colonel

K handed out candy and soccer balls to children, something an Iraqi colonel would never do. A few weeks before, at the council building, when a woman in a broken wheelchair asked for help, Colonel K brought her a new wheelchair the following day. "Thank you," the woman had said, overcome with surprise, and Izzy, interpreting, had felt very good about that.

His doubts were simply about whether anyone would know what to do.

"*As-Salamu Alaykum*," Kauzlarich said, walking into Qasim's office. "*Shaku maku?*"

Qasim rose to greet him. He was the only one there. The office was dark—not to obscure anything, such as people hiding behind a couch about to yell, "Surprise," but because the electricity was out.

"Please. Sit. Down," Qasim said in the English he had been trying to learn.

Kauzlarich sat. Izzy sat. Cummings sat. A few of the soldiers from the security detail sat. And that appeared to be it. A few minutes later, two of the people Kauzlarich often met with from Kamaliyah and Fedaliyah wandered in and sat. Izzy interpreted: they were complaining about someone they knew who had been detained the night before on suspicions that he was part of an EFP cell.

"Okay. I will release him today," Kauzlarich said facetiously.

The two were surprised.

"I don't think so," Kauzlarich said, the facetiousness gone, and as the two resumed complaining, he felt himself being overtaken by a feeling of lonesomeness. It wasn't the absence of a party. Some days just had a built-in feeling of rootlessness, or maybe it was yearning. Christmas. Thanksgiving. All the holidays, really, even though there'd be decorations in the DFAC. Cardboard cutouts of turkeys. Cardboard cutouts of fireworks. Maybe the cardboard cutouts made it worse. And birthdays, for which there were no decorations. Just before leaving, he had checked his e-mail and there'd been nothing new from Kansas, so this was what his birthday would be: this dark room and these oblivious strangers, none of whom would be in his life if there hadn't been the surge.

The door opened, and in came one more, a member of Qasim's National Police battalion, balancing a tray filled with cans of 7UP. In meeting after meeting, serving 7UPs was all he ever seemed to do. He was young and timid and so obviously unworldly that a few of Kauzlarich's soldiers had taken on his maturation as a personal project, one day presenting him with a gift they had ordered for him online. It was a sex toy product called a "pocket pussy." He had looked at it quizzically and then with some embarrassment, but since it was a gift from guests, he had accepted it graciously and never spoken of it since. Now, just as graciously, he went around the room serving cans of soda, and when he was done, he put the extra cans in a refrigerator in a corner of Qasim's office.

The door opened again and in came Mr. Timimi with two more of the chronic complainers, both of whom took seats and started right in. There were two large windows on the far side of the room, and as sounds came through them of more men gathering, Cummings seemed to be looking at the drapes covering them, wondering perhaps if they would suppress a grenade.

Now the doorknob rattled and someone came in with a camera, and Qasim walked across the room to his desk.

The door opened yet again, and two more of Qasim's men wrestled a giant table inside. They were followed by men bringing in plates of chicken and bread and salad. It was the same meal Kauzlarich had been served many other times—no utensils, everyone reaching in with their wet fingers, leftovers taken out at the end for the policemen waiting outside the closed door—and so it wasn't until what happened next that Kauzlarich realized this was different.

Qasim reached under his desk, pulled out a square box with the word *Crispy* on top, placed it on the table, and said to Kauzlarich in perfect English, as if he had been practicing the sentence:

"This is your pizza."

And it was. It was a pizza.

It had tomatoes on it, and cheese, and probably sausage, and almost certainly that was chicken.

"I have never had Iraqi pizza," Kauzlarich said, beginning to laugh, and as a second pizza came out from under the desk, Qasim declared with pride, "Iraq is the first country in everything. In insurgency. In food."

In broken promises, too, it could seem. But on this day, one was being kept. Kauzlarich was getting his birthday party.

"It's a small thing," Qasim said, standing off to the side now, looking pleased. He had paid for this himself, even though in his haphazard life he had no money to spare. "Colonel K deserves much more than this."

Someone blew up three balloons, which Izzy taped to the ceiling.

There were gifts: A pen. A watch. A knife. A framed rendering of the Gates of Babylon. A *dishdasha*.

The complainers stopped complaining and offered congratulations.

"Colonel K. One of our dearest friends," one said.

"Do you think America and Iraq have a long future together?" another asked.

"I think we'll be friends forever," Kauzlarich said.

"Friend," Mr. Timimi said, kissing Kauzlarich on the cheek.

"Friend," Kauzlarich said back.

Most astonishing, though, more so than even the pizza, was the cake. It was three chocolate tiers that were covered in icing shaped into swirls and flowers. Each tier had candles, and sparklers, too, and propped on the very top was a big cardboard heart with writing on it.

"HAPPY Birthday KoLoNiL K!" it read.

Out came cigarette lighters to light the candles and sparklers, and as the candles flared, and the sparklers burned, and some people began singing "Happy Birthday," and some grabbed aerosol cans of artificial snow and sprayed them into the air, only a cynic wouldn't have been delighted. And since turning forty-two, Kauzlarich had yet to become a cynic.

"Unbelievable," he said as the artificial snow came down on his head. He ate cake. He posed for photographs. "This will go down as the very best birthday I've had in Iraq," he said, and then it was time to go.

He walked over to Qasim to thank him and kissed him on each cheek.

"When is your birthday?" he asked.

"The first of July," Qasim said.

Body armor on now, Kauzlarich headed outside. He had his gifts and balloons with him, and as he turned a corner, he was all of a sudden face-to-face with the Iraqis that Cummings had heard gathering outside of the windows. There were several dozen of them. They were Qasim's soldiers, some Sunni, some Shi'a, some trusted by Qasim and some not, and when they saw Kauzlarich and his gifts and balloons, many of them began to shout.

Kauzlarich kept walking. So did Cummings and the other soldiers.

And so did Izzy, who once again found himself in the middle of the Americans he worked for and the Iraqis he lived among.

Such was the life the war had given him. But for once in that life, he felt neither conflicted nor ashamed. Instead, as their shouting continued, he laughed.

"Christmas! Christmas!" they were shouting to KoLoNiL K.

9

DECEMBER 11, 2007

This month, more of our troops will return home as a result of the
success we're seeing in Iraq. People are coming home.
—GEORGE W. BUSH, *December 3, 2007*

Jeffrey Sauer was about to be one of them. All he had to do was get
through a few more weeks.

A lieutenant colonel like Kauzlarich, Sauer commanded another
battalion on the FOB that had arrived a few months before the 2-16
and always seemed to be that much ahead of whatever Kauzlarich and the
2-16 were experiencing. When Cajimat died in April, for instance, Sauer
and his battalion were in the midst of a period in which nine soldiers
were killed in thirty-one days. "Look at these kids," he had said after the
ninth, going through their photographs one by one. "A great kid . . . Had
a fiancée . . . Four hundred push-ups, four hundred sit-ups . . . Frigging
Silver Star winner . . .

"We all come here thinking we can achieve a lot," he then said, knowing something that Kauzlarich at that point did not.

Now, in November, knowing even more about the limits of achievement, he was just about done. "Am I counting the days?" he said one day,
which soldiers weren't supposed to do, because it was as much of a jinx
as picking up the white tray at the DFAC rather than the brown one, or
stepping through a doorway with their left foot rather than their right
foot. "Yes." But he couldn't help it, he said. Home was so close now that
every soldier of his was thinking, "I don't want to be the last guy," he said,
and he was thinking it, too, because for the first time since arriving, he'd

Adam Schumann

finally had the EFP nightmare, the one where you see the explosion coming at you, and then everything goes blank. "Oh, it fucking woke me up,
for sure."

A few days later, as he drove along Route Predators, the explosion
actually occurred, and it was just as he had dreamed. It came from the
left, enshrouding the Humvee in dust until he couldn't see, and afterward
he said that he now knew the answer to the question of whether a person
hears what might be the moment of his death: no.

Then, a few days later, came another explosion, of which he hadn't
dreamed and he couldn't help but hear.

It happened soon after sunrise on a quiet Sunday morning and shook
every building on the FOB. Doors bowed from the concussion. Windows
broke and blew out. It wasn't the usual rocket or mortar, but something
louder and scarier. There'd been no siren, no warning at all, just a sudden
explosion that felt like the end of the world had arrived, and before anyone had a chance to do anything, such as run for a bunker or crawl under
a bed, there was a second explosion, and a third.

The day of the lob bombs, this would be called. Soldiers counted fifteen explosions in all, although some may have been mixed in with the
roars of missiles being fired from Apache gunships or their own racing
hearts. Whatever the true number, the explosions went on for twenty
minutes, and only as calm returned did the audacity of what had just happened become clear.

There had been two long dump trucks. They had pulled off Route
Pluto across from the FOB, into a dirt area beyond which was a cement
factory. Each was carrying a load of thousands of brightly colored bags of
chicken-flavored potato chips that had been manufactured in Syria, but
hidden beneath were propane tanks on launching rails, which became
visible only as the backs of the trucks rose and the bags of potato chips
fell away.

These tanks were the bombs. Each had been packed with ball bearings
and explosives. A 107-millimeter rocket booster attached to the bottom
was just strong enough to lob a tank over the high wall surrounding the
FOB, at which point it turned nose down and plummeted onto its deto-
nator, exploding with the noise and force of a five-hundred-pound bomb

and spraying shrapnel and ball bearings in every direction for hundreds of yards. One after another, the bombs exploded in terrifying succession, until the two launching trucks were finally destroyed by Hellfire missiles, and when the wreckage had cooled enough to be searched, soldiers discovered an inscription on one of the trucks that read, when translated: "A statement from the Holy Koran. Victory is coming from God, and the entire triumph is near." Other statements had been left, too, in the form of text messages on cell phones. "Little Hiroshima is going to happen to you," was one. "How was your morning now? Surprises are coming."

This was the very first use in Iraq of a weapon that would eventually spread across much of Baghdad and be described by the military as "the greatest threat right now that we face" because of its capacity to kill "scores of soldiers" at once. If there was any good news to this first attack, it was that no one was seriously injured. But the damage to the FOB was significant, perhaps in the millions of dollars, and after the attack ended, Kauzlarich went to survey the extent of it, eventually arriving at a collapsed trailer outside of which stood Jeffrey Sauer.

The trailer had been his. He had been inside, waking up, when the lob bombs began landing nearby. Blast walls surrounding the trailer had stopped the shrapnel, but concussions caved in the roof and walls, and as the trailer came down he covered his head and waited to die. Explosion after explosion—this time Sauer heard them all. Finally, he crawled outside into a smoking landscape of broken buildings and vehicles, and when Kauzlarich arrived, he was standing with a dazed expression, staring at something crawling across the ground.

"See that bug?" he said to Kauzlarich.

Kauzlarich nodded.

"A week ago, I would have crushed it. But it's Sunday, and I almost got my ass waxed, so I'm gonna let it live," he said, and as he continued to watch the bug, Kauzlarich continued to watch the face of a man who soon would be going home.

Home: it was less a place than an act of imagination now, a realm fundamentally disconnected from what life had become. The time difference was part of it—dawn in America was dusk in Iraq—but after nine months it was more than that. Soldiers had a hard time explaining Iraq to one another; how could they explain it to someone whose life had nothing to do with the pucker factor of climbing yet again into a Humvee? Or being caught in a flimsy-walled shitter during a rocket attack? Or busting into a building at 3:00 a.m. and finding a little torture room with blood-spattered walls and a bloodstained mattress and a rubber hose and scratchings on a wall of a crazed face and a partly eaten piece of bread? Or touching the bread with a boot and realizing with additional horror that it was still fresh? Or developing the absolute need, as Brent Cummings had developed, of never, never, *ever* standing in his room with half of his foot on the floor and half of it on the cheap rug he'd bought to make his room feel homier, because the one time he stood that way was the day of a KIA?

If Cummings told his wife that, was there any way she would understand?

If he told a soldier that, was there any way he wouldn't?

Nine months along, where *was* home now? Was it back there, where Kauzlarich's wife, Stephanie, recorded a video for him of their three children on his birthday, or was it here, where he interrupted the rhythms of a day in order to watch it?

"Happy birthday, cha-cha-cha," they sang.

"My little buddies," he said. He played it again. And again, amazed at how much taller they had become.

Was home the place where children grew so steadily it was invisible, or here, where their father noticed it in increments, like a distant relative?

Jumpy videos, slapdash e-mails, occasional phone calls, Internet messaging—these were the tether lines from here to there, and there to here, that were becoming ever more frayed by distance and time.

"The weather this weekend has been glorious!" Kauzlarich's mother wrote in October. "The leaves are all turning color, no wind, and temperatures in the upper 60's, low 70's! Are there any other signs of Fall in Iraq except the more reasonable temperatures? Your lovin' Mom and Dad."

"Dear Mom and Dad," Kauzlarich wrote back. "It's still 100 degrees here. The leaves are not turning color. Love, Ralph."

"Hi Love! I Love you! Well, today I've spent in vacation research craziness . . ." Stephanie began an e-mail in early December, and she went on from there to describe different scenarios for Kauzlarich's upcoming leave and their plans to go to Florida. She had found flights, ticket packages, hotels, and resorts, and she laid out the prices of each. Would he prefer this hotel or that hotel? Standard room or suite? A hotel or a condo? With meals or without meals? Disney or Universal? And what about Sea World? "SOOOO THOUGHTS???????"

"Stephanie Corie," he wrote back. "As long as I get to spend all the time with you and the kids we can do it in a bungalow upside down for all I care. Money ain't an issue. Do need a heated pool. Your choice on all . . . Hugs, Ralph Lester."

"OK!!" she wrote back, and before he could fully absorb that she hadn't started with the word *love*, he was reading: "I stayed up 2 extra hours last night to get all the details straight for you so that you could be a part of making the decision on our trip. I know you're making lots of decisions over there & I shouldn't bother you with this. I've been making all the decisions here for 10 months by myself . . ."

Meanwhile, Brent Cummings called home and didn't know whether to laugh or cry as his wife, Laura, told him she had just come back from taking their two daughters to the sports bar the family would go to every Friday afternoon when he was there. It was a tradition of theirs, and it moved him that she had done this, but then Laura was saying that their four-year-old daughter, who has Down syndrome, began vomiting all over herself at the table, and their eight-year-old daughter kept saying, "Gross gross gross," and the waitress was horrified, and Laura couldn't find enough napkins, and as the vomit kept coming, people all over the sports bar were averting their eyes and covering their mouths and noses as they realized it wasn't the aroma of French fries drifting their way . . .

Meanwhile, a soldier who was one of the snipers was storming around in a rage because he had telephoned his wife at one o'clock in the morning her time and no one had answered and *where the hell was his wife at one o'clock in the morning?* So he called her again at two o'clock in the morning and she didn't answer *and where the hell was she at two in the morning?*

"For a lot of soldiers, home is a place of disaster right now," a mental health specialist named James Tczap, who worked in Combat Stress and was a captain, said one day. "It's a broken relationship, a fractured relationship, a suspicious relationship. Even the functional relationships are challenged by the disconnect." Worse, even, he said, was the belief soldiers held that when they went home on their mid-deployment leave, everything would be better than it ever was. "There's an anger in guys when they go back. They want to go home and be normal, and they're not quite normal," he said, and added, "Coming back from leave is the worst part of the deployment."

On their leaves, they got eighteen days at home to not wear camouflage, not wear armor, not wear gloves, not wear eye protection, and not drive around wondering what was in that pile of trash they were passing, although most of them did wonder, because eighteen days is not enough time to shake such a thing. It was a point of honor with Kauzlarich that he would be among the last to go, and so he stayed put month after month as his soldiers disappeared on helicopters and returned three weeks later with all manner of stories to tell.

A specialist named Brian Emerson ended up in Las Vegas at the Sweethearts Wedding Chapel with his girlfriend of two years, getting married as her mother listened in on a cell phone. He spent $5,000, he said when he got back, ring not included, much of it at the Bellagio. "The penthouse suite," he said proudly. "It was like five-hundred-and-something dollars a night. We stayed for two." And then it was time to go. "Worse than leaving the first time," he said.

Sergeant Jay Howell ended up in Branson, Missouri, at a place called the Dixie Stampede. "It's like a rodeo while you're eating, but the theme is the Civil War," he said. "You go in, you pick a side, North or South, they do some singing and dancing, then they do some horse races; they got weapons, they have pigs even; then they pull out kids from the audience and the kids chase chickens. The North versus the South. We've been there a few times, and it always ends in a tie. The kids love it." And then it was time to come back.

Sergeant Major Randy Waddell simply went home, and as glad as he was to be there, his heart sank when he saw that his seventeen-year-old son, Joey, was driving around in a truck that had 160,000 miles on it, was leaking oil and transmission fluid, and had a plastic bag taped over a broken-out window.

"So we go looking for a truck," Waddell, back now, told Brent Cummings of what he had done on leave, "and golly, these cars are so expensive." The one they liked the most was at a Toyota place, he said, a used gray Dodge with 25,000 miles on it, but the price was $17,000. *Only* $17,000, the salesman, a little ball of energy, had said, but there was no *only* about it.

Cummings shook his head in sympathy.

"And one night I was sitting out on the porch by myself and I was thinking about it," Waddell continued. "I was thinking, 'You know, Randy, if you don't make it back, for whatever reason, if you don't come back, what will Joey have to drive if you don't get him something before you leave?'" Alone on the porch, he went back and forth, he told Cummings. Fix the old truck? That he could afford. "Or I could go buy him something and be done with it, and at least when I go back to Iraq I'll have a clear conscience that I did the right thing when I was home.

"So I bought him a seventeen-thousand-dollar truck."

"Wow," Cummings said.

"And let me tell how I did this," Waddell said. "This is great. This is how I surprised him. We find this truck and we drive it and then we go away for a couple of days, and I do all the paperwork while he's at school. So the day that we're ready to sign all the paperwork—because I did it over the phone—I said, 'Joey,' I said, 'Let's drive back up to the Toyota place and see if that truck's still there.' He said, 'There ain't no need in going up there, Dad. We can't afford it. We've already talked about it. It costs too much.' I said, 'Well, let's go talk to him. Let's see if we can get him down to fifteen instead of seventeen.' So we pull up there, and the truck's moved, because they're getting it ready for me to pick up. So we walk up to one of the salesmen, and that guy didn't know me. I said, 'So, what's going on with that gray Dodge?' 'Oh, somebody came by this morning and bought it.' Aww, you shoulda *seen* Joey's face. 'I told you,

Dad! I told you somebody already bought it! I told you!' I said, 'Well let's go in and talk to the guy and see.' So we go inside, and the little guy comes running up to me, 'Hey, Mr. Waddell, how you doing? Blah blah blah.' And I said, 'So, I hear you sold that truck out there today.' He said, 'Yeah. We did. We sold it to *you!*' And Joey turned around and looked at me, and I said, 'Oh yeah, you own that truck outside.'

"And that's how we got the truck."

"That's awesome!" Cummings said.

"It turned out well," Waddell said.

"I spent seven grand," said Jay March, who was just back from leave and once again beneath the tree from which hung the sack of poison filled with dead flies.

"You're shittin' me," a sergeant he was sitting with said.

"Nope," March said, and then went on to describe what he had done after he turned twenty-one, left James Harrelson's memorial service, and went home to Ohio in search of new slides for the continuing show in his head.

"The first thing I did was take fifteen hundred dollars and take my two brothers to the mall," he began, and then backtracked to say that the very first thing he did was strip off his uniform in the airport parking lot, put on shorts and a T-shirt that his brothers had brought him, and then go to the mall. For three hours, they bought whatever they wanted, sale or no sale, as if they weren't poor, and what he bought were new pants, a new shirt, and new athletic shoes, all in white, pure white, because he wanted to feel clean.

From the mall, he went home to see the rest of his family, where the questions began. "So what do you do?" they asked. "Well, we go out," he said, and unsure of how to describe it, he showed them photographs instead. There was Harrelson's Humvee, on fire. There was Craig's Humvee just after Craig died. There were some kids in Kamaliyah. "And my grandma started crying," March said. "She knew about the deaths, but this was seeing how people lived. The shit trenches and stuff. I showed her a picture of a Humvee stuck in a shit trench, and she asked if that was mud, and I tried to explain it was shit, and that those lakes on the sides were shit and piss, and she didn't want to see anymore. She got up and went in the other room and she got busy ordering me my favorite dinner, which is chicken Parmesan."

And his first day went from there, he said. He ate some marvelous chicken Parmesan, he bought his first legal six-pack of beer, and then he went with his brother and some friends to a place called the Yankee Bar and Grill for the Friday night wet T-shirt contest.

He danced. He drank a beer. He drank tequila. He drank Crown Royal. He drank another beer. He drank a Flaming Dr Pepper. He drank something else: "I don't even know what the fuck it was, but they put something on fire and dropped it in the beer."

He danced with a girl and mentioned he was home from Iraq, and danced with another girl and mentioned it again. He was wearing his new white shirt and white pants and white shoes and was feeling pretty good about things, and yes, he was drunk, totally drunk, but not so drunk that he didn't hear them calling out his name and telling him to come up on the stage.

So he and his brother went up onstage and sat back to back in two chairs with a stripper's pole in between, and as six women in T-shirts came onstage and began dancing in a circle around them, he yelled to his brother, "Dude, there's no fucking way." Here came the water hoses now, and soon the women were soaked head to toe and dancing through puddles while pulling off their shirts, and was that the moment he had a new slide for the show inside his head, or was it from what came next? Because now one of the women was stepping onto his new white shoes and leaning toward him and pushing her chest toward his face, and now she was climbing onto his lap and standing on his thighs with her wet dirty feet to get to the stripper's pole, and now she was trying to step onto his shoulders, and now, drunk as he was, all he could think about was:

My new white shoes!

My new white pants!

My new white shirt!

Once again, he was filthy.

"But I remembered it didn't matter," he said. "I had more money. I could buy more clothes tomorrow." So he began laughing, and then cheering as someone yelled into the microphone, "Welcome back from Iraq," and then a woman was saying, "I'll give you a ride home tonight," and then they were in front of his house kissing, and then she was removing her shirt, and then "I passed out on her chest. Drunk. Done. She woke me up. 'Maybe we should do this another night.' 'Yeah.'"

So he went inside, passed out again, and dreamed of an explosion.

"Dude, what's wrong?" his brother said as he sat up wide-eyed.

He passed out again and then the phone began ringing.

"They're trying to call me! They're trying to call me!" he began screaming, and then he had a cigarette, and then he passed out again, and then it was morning and his grandmother was the one leaning toward him, saying, "Here's some orange juice," and he was thinking:

Seventeen days to go.

In the first hours of his leave, Nate Showman walked through the Atlanta airport and couldn't look anyone in the eye. The businessmen on cell phones, the families on vacation—all of it was too strange. The normal abnormal, Cummings called Iraq, but this was exactly the opposite: the abnormal normal. Eyes down so he wouldn't betray any emotion, Showman made his way to a connecting flight home and a girlfriend he wasn't sure he knew how to talk to anymore.

In the final hours of his leave, he ended up getting married, the last thing he had gone home intending to do.

Showman was the twenty-four-year-old lieutenant whose earnestness and optimism about the war had made people think of him as a young version of Kauzlarich. But by the time he headed home, that optimism had been tempered. After being in charge of Kauzlarich's personal security detail for the first few months of the deployment, he was promoted to a platoon leader in Alpha Company, directly responsible for the lives of two dozen men who in horrible June, and horrible July, and horrible August, and horrible September, would roll their eyes at Kauzlarich's "It's all good" pronouncements. Over time, he began to see their point. "I think it's difficult for them, and difficult for me, to hear about these strides we're making, these improvements we're making, when we know—when *I* know—for a fact, that this place hasn't changed a damn bit since we set foot here in February," he said one day.

Mid-August was the worst of it, when two of his soldiers were severely wounded in an EFP attack. Two days later, the rest of his soldiers decided they'd had enough. They were tired of waiting to be blown up, they were tired of being mortared every day at the COP, they were tired of being told they were winning when they knew they weren't. Among themselves, they decided that the following morning they weren't going to go out of the wire. Maybe they would sabotage their Humvees. Or maybe they would just refuse orders to go, even if it meant charges of insubordination. Either way, when Showman heard whispers of it, he realized he had a potential mutiny on his young hands, and he went to Kauzlarich for advice.

"Fix it," Kauzlarich suggested.

He did in the end, by hatching a plan with two of his platoon sergeants to wake up the soldiers in the middle of the night, when they would be at their groggiest, and get in their faces until they were on their way. It would not go down in military history as the most sophisticated plan of all time, but to Showman's relief, it worked. One sleepy soldier headed toward a Humvee, another followed, then another. Problem solved. But of course it was not.

By the time Showman flew to the United States at the end of September, an effusive young man who would write earnest letters home—"We are holding a snake by the tail here . . . Keep the faith . . . Let us finish the fight"—had become largely silent. He and his girlfriend headed to a cabin deep in the woods, but even there, safe and sealed off, he was reluctant to talk. One day he did, though, and when he found himself unable to stop, as if he had become one more war wound in need of a tourniquet, he came up with another plan, this one more elaborate.

It involved a limousine to a restaurant and a bouquet of roses waiting on a chair. Out came a bottle of wine and two glasses, one etched with the words *Will you marry me?* and the other with *Say yes.*

"Yes," she said. "Yes."

"What if we did it now?" he said.

"What if we did it now?" she repeated, and so it was that on day seventeen of his leave, in the backyard of her house, as their families and a few friends watched, Nate Showman's optimism returned.

They spent one night together, and then they were at the airport saying goodbye. It would be six months before he would see her again, and he wanted to find the right words that would last that long, or if it were to come to that, longer.

"My wife," he finally said, saying those words for the first time.

She laughed.

"My husband," she said.

And then he came back.

Adam Schumann was going home, too. But unlike the others, he was not coming back. Five months after carrying Sergeant Emory down the stairs in Kamaliyah, his bad-news vessel, as David Petraeus might describe it, was no longer able to drain.

This was Schumann's third deployment to Iraq. He'd been here thirty-four months by his own count, just over a thousand days, and it didn't matter anymore that he was one of the 2-16's very best soldiers. His war had become unbearable. He was seeing over and over his first kill disappearing into a mud puddle, looking at him as he sank. He was seeing a house that had just been obliterated by gunfire, a gate slowly opening, and a wide-eyed little girl about the age of his daughter peering out. He was seeing another gate, another child, and this time a dead-aim soldier firing. He was seeing another soldier, also firing, who afterward vomited as he described watching head spray after head spray through his magnifying scope. He was seeing himself watching the vomiting soldier while casually eating a chicken-and-salsa MRE.

He was still tasting the MRE.

He was still tasting Sergeant Emory's blood.

He needed to go home. That was what Combat Stress had said after he finally gave in and admitted that his thoughts had turned suicidal. The traveling psychiatrist who spent a few days a week on the FOB diagnosed him as depressed and suffering from posttraumatic stress disorder, a diagnosis that was becoming the most common of the war. There had been internal studies suggesting that 20 percent of soldiers deployed to Iraq were experiencing symptoms of PTSD ranging from nightmares, to insomnia, to rapid breathing, to racing hearts, to depression, to obsessive thoughts about suicide. They also suggested that those symptoms increased significantly with multiple deployments and that the cost of treating the hundreds of thousands of soldiers suffering from them could eventually cost more than the war itself.

Every study that had been done indicated the seriousness of this, and yet in the culture of the army, where mental illness has long been equated with weakness, there remained a lingering suspicion of any diagnosis for which there wasn't visible evidence. A soldier who lost a leg, for instance, was a soldier who lost a leg. Losing a leg couldn't be faked. Same with being shot, or pierced by shrapnel from a lob bomb, or incinerated by an EFP. Those were legitimate injuries. But to lose a mind? Early in the deployment, a soldier had one day climbed onto the roof of an Iraqi police station, stripped off everything he was wearing, then ascended a ladder to the top of a guard tower, and in full view of a busy section of New Baghdad began hollering at the top of his lungs and masturbating. Was it an act of mental instability, as some thought, or was it the calculated act of someone trying to get home, which was Kauzlarich's growing suspicion? Trying to figure it out, Kauzlarich kept returning to the fact that the soldier had paused in the midst of his supposed meltdown to remove sixty pounds of clothing and gear before climbing the ladder, which suggested a deliberateness to his thinking. Perhaps he hadn't been so out of control after all. Perhaps he was just a lousy, disloyal soldier. And so, in the end, he was sent home not with a recommendation for treatment, but for a court martial and incarceration.

Kauzlarich himself was another example of the army's conflicted attitude about all this. On one hand, he endorsed the idea of his soldiers being debriefed by the FOB's Combat Stress team after witnessing something especially traumatic. But when Kauzlarich was the one in need of debriefing after he saw the remains of three of his soldiers scattered along the road on September 4, he made it clear that he needed no help whatsoever. "I don't need that bullshit," he told Cummings, and so Cummings, who knew better, discreetly arranged for a Combat Stress specialist to casually drop by Kauzlarich's office. An hour later, he was still leaning in Kauzlarich's doorway, tossing out questions, and afterward Kauzlarich mentioned to Cummings that he was feeling a lot better. He understood what had just happened and was glad for it, and yet even with that he had no intention of ever being seen walking into the aid station and disappearing through the doorway marked COMBAT STRESS. And as reports of soldiers supposedly having problems continued to reach him, he continued to reduce some of those reports to the infantry's historically preferred diagnosis: "He's just a pussy."

With Schumann, though, there was no such pronouncement, because it was obvious to everyone what had happened, that a great soldier had reached his limit. "He is a true casualty of battle," Ron Brock, the battalion's physician assistant, said one day as Schumann was preparing to leave Rustamiyah for good. "There's not a physical scar, but look at the man's heart, and his head, and there are scars galore."

You could see it in his nervous eyes. You could see it in his shaking hands. You could see it in the three prescription bottles in his room: one to steady his galloping heart rate, one to reduce his anxiety, one to minimize his nightmares. You could see it in the screensaver on his laptop—a nuclear fireball and the words FUCK IRAQ—and in the private journal he had been keeping since he arrived.

His first entry, on February 22:

Not much going on today. I turned my laundry in, and we're getting our TAT boxes. We got mortared last night at 2:30 a.m., none close. We're at FOB Rustamiyah, Iraq. It's pretty nice, got a good chow hall and facilities. Still got a bunch of dumb shit to do though. Well, that's about it for today.

His last entry, on October 18:

I've lost all hope. I feel the end is near for me, very, very near.

Day by day my misery grows like a storm, ready to swallow me whole and take me to the unknown. Yet all I can fear is the unknown.

Why can't I just let go and let it consume me. Why do I fight so hard, just to be punished again and again, for things I can't recall? What have I done? I just can't go on anymore with this evil game.

Darkness is all I see anymore.

So he was finished. Down to his final hours, he was packed, weaponless, under escort, and waiting for the helicopter that would take him away to a wife who had just told him on the phone: "I'm scared of what you might do."

"You know I'd never hurt you," he'd said, and he'd hung up, wandered around the FOB, gotten a haircut, and come back to his room, where he now said, "But what if she's right? What if I snap someday?"

It was a thought that made him feel sick. Just as every thought now made him feel sick. "You spend a thousand days, it gets to the point where it's *Groundhog Day*. Every day is over and over. The heat. The smell. The language. There's nothing sweet about it. It's all sour," he said. He remembered the initial invasion, when it wasn't that way. "I mean it was a front seat to the greatest movie I've ever seen in my life." He remembered the firefights of his second deployment. "I loved it. Anytime I get shot at in a firefight, it's the sexiest feeling there is." He remembered how this deployment began to feel bad early on. "I'd get in the Humvee and be driving down the road and I would feel my heart pulsing up in my throat." That was the start of it, he said, and then Emory happened, and then Crow happened, and then he was in a succession of explosions, and then a bullet was skimming across his thighs, and then Doster happened, and then he was waking up thinking, "Holy shit, I'm still here, it's misery, it's hell," which became, "Are they going to kill me today?" which became, "I'll take care of it myself," which became, "Why do that? I'll go out killing as many of them as I can, until they kill me.

"I didn't give a fuck," he said. "I wanted it to happen. Bottom line—I wanted it over as soon as possible, whether they did it or I did it."

The amazing thing was that no one knew. Here was all this stuff going on, pounding heart, panicked breathing, sweating palms, electric eyes, and no one regarded him as anything but the great soldier he'd always been, the one who never complained, who hoisted bleeding soldiers onto

his back, who'd suddenly begun insisting on being in the right front seat
of the lead Humvee on every mission, not because he wanted to be dead
but because that's what selfless leaders would do.

He was the great Sergeant Schumann, who one day walked to the aid
station and went through the door marked COMBAT STRESS and asked for
help from James Tczap and now was on his way home.

Now he was remembering what Tczap had told him: "With your stat-
ure, maybe you've opened the door for a lot of guys to come in."

"That made me feel really good," he said. And yet he had felt so awful
the previous day when he told one of his team leaders to round up
everyone in his squad.

"What'd we do now?"

"You didn't do anything," he said. "Just get them together."

They came into his room, and he shut the door and told them he was
leaving the following day. He said the hard part: that it was a mental
health evacuation. He said to them, "I don't even know what I'm going
through. I know that I don't feel right."

"Well, how long?" one of his soldiers said, breaking the silence.

"I don't know," he said. "There's a possibility I won't be coming
back."

They had rallied around him then, shaking his hand, grabbing his arm,
patting his back, and saying whatever nineteen- and twenty-year-olds
could think of to say.

"Take care of yourself," one of them said.

"Drink a beer for me," another said.

He had never felt so guilt-ridden in his life.

Early this morning, they had driven away on a mission, leaving him
behind, and after they'd disappeared, he had no idea what to do. He stood
there alone for a while. Eventually he walked back to his room. He turned
up his air conditioner to high. When he got cold enough to shiver, he put
on warmer clothes and stayed under the vents. He started watching *Apoc-
alypse Now* on his computer and paused when Martin Sheen said, "When
I was here, I wanted to be there; when I was there, all I could think of was
getting back into the jungle." He backed it up and played it again. He
packed his medication. He stacked some packages of beef jerky and mac-

n-cheese and smoked oysters, which he wouldn't be able to take with him, for the soldiers he was leaving behind and wrote a note that said, "Enjoy."

Finally it was time to go to the helicopter, and he began walking down the hall. Word had spread through the entire company by now, and when one of the soldiers saw him, he came over. "Well, I'll walk you as far as the shitters, because I have to go to the bathroom," the soldier said, and as last words, those would have to do, because those were the last words he heard from any of the soldiers of the 2-16 as his deployment came to an end.

His stomach hurt as he made his way across the FOB. He felt himself becoming nauseated. At the landing area, other soldiers from other battalions were lined up, and when the helicopter landed, everyone was allowed to board except him. He didn't understand.

"Next one's yours," he was told, and when it came in a few minutes later, he realized why he'd had to wait. It had a big red cross on the side. It was the helicopter for the injured and the dead.

That was him, Adam Schumann.

He was injured. He was dead. He was done.

"You okay?"

Laura Cummings asked this.

"Yeah. Just watching the storm," Cummings said. He was home, too, now, sitting on his front porch since waking up in the dark to the sound of explosions. Just thunder, he'd realized, so he'd gone outside to see his first rainstorm in months. He'd watched the lightning flashes come closer. He'd felt the air turn moist. The rain, when it came down on the roof, and fell through the downspouts, and washed across his lawn, and flowed along his street, sounded musical to him, and he listened to it, wondering what time it was in Iraq. Was it two in the afternoon? Three in the afternoon? Had anything happened? Unlikely. Anything bad? Anything good?

"We're going to have to get the umbrellas out for the girls," Laura said now, and he wondered whether the umbrellas were still kept in the same place as when he had left.

At Radina's, the coffee shop he liked to go to, one of the regulars clapped him on the back and motioned to a friend. "Come on over and meet Brent Cummings," he said. "He's just back from Iraq. He's a hero."

Before a Kansas State University football game, as he stood in the stadium parking lot, dressed in school colors, just like always, and wondering if he would ever again think of a football game as life and death, people had questions.

"How are things in Iraq?"

"It's been difficult—but we're doing good," he said.

"Is the war worth it?"

"Yeah, I think it's worth it," he said.

"You can ask him," he overheard a man saying to a woman, who then asked, "Is Bush a good man?"

Sometimes he would look at his daughters and think about the day that a little Iraqi girl waved at him and a man standing next to the girl saw this and slapped her hard across the face, and he grabbed the man and called him a coward and said if he ever did that again he would be arrested or killed. "It felt good to say it," he had said that day, right afterward. "It felt good to snatch him off the street in front of people. It felt good to see the fear in his eyes. That felt good."

He would sit on the porch and listen to the automatic lawn sprinklers that Laura had mentioned in an e-mail that she was having installed.

He would sit in the living room and listen to his daughters play the piano that Laura had mentioned she was thinking of buying.

Back at Radina's, someone said, "We saw a few soldiers in the paper," and he knew what they meant and wished they would talk about something else. And soon they did. The conversations were once again about football or vacations or the weather or, for the thousandth time, how good the coffee was, and he was grateful.

One day he said to Laura, "How much do you want to know?"

They were in the bedroom, just back from a memorial service at the Fort Riley chapel, where he had delivered a eulogy for Doster, who had died a few hours after Cummings had flown out of Rustamiyah to begin his leave. "Whatever you do, when you get up to speak, don't look at the family," the chaplain had said beforehand, advising Cummings on how not to lose his composure, and he hadn't looked, but he had heard them, as had everyone in the chapel, including a few of the 2-16 soldiers who had been injured and sent back to Kansas. The soldier who had been shot in the chest at the gas station and dragged to safety by Rachel the interpreter was there. A soldier who had been shot in the throat and appeared to Cummings as if he were in the midst of a perpetual flashback was there. A soldier who had been in Cajimat's Humvee way back when and now spent his days watching one of his arms wither away was there. There were five in all, and Cummings had made plans after the service to see them again, maybe for lunch, and then he and Laura had gone home to the one place in the world where he didn't worry about whether his foot was halfway on the carpet and halfway on the floor. "How'd I sound?" he'd asked as he hung up his uniform. "You were good," Laura had answered, sitting on the edge of the bed, looking at him, and suddenly he was crying and saying, "It's so stupid, Laura, it's so stupid, it's so stupid," and feeling as if the rainstorm he had watched the first night was now moving through him.

He felt better after that. He went for bike rides. He got his daughters ready for school. He drank the best beer he had ever tasted. He went to the gym with Laura. He sat on his porch with his dogs. He went to Radina's and saw the man with the big beard who always sat in the corner reading a novel, there as ever, as if there weren't a concern in the world.

"Oh man, it was so good, just to be home," he said, back in Baghdad now, about to take an Ambien, hoping he would be able to sleep. "It was the best time of my life."

He had not seen the injured soldiers again, even though he'd intended to.

He'd also intended to go to the Fort Riley cemetery and visit the grave of the lone 2-16 soldier who had been buried there. Back in the war again, he wondered why he hadn't.

But he hadn't.

The grave was that of Joel Murray, one of the three soldiers who died on September 4 and whose home now was an old cemetery filled to its edges with dead soldiers from half a dozen wars. On December 11, his grave and that cemetery were covered in ice from a massive storm that was blowing through Kansas on its way from the Great Plains into the Midwest. Seventeen people so far were dead. Hundreds of thousands were without electricity. Trees were crashing down everywhere. Down came a huge limb in the cemetery, collapsing onto a line of headstones and just missing Murray's. Down came more limbs all over Fort Riley, including in the front yard of a house near the cemetery, where a sign out front read, LT COL KAUZLARICH and where the morning newspaper with a story about the two most recent battle deaths in Iraq was buried under a layer of ice.

Stephanie Kauzlarich would get to the paper eventually, but at the moment she had too much to do.

"Next time I'll buy the Jungle Pancakes," she was saying to Allie, who was eight years old now and bored with her Eggos.

"You want more syrup?" she was saying to Jacob, who was six now.

"You gonna eat breakfast?" she was saying to Garrett, who was four now and racing around the house in a T-shirt and underpants while screaming, *"I can't stop running!"*

Last night's pizza slices were still in the sink. Flash cards were on the counter. Lego pieces were everywhere. Stephanie opened the refrigerator and the orange juice came tumbling out, which somehow caused the Eggos to fall out of their box and go skidding across the floor. "It's snowing waffles!" Jacob hollered as Stephanie, who had turned forty since the deployment began, ran after them.

Here was home in its truest form, when the soldier who lived there was not on the front porch watching a thunderstorm, or proposing, or passing out on the couch, or buying a truck, but was still in Iraq. It was what home was like not on the eighteen days that Kauzlarich would be there, but on the four hundred days he would not.

It was boxes of Christmas decorations that Stephanie had hauled down from the attic and needed to put up. It was thickening ice on the sidewalk and steps, and where in the world was the big bag of ice melter they bought last year? It was the lights flickering in the storm, and where were the AA batteries for the flashlight, in case the electricity went out? Here were the C batteries. Here were the AAAs. But where were the AAs? The framed photograph of Ralph on top of the refrigerator also needed batteries to power the motion sensor that triggered the memory chip on which he had recorded a message so the kids wouldn't forget his voice. "Hey. Whatcha doin' over there? I seeeee you," he had recorded, trying to be funny, after Stephanie had said that his original message, about how much he missed them, might be too sad. And it worked. He got on a plane to go to Iraq, and the kids came home and walked into the kitchen and heard him saying, "I seeeee you." They went out and came back in. "I seeeee you." They woke up the next morning and came into the kitchen for breakfast. "I seeeee you." Every morning, there he was, even before Stephanie had coffee. "I seeeee you." She went upstairs to get dressed and came back. "I seeeee you." She went to get the mail and came back. "I seeeee you." She began ducking when she came into the kitchen. "I seeeee you." What could she do, though? She couldn't turn the photo upside down. She couldn't take the batteries out, or cover the sensor, or do anything that would seem disrespectful of the circumstances that had led to the buying of the frame and the recording of the message. "I seeeee you." "I seeeee you." "I seeeee you." "I seeeee you." And then, one day, the batteries ran out, and she meant to replace them, but now it was months later, and anyway they were probably AAs, and if she could find any AAs she'd better put them in the flashlight, because the storm was getting worse. Down came a branch. "I wonder if I should move the car," she said. But it was miserable out there. Down came more branches. "I should move the car," she said.

His war, her war. They were vastly different and largely unshared with each other.

In April, when he wrote to tell her that Jay Cajimat died, he didn't go into detail about learning what an EFP could do, and when she wrote back she didn't go into detail about painting Easter eggs with the kids.

In July, when the 2-16 was being attacked several times a day, she didn't dwell on her own drama: that she and the kids were driving home from out of state, and the car died and had to be jump-started, and they went to a Wendy's, and the kids had to go to the bathroom, and she couldn't turn off the car because she was afraid it would die again, and she couldn't let them go in by themselves . . .

In September, she didn't tell him much about the colonel's wife who'd approached her and asked, "How are you doing?" "I'm doing okay." "Are you sure?" "Yes." "Are you *sure?*" "Yes, I'm doing okay." "No, you're *not*. You're *not* doing okay." It would have been an uncomfortable conversation anytime, but making it worse was the setting: the memorial service for the three dead soldiers. "And what am I supposed to say?" she said now, sitting in her kitchen. "I'm sick of being a single parent? I'm sick of not having sex? Is that what I say? That life sucks?"

Instead, she kept anything like that to herself. She wasn't going to tell a colonel's wife that, and she wasn't going to tell Ralph, who she was sure needed her to be nothing other than upbeat.

"Happy birthday, cha-cha-cha," the kids sang, and there was no way she was going to tell him how much work those videos were: that the boys preferred to be watching TV or playing with friends, that no one would say anything and she'd have to prompt them with whispered commands.

"Hi Love! Well, guess who loves you! Me & A, J, & G!!!!! I hope that you enjoyed the pictures I sent earlier . . . quite a remarkable storm!" was how she began her e-mail to him the night of the storm, after getting the kids into bed.

She didn't tell him about the branch that just missed the car, or the way she attacked the ice on the sidewalk, with a hammer and knife, because she couldn't find the melter, or that when she sent the pictures, she was sure he would notice that she hadn't brought in the garden hose for the winter.

She didn't tell him that before she could find a moment to write to him, the night had been a parade of footsteps and flushing toilets and coughs and a tired mother trying to soothe some anxious little boys by saying, "Good night, my handsome men."

She came back downstairs. She looked at the silent photograph on top of the refrigerator. He was in a white shirt. They had all worn white shirts that day and gone to Sears to be photographed. It was right before he left.

Almost eleven months later, of course she missed him, but it was more than that. "I think it's hurt. Deep down personal hurt. Resentment. That it's fifteen months. That I'm parenting alone. That I'm just doing life alone," she said.

"I hate the war and what it has done to my life."

She didn't tell him that, either. Instead, giving no indication of her exhaustion, except for the time stamp on the e-mail that said it was sent at 12:44 a.m., she wrote, "Schools are closed again tomorrow. Some more precipitation fell, and well I think that perhaps we may be able to hit the slopes and go for some ice sledding! WOW! That would be fast & fun. Yes a perfect way to introduce the kids to Extreme Sports!!! I've been waiting for this opportunity to live on the edge!! ha-ha! Yea I know without you it won't be quite as fun, but about living on the edge—I bet we can accommodate that feat in January!!!"

January was when he would be home. He was due to leave Baghdad in sixteen days.

"I'm worried about January," she said. "Who will he be?"

"I'm proud of you!" she wrote to him. "Your wife, Stephanie."

And now it was his turn.

Home.

He couldn't wait.

He flew out at 1:00 a.m. on December 27. He would go to Fort Riley first, then to Orlando, then to Fort Riley again, and then back to Baghdad, with a stop at the end at Brooke Army Medical Center in San Antonio, so he could visit some of his most seriously injured soldiers. Next to seeing his family, he was looking forward to that most of all.

A few other soldiers from the battalion had already made such a visit to BAMC and had come back shaken from what they had seen. One was a specialist named Michael Anderson, who on September 4 was three Humvees behind the Humvee that was hit. A month later, on leave, he went to BAMC to visit Duncan Crookston, one of the two soldiers in the Humvee who had survived. "And it was heartbreaking," Anderson would say, "because I remember Crookston being a grown man. I remember seeing what he looked like, and when I saw him, he honestly looked like a kid. You couldn't tell that he used to be a grown man. He didn't have his legs. He didn't have his right arm. He didn't have his hand. He was completely wrapped up. He had goggles on. His body was like in this mesh. It was, honestly, I don't want to say creepy, but it was honestly creepy, seeing my buddy like that. It was just not right. It was September fourth all over again."

Crookston was one of the soldiers Kauzlarich wanted to see. There were fourteen in all there, including six Nate Showman met with when he was on leave and spent an afternoon at BAMC. One of the soldiers had lost both of his legs below the knee. One had lost an eye. One had lost much of his left foot. One had lost much of his right foot. One had lost his lower right arm. One had lost his right hand. They met in the cafeteria for lunch, and at one point Kauzlarich's name came up.

"I don't ever want to see that motherfucker again," one of the soldiers said.

10

JANUARY 25, 2008

Here's what I tell people. I tell people here in America that an Iraqi
mother wants the same thing for her children that an American mother wants,
a chance for that child to grow up in peace and to realize dreams, a chance
for the child to go outside and play and not fear harm.
—GEORGE W. BUSH, *January 4, 2008*

The guys are real excited to see you, sir," the BAMC escort told Kauzlarich.

It was a windy, drizzly, bitingly cold day, especially for someone who had spent ten months in Iraq and ten days in Florida. During the leave, Stephanie kept her thoughts about the war mostly to herself, and so did Kauzlarich, until his last night home, when he confessed that there had been a few times in Orlando when he was driving and felt himself in a Humvee and here came the flash, the boom, the dirt. But only a few times, he said, and after a moment or two he was back in a rental car with his family. "How are you doing?" they asked each other, and the true answer was that they were doing fine. His being home had rejuvenated both of them, even during the worst of it, at Disney World, as he was steering the rental car into the Dopey parking lot and Garrett socked Allie in the nose. Allie screamed. Blood poured from her nose onto her clothing. Stephanie couldn't find tissues. Kauzlarich began mopping up the blood with Garrett's jacket, figuring it would teach him a lesson. In the chaos of the car, it seemed like a good idea, except instead of grabbing Garrett's jacket, he accidentally grabbed Jacob's, and now Jacob was upset, and Garrett was upset, and Allie was upset, and Stephanie was upset, and Kauz-

Joshua Atchley

larich was in the midst of saying, "You can't hit girls, never hit girls," when Allie began choking and spitting up blood, which went all over Garrett's jacket.

War? What war?

But soon it was back again as Kauzlarich flew to San Antonio and was escorted to the fourth floor of the hospital at BAMC, where a sign read, U.S. ARMY INSTITUTE OF SURGICAL RESEARCH BURN CENTER.

He had decided to start with Duncan Crookston.

He put on a protective gown, protective boots, and protective gloves and walked toward a nineteen-year-old soldier whose left leg was gone, right leg was gone, right arm was gone, left lower arm was gone, ears were gone, nose was gone, and eyelids were gone, and who was burned over what little remained of him.

Michael Anderson had been right. It was September 4 all over again.

"Wow," Kauzlarich said under his breath. And then, taking it in: "Bastards."

Here it was, then, the view of the war at its far end, and not only in the first startling view of Duncan Crookston, but in a series of first views that Kauzlarich would absorb throughout the entire BAMC complex. There had been more than thirty thousand injuries to American troops so far in the war, and several thousand of the worst of them had been sent to this corner of Texas to recover, or, every so often, to die. The severe burns came here. Many of the amputations came here. The stays could last weeks, months, a year, whatever it might take, and the medical care was widely regarded as extraordinary.

But just as extraordinary was the culture surrounding the care, which could feel as determinedly hopeful as the other place Kauzlarich had been to on his leave, Disney World. Injured soldiers were referred to not as injured soldiers but as Wounded Warriors, with the *W*s always capitalized. When they arrived they were given a Warrior Welcome Packet and a Hero Handbook. They and their families got assistance in the Warrior and Family Support Center, a Returning Heroes Home was being built, and amputees received specialized care in a new facility called the Center for the Intrepid, which, by coincidence, was dedicated on the same day in January 2007 that Duncan Crookston was in his little apartment in Fort Riley, saying into the phone "buried" and "Battle Hymn of the Republic," as his parents and new nineteen-year-old wife listened. "Just planned my funeral," he'd nonchalantly told them after he hung up, and meanwhile, at the Center for the Intrepid, the chairman of the Joint Chiefs of Staff was saying in a dedication speech, "There are those who speak about you who say, 'He lost an arm. He lost a leg. She lost her sight.' I object. You *gave* your arm. You *gave* your leg. You *gave* your sight. As gifts to your nation. That we might live in freedom. Thank you."

And that in a nutshell was what BAMC was about—no pity, all hooah and gratitude. Kauzlarich would have two days to tour various parts of BAMC to get a sense of how much was being done for America's emerging generation of burn victims and amputees. At the Center for the Intrepid, he would see the prosthetics lab, the wave pool, the climbing wall, the driving simulator, and the shooting range. Most impressive of all was a room with a computer-controlled tilting floor to help soldiers regain equilibrium. The floor was so sensitive to changes of weight, and so quick to adjust to them, that according to the tour guide it could balance a pencil standing on its end.

But two other sights, not on the tour, were also crucial to see.

One was a gazebo. It was empty when Kauzlarich happened to walk by it in the morning, but at night it was packed with mothers and wives who couldn't get to sleep, even though it might be four o'clock in the morning. In mentioning this to Kauzlarich, Judith Markelz, the program manager for the Warrior and Family Support Center, said that there might be as many as twenty women in the gazebo, no matter the season, no matter the weather. "[A] chance for that child to grow up in peace and to realize dreams," is what President Bush said any mother wants, but in the gazebo their wishes had been updated. Some would smoke. Some would drink. Some were on medication for indigestion, and most were on antidepressants. "Whatever it takes for a mother who spends twenty hours a day in the burn unit watching her son scream," Markelz explained.

As for the second sight, it was the waiting area outside of the burn unit, where as Kauzlarich waited to visit Duncan Crookston, he met one of those mothers, Lee Crookston, and one of those wives, Meaghun Crookston. Both had been living at BAMC since Duncan arrived on September 6. Four and a half months later, they were used to everything about the place, but they were also aware of what seeing Duncan for the first time could be like, and they wanted to prepare Kauzlarich.

"A lot of the time you just don't know what he's saying," Meaghun, who was twenty years old and had married Duncan a few months before his deployment, said. "He can't bring his lips together yet."

"He's working on it, though," Lee said.

"Well, the last time I saw Duncan was right after the, I mean, right after . . ." Kauzlarich began to say, and then paused when he saw one of the other patients on the ward moving along the hallway. His face appeared to have been burned almost entirely away. He was moving so slowly it was as if the merest bit of air moving against his skin would hurt. "How's it going?" Kauzlarich's escort said to the man as he got close. "All right," he answered, and as he moved past, Lee Crookston smiled at this vision of what her son could one day become. "He's a real success story," she whispered. Hope at its most warped and willful—that was the waiting area, where Lee and Meaghun now took turns telling Kauzlarich how many surgeries Duncan had been through and how many times he had nearly died.

"The doctors are like, 'I'm not even going to guess anymore. I'm not even going to tell you,'" Meaghun said.

"They say, 'We're not going to predict anything anymore when it comes to Duncan, because he always proves us wrong,'" Lee said.

"Well, I heard he is like one of only three guys that has been this seriously wounded to survive," Kauzlarich said.

"Yeah, that's what we were told, too," Lee said.

"Unbelievable," Kauzlarich said. "You guys pray a lot?"

"Yeah."

"All the time."

"He's just a fighter," Meaghun said.

"He's like a cat with nine lives," Lee said. "You kind of wonder how many he's got left, you know?"

"Yeah," Kauzlarich said.

"But it is looking better. It's looking much better than it was three or four weeks ago for him," Lee said.

"When he first got here, we were told that we needed to be careful of what we tell him because what could happen is we could tell him stuff and then he'd go to sleep and forget it and we would have to go over it all over again," Meaghun said. "And then one day, at the beginning of October, he was asking all these questions, and I was like I *have* to tell him. And so we got together, and we were bawling when we were telling him—"

"We were both really a mess—" Lee said.

"—and we explained to him, 'You had, you know, both of your legs amputated.' And he said, 'Both of them?' 'Yeah. And your right arm, and your left hand.' And he said, 'Okay, look, I want details.' And so we told him everything we knew about it, and then he wanted to know the whole process of how they told us, and how we got down here, and then we told him about his friends that passed away, and his mom told him that we didn't want him to feel guilty—"

"—that he was still here and they weren't—" Lee said.

"—and he said he doesn't think of death that way, that those men died honorably. And his mom goes, 'Well, you got injured honorably,' and he goes, 'Yes, I did.'"

"I think he knew that he was hurt bad," Lee said. "But he was so drugged all the time—"

"We thought he was going to take it a lot harder than he actually did," Meaghun said.

"We were worse off than he was," Lee said.

"He said that from time to time he gets depressed, but he gets over it," Meaghun said. "He said for a while there it was hard to wake up and just realize that this was his reality. Sometimes he wished he was back in Iraq, because he'd have his arms and his legs."

"He said, 'If I was back in Iraq, it would mean that this didn't happen to me,'" Lee said. "And I said, 'Well, it did, and I know that you can handle it. You're a tough kid, and you've proven that over and over again.' And I said, 'You know we'll do everything we can to help you through whatever you need.'"

"Yeah," Kauzlarich said and paused again as another burn victim moved along the hallway, his entire head wrapped in bandages except for eyeholes.

"So he just, I don't know . . ." Meaghun said, watching that one go by.

"The military guys that came and talked to us told us about the actual bomb; they said it was huge," Lee said. "I mean just a gigantic explosive."

"Well, the bomb was a ten-inch copper plate, concave shape, so when it blows up there's about fifty pounds of explosives behind it; it just goes like this and forms and shoots right through the vehicle," Kauzlarich said.

"It's made to penetrate," Lee said.

"It's made to penetrate," Kauzlarich said, nodding. "It went right through the vehicle. It immediately killed Murray. Murray didn't even know what hit him. Shelton didn't know what hit him. It immediately amputated Duncan's legs. It went through the back of David Lane. So he bled out pretty quick."

"They said they got him out of the car," Meaghun said.

"They got him out, but he had already—he looked fine, but it was behind him that they couldn't see," Kauzlarich said. "And it blew Joe Mixson, who is six foot six, completely out of the vehicle, and he was laying on the ground, rolling around, and I'm like, what in the heck? I mean we've been hit by single EFPs and then multiple arrays, like six of them all together. This one was one single, and it hit exactly—"

"In just the spot that could do the most damage," Lee said.

"In just the spot," Kauzlarich said. "And it did."

They began walking down the hallway now, toward Duncan's room. Four and a half months later, there was still so much about September 4 that Lee and Meaghun didn't know. That Duncan's platoon circled up and prayed before every mission. That his body armor was still on fire when he was loaded into a Humvee. That his hands were so black that Michael Anderson thought he was still wearing his gloves. That as Anderson cradled his head in the back of the Humvee, Duncan, hair and eyebrows and so much else of him gone, began to talk.

"Who is this?"

"It's Anderson. Can you hear me?"

"How's my face?"

"Don't worry. It looks good."

"Ow, it hurts. It hurts. It burns. And my legs hurt."

"Don't worry. Don't worry. I got you. Just rest your head in my hands. It's okay. It's okay."

"Give me some morphine."

"It's okay."

"Morphine."

"It's okay."

"I want to go to sleep."

"Stay awake. Don't close your eyes."

"I want to go to sleep."

"Keep talking to me, buddy. You love your wife, right?"

"I love my wife."

"Well, don't worry, man. She's gonna be waiting for you, man."

"I LOVE MY WIFE."

"You're safe. You're here with us. We got you."

"I LOVE MY WIFE. I LOVE MY WIFE."

"Nothing's gonna happen to you. You're safe. You're fine."

"I LOVE MY WIFE. I LOVE MY WIFE."

He shouted that again and again, all the way to the aid station. They didn't know that, either, but from the moment he reached BAMC, they knew everything from then on, because this was their life now. His infections. His fevers. His bedsores. His pneumonia. His bowel perforations. His kidney failure. His dialysis. His tracheotomy for a ventilator tube. His eyes, which for a time had to be sutured shut. His ears, which were crisped and useless when he arrived, and subsequently dropped away. His thirty trips so far to the operating room. His questions. His depression. His phantom pains, as if he still had two arms and two legs.

"I mean, we weren't even married for a year," Meaghun said as they neared the room.

"I know," Kauzlarich said, and now he was looking through the window at the sight that Anderson had called honestly creepy, but even that didn't begin to describe what he was seeing. There was so much of Duncan Crookston missing that he didn't seem real. He was half of a body propped up in a full-size bed, seemingly bolted into place. He couldn't move because he had nothing left with which to push himself into motion except for a bit of arm that was immobilized in bandages, and he couldn't speak because of the tracheotomy tube that had been inserted into his throat. Every part of him was taped and bandaged because of burns and infections, except for his cheeks, which remained reddened from burns, his mouth, which hung open and misshapen, and his eyes, which were covered by goggles that produced their own moisture, resulting in water droplets on the inside through which he viewed whatever came into his line of sight. "Bastards," Kauzlarich said quietly as into those droplets Meaghun now appeared.

"Do you want the music on or do you want me to turn the music off?" she asked, and when there was no response from him, she patiently tried again.

"Do you want me to turn it off?"

No response.

"Off?" she said.

No response.

The room was hot. The sounds were of the ventilator, IV drips of pain medication, and monitoring machines whose beeps and numerical read-outs were the only indication that inside those bandages life continued to go on.

Now Lee swam into Duncan's view.

"Is that better?" she said as she put a pillow on the board that was supporting the remains of his arm.

No response.

"Yeah?" she said as she fluffed it into shape.

No response.

And now it was Kauzlarich.

"Hey, Ranger buddy. It's Colonel Kauzlarich. How are you doing?" he said as he stood at the side of the bed.

No response.

"You hanging in there?"

No response.

"Can you hear him? Yes or no?" Meaghun said.

No response.

"All the guys in Iraq want to let you know that they appreciate what you're doing," Kauzlarich said. "I appreciate what you're doing."

No response.

"We're doing good. We're winning," he said, and soon after that, after listening to Meaghun talk about Duncan's upcoming twentieth birthday and their plans to someday live in Italy, and then listening as she suctioned saliva out of his mouth, he left, promising to be back.

The following day, January 18, Kauzlarich saw the rest of his soldiers, including the one who had told Nate Showman that Kauzlarich was the motherfucker he never wanted to see again.

In fact, several soldiers had been talking among themselves about snubbing Kauzlarich during his visit because of how angry they were. But in the end, they all showed up to see him, and as they rolled toward him in wheelchairs, and walked toward him on artificial limbs, and sat with him at a long table in the hospital cafeteria for lunch, they were a remarkable portrait of how much violence the 2-16 had been through so far.

Joe Mixson was here—he was the fifth soldier in the Humvee on September 4, and now he was trying to adjust to life with two legs amputated above the knee.

Michael Fradera was here—he had lost both of his legs below the knee in August.

Joshua Atchley was here—he was the one who in June had screamed to Sergeant Gietz, "They got my fucking eye."

John Kirby was here—he had been sitting next to Cajimat way back in April when Cajimat died, and in May had taken a bullet in an arm.

And around the table it went—a lost foot (he *gave* his foot), shrapnel in the groin (he *gave* his groin), another lost foot—until the far corner, where a soldier with an asymmetrical head sat cockeyed and silent in a wheelchair. It was Sergeant Emory. Nine months after being shot in the back of the head, he was here at BAMC. Kauzlarich had seen him earlier, unexpectedly, during one of the tours he was being given of a facility where soldiers there for the long haul could stay with their family. "I love you, Sergeant Emory," he'd said in a quick conversation and promised that after lunch he would tell him the details of that day in Kamaliyah. And so here Emory was, his right leg shaking as if from tremors, waiting to at last find out what had happened on the roof.

Emory's leg shook, Andrew Looney chewed on his fingers, Kirby still had nervous eyes. Leland Thompson showed up wearing his Combat Infantryman Badge, which all of them had been awarded for being under fire, and Atchley showed up wearing a fake eye that had been designed to look not like a normal eye but like crosshairs through a rifle scope. In every case, they were not the soldiers they had been as they left Fort Riley, but Kauzlarich didn't have to be told who any of them were. He recognized every one of them immediately. Part of command is to know a soldier only well enough to send him into battle, but once an injury occurred, that soldier became to Kauzlarich unforgettable. He knew the names, the injuries, the dates. He knew the sounds some of them had made in the aid station and the absolute silence of others. He knew their blood and their insides and what their eyes were doing as they became imprinted in his mind. When they died, he knew the voices of their wives and mothers and fathers when he telephoned them and said words such as *instantly*. Every bit of their damage had become part of him, as clear in his mind as the spoke-and-wheel chart he had shown to General Petraeus, but this was a chart of a different sort, not a tactical one of "Our Fight," but of his very own war. He had come to realize that long after Iraq was over and forgotten, this was the war he would be left with, and now, adding new spokes and wheels, he looked around the table.

"It's Wacky World," he said with tenderness.

He turned to Kirby and asked how he was, and to answer, Kirby removed the brace on his arm and demonstrated how floppy and useless his hand was. "After we eat, I'll show off my scars," he said.

He turned to Joshua Wold. "What'd they do? They ended up amputating half of it?"

"Yes, sir," Wold said.

"So you have a club foot now?"

"Yes, sir."

He turned to Fradera. "Have you walked on your hands yet?"

"Many times," Fradera said. "I tried doing it to get to the toilet a couple of times."

"Yeah?" Kauzlarich said.

"Not a good idea," Fradera said.

"Not a good idea." Kauzlarich laughed.

"It's crazy when you see fellow amputees, like, doing push-ups," Looney said.

"Yeah, they do push-ups; their whole body is elevated in the air," Fradera said. "It's easier for guys that have above-the-knee to do it."

"I can't do it," Mixson said.

"Give it time," Fradera said. "How long you been here?"

"Since September," Mixson said.

"September. Give it time. You'll be able to do it, man," Fradera said.

Even though all the soldiers lived at BAMC now, they didn't see one another that often, not all at once like this. Rehabilitation was mostly a private affair, and as they continued to talk, catching up and comparing injuries, no one seemed angry or embittered in the least. Away from here, it was different, though. In Atchley's room, for instance, was a specimen cup with a growing pile of shrapnel in it, some plastic, some copper, and all pulled out of Atchley by Atchley himself. The doctors seemed not to want to go after the pieces still inside of him, and so every so often he would stand in his bathroom, where the light was the brightest, take out a knife and tweezers, and start cutting, digging, and pulling. He still had a lot of shrapnel in his right arm and leg, and in his left hand, too, he had just discovered, because the most recent thing he pulled out was a piece of copper from the webbing between two fingers. "Once you get started, it doesn't hurt," he insisted, but even if it did, he would have done it regardless. "I take it out because I don't want a dirty piece of Iraqi anything in me," he said, and in that attitude was also the explanation for why he wore short-sleeve shirts even though his right arm was terribly scarred: "I want people to know the price of war." And what he thought of the war: "It's bullshit. This war is complete bullshit." And why he wore a fake eye with a crosshair pattern: "Because I don't like pretending I have an eye."

In the cafeteria, though, there was no such edginess. Instead, very seriously, Atchley told Kauzlarich that he had a total of four fake eyes— two that looked like regular eyes, one that glowed in the dark, and the one he was wearing. He reached up. He popped it out. He held it out toward Kauzlarich, and everyone at the table started to laugh.

"Put that back in!" Kauzlarich said, laughing, too, and then he decided to give a short speech, the type that soldiers would sometimes make fun of when they talked about him in his absence. Not this time, though. This time they soaked up every word.

"Everything that you guys have done will not be in vain. That's my sole purpose in life—fighting and winning. But each of you, your sole mission in life is to get better," he said. "The bottom line is I'm on your team, and I always will be. We are a family. You fought for me; I'll fight for you the rest of my life. Okay? Is that a deal?"

They nodded.

"Anybody want to come back with me on Sunday?" he asked.

Wold raised his hand.

Mixson, with his two above-the-knees, did, too. "I would go back. I would. Dead serious. I would," he said.

Kauzlarich got up and thanked them one by one. "It's all good," he said when he was finished going around the table, and then, keeping his prom-ise, he went off with Sergeant Emory and his wife, Maria, to tell them everything he knew about what had happened in Kamaliyah, from the moment of the gunshot, in as much detail as they wanted to hear.

"You guys were on top of a roof," he began.

"I don't know if it makes you feel any better," he said when he was done.

Maria Emory, crying, shook her head.

"It changed our lives forever," she said.

"It's changing everybody's life forever. That's what this war is doing to us," Kauzlarich said, and as he continued to talk about how that day was the day that people in Kamaliyah found hope, Maria Emory was floating backward, having another moment like the one she'd had when she met President Bush.

She wondered: Should she tell him what *she* knew?

How depressed her husband was?

That one day he had tipped himself over onto a hard tile floor, telling her when she found him that he'd wanted to hit his head and die?

That another day he had begged her to get him a knife?

That another day he had asked for a pen so he could push it into his neck?

That another day, instead of asking for a knife or a pen, he'd tried to bite through his wrists?

She kept crying as her husband said something now to Kauzlarich. His voice was soft and still a little slurry.

"What?" Kauzlarich said, unable to make out the words.

"Have a good trip back," Emory repeated.

"These guys got me all fucking motivated," Kauzlarich said once he was outside. He meant Emory. He meant Mixson and Atchley. He meant every one of them, including Duncan Crookston, whom he had seen again just before lunch.

By the time he walked into Crookston's room for the second visit, Lee and Meaghun Crookston were deep into their daily routine. Lee was usually the first awake, and once the realization seeped in that she was still at BAMC rather than home in Denver with her husband and five other sons, she was out of bed, on her way to the hospital, and moving through the lobby past the portrait she saw every morning of a smiling George W. Bush in front of an American flag.

Duncan had a flag portrait, too, of course; every one of the soldiers did. Some had been taken at Fort Riley and some at Rustamiyah, but the process was always the same: someone would attach a flag to a wall for a backdrop, and one by one, soldiers would stand in front of it while another soldier snapped away with whatever digital camera was handy. None of them had any illusions about what the portrait was for. "I don't plan on dying, so you don't need a picture of me," one soldier protested during one of the sessions. "I'm already dead, so what does it matter what I look like?" another said, laughing and making faces.

Unlike that soldier, or Bush, for that matter, Duncan was solemn in his photograph. He took his place in front of the flag and stared straight into the camera. He had a good, straight nose, ears that slightly protruded, freshly cut hair, and a mouth that closed into a tight, serious expression. He was a handsome young man with a delicateness to some of his features that came directly from Lee, which Kauzlarich had noticed the day before, when he was standing next to Duncan's bed. "Looks like his mom," he had said, and it was true. Duncan was very much his mother's son.

Up the elevator now to the burn unit, and Lee was ready for her 134th day at her son's side. "I'm here, and I'm going to be here," she had promised Duncan when she first saw him on September 6. She had said it aloud, even though Duncan was sedated and couldn't hear, and when Meaghun made a similar promise, Lee worried about the life that this nineteen-year-old woman was promising herself to. Meaghun wasn't a middle-aged mother, after all, but a girlfriend who had married her boyfriend ten and a half months before because the boyfriend realized he was about to go to Iraq. One day he mentioned it, and the very next day they were married and going to Red Lobster to celebrate, and then he was deploying, and then it was September 4 and her phone was ringing, and then she was making a promise into her husband's blackened ears. "I'm here, and I love you, and I'm in for the long haul," she had declared, and the single time she had wavered since then was when she said to Lee one day, sounding defeated, "How do you decide when to freak out?"

"Not until they come to me and tell me there's nothing else they can try," Lee answered.

So it was the two of them, the mother and the wife. Over the months, other family members had come to BAMC as they were able to, but Lee and Meaghun had been the ones to stay. Every day they tended to Duncan, and at night they called home with updates, which Meaghun's parents would occasionally post on a website for a small circle of people who had become interested in Duncan's progress—family, friends, friends of friends, even a kids' football team in Colorado that had heard about Duncan and decided to dedicate their season to him. They played wearing his name on their helmets. They took a photograph of themselves that maybe he would see one day in which they were all yelling, "Freedom!" as the shutter snapped. That picture was posted, too, and to see it was to think of how the war really had come to stitch the nation together, that from coast to coast and border to border there were thirty thousand knots of people screaming "freedom" into a camera because they knew somebody, or knew somebody who knew somebody, who had been injured in Iraq.

September 19: "Dear Family & Friends," Meaghun's parents wrote, "our soldier is losing the battle. Infection has set in throughout his body and spreading."

October 11: "Duncan was in surgery yesterday and the doctor has given us FABULOUS news. The mucor infection which set in last month and was eventually going to take his life is now 'OUT OF THE PIC-TURE,' says the doctor," they wrote. "Of all the patients Dr. White has seen, there was only one other soldier to survive this type of infection. We can now say Duncan is no. 2!"

November 5: "Duncan is amazing, amazing, amazing. He is what you define a true soldier."

December 10: "Please please please pray for Duncan. He took a turn for the worst last night . . ."

"Ups and downs," was how Duncan's days were described, and so they went, from the best day, in early October, when he first spoke, to the worst day, December 10, when as Lee described it, "It was the closest he came to dying in front of us." The night before his blood pressure had dropped, and when Lee and Meaghun were called to his room early the next morning, his organs had begun shutting down and he was unconscious and in septic shock. Meaghun, seeing this, became so nauseated she nearly passed out, and Lee began to cry because the moment of no options seemed to be at hand. Then some doctor came up with an antibiotic that might save him from infection, but might also thin his blood to the point where he would develop brain bleeds and die. "Okay, if we don't give him the drug, does he have any chance of survival?" Lee asked. "No," the doctor answered, and so they gave him the drug, and he didn't die, and that was the thing about Duncan, Lee said now: he kept finding ways not to die.

Some of Duncan's fellow soldiers following the updates in Iraq wondered if it would have been better if he had died right away. As Michael Anderson had said after visiting him, "All he's going to be able to do is be left with his thoughts. He's laying on that bed, not being able to do anything."

But Lee said that anyone who thought that Duncan would be better off dead was someone who hadn't been with Duncan every day, as she and Meaghun had been. "Those people haven't seen this place and what can be done. We have," she said, and because of that it wasn't difficult for her to imagine Duncan's future.

First he would get an artificial left hand and learn to use it.

Then his legs.

Then his right arm.

Then, with rehabilitation, he would become the soldier moving slowly down the hallway as people whispered, "He's a real success story."

And then, maybe in five years, or ten, if it took ten, he would be the husband living with his wife in Italy, or Denver, or wherever they decided to settle to raise a family.

"So there's hope there," Lee said, and got busy with another day.

She put on her protective clothing. She turned on the TV and read to Duncan from the news crawl. She told him what the weather was like in Denver. She read to him from a book written by a concentration camp survivor, called *Man's Search for Meaning*. Meaghun came in and read to Duncan, too, and then she and Lee talked about what to get him for his twentieth birthday, which was eight days away, and then Kauzlarich arrived.

He had come back to award Duncan some medals, and as he moved toward the bed, Lee called out, "Are you awake? Duncan? Can you hear us? Duncan, can you hear us?" She turned to Kauzlarich. "He's still a little bit—"

"Yeah," Kauzlarich said. At the side of the bed now, he looked down at Duncan, who looked exactly as he had the day before. Unmoving. Unreal. "What's up, Ranger buddy?" he said. "Good morning. Well, I guess it's afternoon right now, isn't it?"

Just like the day before, there was no response, but Kauzlarich went ahead anyway, holding up one of the medals in front of Duncan's goggle-covered eyes. "Hey, Duncan, what I have right here is what every infantryman wants. The Combat Infantryman Badge. Right? You can see it right here. That's yours. When you get out of here, you can put it on your ACUs. All right?"

He moved the medal closer to the goggles, but the eyes behind them didn't seem focused on the medal, or Kauzlarich, or anything at all.

"It says here the reason: 'For participating in ground combat operations, under enemy hostile fire, to liberate Iraq, in support of Operation Iraqi Freedom,'" Kauzlarich continued, reading the citation. "And like we talked about yesterday, it was your efforts that have allowed Task Force Ranger to do what we do, and we are winning right now. And you're inspiring us every day to do what we do, so your injuries weren't in vain."

Now he held up a second medal.

"The other thing I want to give you is the Army Commendation Medal. And you know what that looks like. Right there. That's one award that you'll receive. You'll also receive the Overseas Service Ribbon and the Iraqi Campaign Medal. So you've got a whole row, actually you got two rows now, of medals for your Class As. So just a small thing that we can do for you today, in front of your family, is to award these to you. And I will give them to Meaghun, and your mother, Lee, and we will take pictures of these for you so that when you're in a little better shape you'll be able to take a look and watch and see this. All right?"

No movement. Nothing, other than eyes looking through droplets of water.

"I appreciate everything you do, brother," Kauzlarich continued. "And you're always in our prayers and in our thoughts. But today I'll go down and see Joe Mixson, who was with you that day, and all the other thirteen guys who are currently at BAMC. It'll be good to get you out of here so you guys can all work together to get healthy, because that's your number one mission right now. It's to get healthy. Okay? And that's a direct order from me, your commander. Are you with me?"

And was that a nod?

"Hooah," Kauzlarich said.

It was. Duncan was nodding.

"Hooah!" Kauzlarich said again.

He was nodding and seemed now to be looking directly at Kauzlarich. Lee was right. He *could* move. He *could* hear. He *did* understand.

"All *right*, brother," Kauzlarich said. "It's good to see you. You're looking good. You're getting better every day. So keep doing what you're doing. You're always in my prayers, big guy. Hooah?"

Another nod.

So he was aware of everything.

Kauzlarich turned away for a moment to hand the medals to Lee and Meaghun.

"Thank you," Meaghun said.

"My honor," he said, and then he turned back to Duncan and reached toward him, searching for a place to touch.

He rested his hand on his side, but only for a moment, and then he lifted his hand, and then left the room, and then left the hospital, and then went to the airport, and then flew back to Iraq, and a week later, on January 25, was in his office in Rustamiyah, back once again on the front lines of a place where an Iraqi mother wants the same thing for her children that an American mother wants, a chance for that child to grow up in peace and to realize dreams, when an e-mail arrived from Lee.

"Dear Friends and Family," it began.

"It is with great sadness I write to you today—Duncan passed away at 3:46 p.m. today after the decision was made to stop heroic measures. Duncan developed another infection over the past two days, the effects of which were causing him a great deal of pain and causing him to run a fever of 108° F overnight. The doctor who treated Duncan said he had never heard of anyone surviving such a high fever, and that normally the body did not allow itself to sustain such a high temperature for even 15 minutes, let alone the two hours Duncan suffered with it. The doctor said it was an indication the hypothalamus of the brain, which regulates body temperature, was damaged.

"He also advised us that even though Duncan survived, he would have permanent and widespread brain damage that would eventually cause his organ systems to fail, and that his kidneys were already dialysis dependent, and he was quickly becoming ventilator dependent. Meaghun and I were asked to make a decision, and we chose to allow Duncan to die a dignified and peaceful death, so he was given a morphine drip and taken off the ventilator. He died about 45 minutes later surrounded by his

217

beautiful wife, his mother, his battle buddy Joe Mixson and the hospital chaplain he had come to know during his stay. It is the closest thing to a 'good death' one could ask for a young man who fought so hard and long, only to have the limits of his body betray him. Once we knew there was no chance of any sort of quality of life, we felt we could not ask this brave young man who lived life to its fullest to spend his remaining days hooked to machines with no chance of recovery.

"Words cannot express the gratitude we feel towards all those who offered support and prayer to Duncan and our families during the past five months. We can take away from this experience the knowledge that good people exist in this world, that evil is worth fighting for that reason, and that Duncan was a proud example of a good person who did not stand by and allow it to flourish by doing nothing. Duncan would have been twenty years old tomorrow—he will be forever nineteen now, and forever missed.

"Love, Lee Crookston."

Twelve dead now.

"Damn," Kauzlarich said.

Just under three months left to go.

11

FEBRUARY 27, 2008

*So I had a choice to make. Do I suffer the consequences of defeat by withdrawing
our troops, or do I listen to my commanders, the considered judgment of military
experts, and do what it takes to secure victory in Iraq? I chose the latter. Rather than
retreating, we sent 30,000 new troops into Iraq, and the surge is succeeding.*
—GEORGE W. BUSH, *February 25, 2008*

In January 2007, when the surge was being announced, 83 American troops died in Iraq. In January 2008, the number was 40.

In January 2007, 647 troops were wounded. In January 2008, the number was 234.

In January 2007, troops were attacked 5,000 times. In January 2008, the number was 2,000.

In January 2007, the number of Iraqi civilians who died was estimated at a minimum of 2,800. In January 2008, the number was a minimum of 750.

In January 2007, some 90,000 Iraqis fled their homes for Syria, Jordan, or other parts of Iraq, joining four million others who had already done so. In January 2008, with the total now approaching five million, the number leaving their homes was 10,000.

". . . and the surge is succeeding," George W. Bush said after a month in which 40 American troops died, 234 were injured, troops were attacked 2,000 times, and at least 750 Iraqis died and 10,000 fled their homes, and meanwhile, at Rustamiyah, where things had been quieter lately, soldiers had been thinking the very same thing as Bush, right up until 5:45 p.m., on February 19, when the second lob bomb attack began.

Jay March

"You guys getting hit?" It was another FOB, calling in to the 2-16 operations center.

"Yeah," said the sergeant who'd grabbed the phone.

"Can you tell us anything about it?"

"Yeah. It sucks," the sergeant said, and slammed down the phone as another explosion shook the walls.

Fifteen soldiers crowded into the room. Some worked the phones and radios, and the rest stood against the back wall, hoping it was thick enough to stop hurtling pieces of shrapnel and ball bearings.

A captain came running in. He had been over by the motor pool, where a dozen vehicles were now on fire. One was a fuel tanker that had been pierced by shrapnel and was leaking. Burning fuel was everywhere. The captain said he had ducked into a darkened storage shed and discovered three private contractors who worked on the FOB. One had a bloody leg, the second had lost his right arm, and the third was missing the back of his head and was dead. "Nothing we could do," he said.

Here came another explosion. There had been eight so far.

"Wham!" a soldier said, imitating the sound and laughing nervously.

"Whoosh . . . BOOM!" another soldier said, laughing, too.

Another explosion. Because of weather conditions, no helicopters were flying, which meant no Hellfire missiles. This was going to go on for a while, and there was nothing to do but wait for the next one. Reports came in of barracks that had collapsed, of a breach in the wall surrounding the FOB, of a second attack a few miles to the north and twenty dead Iraqi National Police who'd been trying to defuse a booby-trapped truck. Now Brent Cummings ran in; he'd been at the motor pool, too, taking cover underneath a truck, his face pressed into gravel, the taste of the dust in his mouth, the shudders of the concussions moving through him, until he saw and smelled the burning fuel headed right at him, at which point he ran. "Good thing we're winning," he said, out of breath. Now some of the soldiers slid down the back wall and compressed themselves into tight balls. "No matter how many times it happens, it's scary," one said. The others looked at him. No one was supposed to say such a thing, even if every single one of them was thinking it.

"It's scary," he repeated.

Everyone looked away, quiet now.

"I don't like it at all," he said, and he didn't say much more until the all-clear sounded several hours later, after which the bomb shelters emptied, the fires burned themselves out, the damaged buildings were patched up, some slightly injured soldiers were treated at the aid station, the badly injured contractors were choppered to hospitals, the dead contractor was bagged for shipping home, and soldiers gradually went back to thinking that George W. Bush was right.

In January 2008, 40 U.S. troops died in Iraq; in February 2008, the number was 29.

In January 2008, 234 troops were wounded; in February 2008, the number was 216.

"Sir, would you please tell us a little bit about your current operations?" Mohammed said in Arabic to Izzy, who translated it into English for Kauzlarich, on PEACE 106 FM.

"Security throughout Iraq, and in particular Baghdad, is the best it has ever been since the fall of Saddam Hussein," Kauzlarich said.

In fact, after the lob bomb attack, things were so quiet as the end of February approached that the battalion went ahead with a contest it did sometimes to choose a soldier of the month.

Thirty soldiers were selected to compete against one another. One at a time, they would appear before a panel of sergeants who would ask a series of questions about anything they felt like asking. Weapons. Current events. First aid. The history of the army. It was an intimidating process that would make one of the thirty so nervous that when he walked in and presented his weapon, he would conk himself in the head with it.

That soldier would not win.

Nor would the soldier who, when asked to name a type of contour line on a map, answered, "Invisible?"

Who would win?

Would it be the soldier who had sweat rolling down his face as he struggled to answer the question "What are the four common points for checking a pulse?"

"The wrist. The neck. The ankle. And the anus," he would say.

"Did he just say anus?" one sergeant would whisper to another.

"All right. Ready?" Four days before the contest, Jay March, who was one of the thirty, was studying with John Swales, who was another.

"What is AFAP?" March said. He had in his hands a 262-page book called the *U.S. Army Board Study Guide*.

"Army Family Awareness Program," said Swales, who had in his hands a big glass of CytoGainer High-Protein Mix.

"Army Family *Action Plan*," March said. "What are the three phases of physical conditioning?"

"Say again?" Swales said.

"What is the maximum range of the AT4?" March said, moving on to weapons.

"Thirteen hundred meters."

"Twenty-one hundred meters."

Four days. Good thing. They'd need it. Swales was a twenty-four-year-old specialist with a college degree who had worked as an accountant, gotten bored, joined the army, ended up in Iraq, and finished second in his one other attempt to be soldier of the month. "It was really, really relaxed," he said, but this time, with a different panel of sergeants, he didn't know what to expect. "I hear they're absolute asses."

Jay March *knew* they were asses. He had competed twice before, and both times he hadn't even made it past the pre-contest inspection. As required, he had shown up fully dressed for combat and stood at attention as a sergeant looked him over for flaws. The first time, he got kicked out because his compression bandage wasn't in its original green wrapper. That's the way his platoon always rolled, though—bandages ready to go, so no time would be lost—but before he could explain this, he was out the door. "Fucking bullshit," he said as he walked away. The second time was even worse. He had shown up early and was waiting outside the room with some other soldiers when the sergeant in charge of the panel brushed past and lost his temper because the doors to get into the room

223

were locked. "Why the hell are the doors locked?" he screamed, and when he was let in by the other sergeants, his screaming only continued. "All we heard was 'fuck this' and 'fuck that,' and we all stood in the hallway and said, 'Fuck,'" March recalled. His luck: that was the sergeant who had inspected him and kicked him out for not properly wearing the plastic pouch that held his drinking water. More luck: that sergeant would be on the panel again.

"I want to win it—but I just want to get *in* so I can go to the promotion board," March said to Swales. That was the ultimate point of the competition—to prepare a low-ranking, possibly quivering soldier to face a promotion board one day in order to become a sergeant—and March, who wasn't as confident as Swales, who wasn't a college graduate, who because of his family circumstances had barely gotten through high school, fell into the category of the possibly quivering. "I wouldn't even get in front of my class to read a book report," he said. "I'd say, 'I'll turn it in to you, but I'm not gonna read it. Give me a D, or whatever.'" So nervous did he get that in his two previous attempts to be soldier of the month, as the sergeant approached him for inspection, he had spent his final seconds trying to will his hands to stop shaking.

"I just want to get in," he repeated, and so for this try he had devised a time line to follow so nothing would go wrong. Two days before the contest, he would spend three hours thoroughly cleaning his weapon, which the sergeants were sure to dismantle and inspect. The day before, he would get his hair cut and clean his weapon again. The day of the contest, he would wake at six, shave, dust the weapon, and dress in the cleanest uniform he had, which would include a helmet he had taken into the shower and scrubbed down with laundry detergent. He would tuck his pants into his boots in such a way that the pants would not blouse past the third shoelace eyelet from the top. He would remove the beaded bracelet his brother gave him as a good-luck charm, which he swore he would never take off. When the time came for his interview, he would knock on the door three times, no more, no fewer, and once inside, he would speak to the sergeants slowly and clearly. He would also keep his goals modest— just finish in the top 50 percent—and to that end, he intended to spend whatever spare time he had between this moment and then studying on his own or with his good buddy Swales.

"Counseling," he said now, flipping to another section of the study guide. "How many human needs are there?"

"Ten," Swales said.

"No."

"Seven."

"No."

"Three."

"No."

"Five."

"No. Four," March said. "Do you know what they are?"

Swales grabbed the book out of March's hands. "All right," he said. "What is DA form 3349?"

"Physical Profile," March said.

"Okay. What is DA form 2442?"

"2442?" March said.

"Not so fucking smart, are you?" Swales said.

Specialist Charles White, a twenty-six-year-old medic, was another of the thirty. Like Jay March, this would be his third attempt just to make it past inspection.

The first time he had forgotten his elbow pads, which he realized as a sergeant closed in on him.

"What are you missing, Ranger White?"

"My elbow pads, First Sergeant."

"What are you going to do about it?"

"I'm going to leave, First Sergeant."

Try number two ended when his platoon sergeant told him what time to show up, and then the time was changed and the guy who was supposed to tell him didn't tell him, and how interesting was it that he was another contestant, and "I was twenty minutes late."

On to number three.

Unlike March, White's goal was to win. "I mean, second place is the first loser," he said, and so he was in his room studying, door locked, not answering any knocks unless it was about a mission. "I'm a loner," he said. "If they come in my room, I'm not studying with them. Not here." He lowered his voice. "Because this is the top-secret area." He had some Motown playing, his study guide open, and he was trying to memorize all of it, right down to the 121-word Soldier's Creed, which he had taken to reciting out loud, even if he was walking somewhere with other soldiers. "To the chow hall, that's five minutes. I can recite the Soldier's Creed four or five times," he said, and if the other soldiers thought he was a little off for doing so, that wasn't going to stop him. "I'm twenty-six. I'm older. They're eighteen or nineteen. They talk about a lot of stupid stuff. 'Look at her tits.' I've done that. I can just talk to myself."

Three days till the competition now, and White was considering what to say when the sergeants asked him to introduce himself. It was an invitation for a soldier to say absolutely nothing more than his name, his birthplace, where he went to school, and his objectives in the army—five sentences, maximum—but White was a thoughtful soldier who wished he could find a way to say something more.

"See, it's kind of weird," he said. "I've noticed when I'm out there and shit goes down, my hand doesn't shake. Later, when it's out of my hands, I do. But when it happens? That's where you find out what you're made of."

Could he say such a thing to a panel of sergeants expecting five by-the-book sentences, assuming he made it past inspection? Not if he wanted to win, he realized, but it was interesting to imagine anyway. "Tell us a little about yourself," the sergeants would say, and he would say, "In Iraq, I found out what I'm made of," and then he would give three examples.

The first was from June 11, when his convoy was passing a mosque and an EFP blew into the gun turret of the Humvee two ahead of him in line. It was 1:55 in the afternoon. One moment he'd been riding along thinking, *'When's it coming, when's it coming,'* like everyone else, and in the next moment it had. "Get the fuck out of my way!" he would remember hollering as he ran past soldiers and through sniper fire, and then he was by the side of a dying Cameron Payne, taking inventory of his wounds. The eyes: a bit of an eyelid was gone. The mouth: a bit of the left side was gone. The ears: behind the left one was a puncture wound straight into the brain. "You're gonna have to move your feet so I can close the door," he said, and when Payne did so, White closed the door and methodically went to work on the wounds. Covered in so much blood that his hands were slippery, he tore open the packaging around the compression bandage with his teeth, pushed the bandage into place, and held Payne in his arms all the way to the aid station, and only afterward, when he began to shake, did he realize that all during it he hadn't.

Joshua Reeves—Rustamiyah fuel station, September—would be his second example. "Two casualties. One not breathing. Life threatening," a soldier yelled into the radio moments after the explosion as White checked Reeves for a pulse. He straddled Reeves and did mouth-to-mouth resuscitation as Rachel the interpreter pushed on Reeves's chest. Thirty compressions, two breaths. No pulse. Thirty compressions, two breaths. No pulse. On it went until they reached the aid station. Reeves was taken inside, Rachel stood in her blood-filled boots, and White, his work on Reeves done, began to shake. But not a moment before.

As for the third example, it involved James Harrelson, who had died on Outer Berm Road, and a woman White had met and married just before he deployed. He was twenty-five then, and she was nineteen. They were married in a small church in northern Kansas where his mother was the minister, and five days later he'd gone to Iraq, leaving his new wife with his most beloved possession, a silver 2006 Pontiac Grand Am. "Blah blah blah blah I wrecked your car blah blah blah blah," he remembered her saying when he got to Rustamiyah and called to say he was safe. "I let her finish with the blah blahs. 'That's nice. Can we go back to the part where you said *you wrecked my car?*'"

And it went on from there, he said. "She wanted me to, like, call her more, and this was when we just got here. Things were crazy. I was calling her once a week, but she wanted more. She'd be all sobby. 'You don't call me enough. I'm the only one talking. You don't care about me. You don't love me.'

"So, whatever. That didn't work," he said. Four months after the wedding, he managed to get it annulled, leaving him with several bad memories and one good one that would forever bring tears to his eyes: having

James Harrelson as his best man. Harrelson had been the first person White became friends with when he arrived at Fort Riley. They roomed together, drove around together, went out dancing and met girls together, and after Harrelson burned to death, White was asked to give the "Soldier's Tribute" at the memorial service, which was more informally known as the speech by the best friend. "I choose to remember him as a friend and fellow brother in arms who died for something he loved, and that was the army and America," he said in his speech, and as his words moved through a chapel overflowing with soldiers of all stripes who were looking at him and listening to him, he didn't shake then, either.

In his imagination, a soldier who deserved to be soldier of the month would be able to talk about examples such as those. "Tell us a little bit about yourself," they would say, and he would tell them not only that he was the soldier who didn't shake until afterward, but also the truth of war, that "shit happens," and that "being paranoid is okay. Because you can get hit anywhere. Paranoid makes you scared, and being scared is okay because it keeps you on edge."

The reality, though, was that the sergeants would not be interested in such things. "What is the seventh sentence of the Soldier's Creed?" they were more likely to ask, and if they did, he knew that he would be able to recite the answer perfectly, and that he would win. He was sure of this. Assuming he was finally able to get in.

Sergeant Mays took Jay March's freshly cleaned helmet, brought it to his nose, and inhaled deeply.

"Tide," he said after a moment, pleased.

He took Swales's helmet and pointed to a frayed strap that would need to be replaced if Swales wanted to make it past inspection. He looked over Swales's ammunition magazines and shook his head. "You got a lot of work to do," he said, and Swales knew this was true, because Sergeant Mays knew everything about becoming soldier of the month.

As the platoon sergeant, Mays was the one who made the nominations, and all of his soldiers understood how seriously he took it. "I just won't send anybody," he said. "I put myself in a private's shoes: Would I want to be led by this guy? Does this guy inspire me? Does he have the passion? And the knowledge?"

March and Swales—those were the guys this time around whose answers came out to yes, yes, yes, and yes, and now it was down to advice time.

How to knock on the door to enter: "Three times. Loud. Like you're in charge."

How to walk in: "You beeline straight to the desk and stop three meters away."

Next: "You salute the sergeant major. You state your name, and you say, 'Reports to the president of the board as directed,' and you hold the salute until he renders the salute."

And: "Ninety percent of it is confidence. The way you sell yourself to the board. The Q&A is just part of it."

The Q&A was actually idiotic, he said, at least the way this panel did it. "It's supposed to be about leadership. Not memorization." But that's what this panel emphasized, so he encouraged March and Swales to study. "If they don't make it in, I don't know, it's horrible," he said, and then softened. "I mean, I would like them to win it, but if they don't win it they're still the best two team leaders in the battalion."

"Don't fidget," he advised them.

"No head movement."

"No eye movement."

"If a fly lands on your nose, you can't swat it."

Two days until the competition now, and Ivan Diaz, another of the thirty, was saying of his first failed attempt to win, "When I walked in there, it was nerve-wracking." That had been at Fort Riley, as the deployment neared and Diaz was wondering about everything that was about to happen: "Do we go out all day?" "Do we get attacked every day?" "Am I ready for this?"

Then, on April 6, he was the gunner in a Humvee being driven by Jay Cajimat, and as he explained now, "It turned out I was ready."

Ten months after that day, Diaz still had pieces of shrapnel in his leg and awakened every morning to a dull pain that reminded him once more of what had happened. "We'll get you out in the fight again ricky tick," Kauzlarich had said to him at Cajimat's memorial ceremony, but it hadn't been ricky tick at all. For the first month he couldn't walk, and in the months after, there was the mental part. "I got nervous for a while," he said. "There were a lot of mortars. The noise got to me more than anything. I couldn't sleep."

He wasn't the only one awake: the inability to sleep was one of the things that had steered Adam Schumann to ask for help from Combat Stress. It was what Sergeant Mays had tried to remedy after the death of James Harrelson by increasing his nightly dosage of Ambien. In Diaz's case, he tried to overcome it using the method Jay March would use to try to get his hands to stop shaking: willpower. "It's going to keep happening," he told himself one day, after another rocket attack had left him on edge. "You have to become fearless here."

"So I became fearless."

Fearless in his case had translated into always seeming to be rock steady. From a wounded soldier, he had repaired himself into being a team leader who was not going to let anyone define him by a few seconds on April 6, even though the fact was that those few seconds would define him for the rest of his life. He rarely talked about them anymore, but he knew better than to describe them as buried. Better to say they now inhabited the area between silence and dreams. He remembered being up in the turret. He remembered seeing an ambulance approaching and hearing John Kirby yell, "Stop!" He remembered swiveling his head to the right. He remembered the flash. He remembered the boom. He remembered the impact. He remembered falling from the turret and onto his back. He remembered trying to run, looking down at his boot, seeing a hole, and thinking his foot must be gone. He remembered Kirby yelling, "Get a fire extinguisher," and hopping around in search of a fire extinguisher. He remembered realizing that still inside the burning Humvee was Jay Cajimat. He remembered everything of that night and all of it since, right up to this moment, in which he was a soldier who once was a few inches away from dying and was now thinking that he needed to scrub the black marks from a long-ago explosion off his helmet if he wanted to be soldier of the month.

So much to do still.

He needed to memorize a set of index cards he had gotten from another soldier as a study guide, and figure out what he was going to answer when the sergeants asked him for his biography. Maybe he would tell them he was engaged to be married. Maybe he would tell them he had a newborn son. He knew he would not talk about April 6 because why would he, but maybe he would mention what he had learned about himself since the day he had wondered if he was ready for this. "There's nothing that can hurt me now," he said.

The night before the competition, Sergeant Mays decided to check March from head to toe. "All right. Put your shit on," he ordered.

On went his clean uniform. On went his Individual Body Armor with optional groin-protector panel. On went goggles, elbow pads, knee pads, throat protector, water source, M-4, eight magazines of ammo, knife, flashlight, compression bandage, tourniquet, earplugs, gloves, and boots, which were a new pair he borrowed from a friend that were two sizes too big. But they were clean.

A sergeant, watching this, walked over to March and swatted him between the legs, right in the optional groin protector, to make sure it was properly positioned.

It was. From groin protector to clown boots to a suddenly blushing face, March was ready to go.

He didn't sleep well. By six, he was getting dressed, even though the contest wouldn't be starting for a couple of hours. He went outside for a cigarette. It had rained overnight, and he tried to keep the mud off his boots as he sat under the tree with the bag of fly poison. He smoked one cigarette and then another. What were the eight steps in the functioning of the M-4 rifle? Whose profile was on the Medal of Honor? What were the four types of burns?

Diaz was up early as well, and so was Swales, who shrugged and said, "So, we'll see." Even if nothing came of it, he was glad to be starting a day differently from the usual ritual that so far had kept him and his closest friends alive: "We tell each other we love each other right before we go out," he said, "and then we jump in the fucking truck." As for White, he awakened to a computer message from his new girlfriend in Texas. "Baby, I know you'll do well," she had written while he was asleep. "Hey, I'm going," he messaged her now, and she must have been waiting for those words back in Texas, because she wrote to him immediately: "Good luck." "Luck is for the ill-prepared," he wrote back, and walked through boot-sucking mud across the FOB to a building where Sergeant Mays, in a final act of kindness, was wiping an anti-fogger cloth on March's and Swales's goggles. "Because they're gonna sweat," he explained.

Several dozen soldiers were crowded into a hallway, and by now, this far into the war, every one of them had some kind of story to tell. What they had seen. Whom they had held. What they had done, and what they had not. But anyway, here they were, that was the point, and every one of them fell suddenly silent when Command Sergeant Major McCoy appeared. "We ready?" he barked and, without waiting for an answer, walked past them and into the contest room, shutting the door behind him. He would be in charge of the panel. The three other sergeants on it were already inside. The soldiers listened through the closed door. A good sign: no one in there was yelling, "Fuck."

A few minutes later, the door opened, and the soldiers were motioned inside. The time had come. Wordlessly, they formed into lines. "All right, men. If you don't pass the inspection, you don't go to the board," McCoy said, and then he and the three other sergeants fanned out to examine them.

One of the sergeants approached March. "Nervous?"

"Yes, sir, sergeant. A little bit," March said.

"We haven't even started asking questions yet. Relax," the sergeant said and began looking through March's ammunition magazines as March's hands started to shake.

McCoy, meanwhile, bore down on White. "When's the last time you cleaned your IBA?" he said, looking at White's armor.

"It's been a while, Sergeant Major," White said.

He looked at White's helmet, which was missing its nametag. He looked at White's compression bandage, which was out of its green wrapper.

"You're done," he said, and just like that White was shaking his head and on his way out the door.

Next McCoy approached another soldier and discovered a small hole in the wrapper of his compression bandage. Two gone.

Make it three: a soldier had a grenade in his pocket. "Where's that supposed to be?" he asked, and when the soldier didn't answer, he looked at the one standing next to him, who was March. "In the vehicle, Sergeant Major," March answered for him, his hands continuing to shake.

Four: when McCoy took his little finger and put it inside another soldier's gun barrel, his finger came out black. "Okay, stud," he said.

Now he approached Diaz and regarded his helmet, which still had streaks on it, even though Diaz had cleaned it the day before.

"You mean to tell me that won't come out if you clean it?" he asked.

In his steady voice, Diaz started to explain its origins, but McCoy cut him off.

So Diaz was done, too, and as he walked out the door, McCoy said to those who were left, "I don't expect your IBA to be spotless. I understand. But if it looks like you haven't fucking washed it since you got here? I mean, I even washed my boots last night to come to this fucking board."

He continued to inspect and continued to kick out. "A little saying," he said. "What's the difference between ordinary and extraordinary? A little extra."

Now he moved toward Swales and gazed with concern at his knees.

"Swales, are those knee pads or elbow pads?"

"Knee pads, Sergeant Major," Swales said and stood still as McCoy examined them, decided they were in fact knee pads, next considered the length of his hair, decided it was an acceptable length, and moved toward March, who had been so upset at the barber who had given him a five-dollar haircut that he stiffed him on a tip.

But his hair was fine. His big boots were fine. Silently, he asked his hands to be still as McCoy ripped open every Velcro'd pocket on his uniform and checked inside. They were fine, too.

"All right, I guess this is it," McCoy said to the soldiers still in the room, and that was how March knew he was one of the eleven to make it through. He stopped shaking and turned visibly red.

Swales, through too, smiled and wiggled his eyebrows.

White, meanwhile, was back in his room and angry. "Have you ever tried to open a bandage when you have blood on your hands?" he was imagining saying to McCoy. "Well, I have. Have you ever had to rip open a bandage with your teeth?"

Diaz was back in his barracks, too, once again trying to clean his helmet with laundry detergent and a brush and wondering: "How do you ever scrub out an explosion completely?"

And March, now in the hallway with the remaining soldiers, watched in silence as the first among them knocked on the door, went inside to be questioned, and was back out three seconds later, sighing deeply and knocking again.

"Hey," March said now to Swales as their turns approached, "what was the maximum effective range of the AT4? Three hundred meters?"

Swales thought for a minute and nodded.

March began pacing.

"Relax," a sergeant said to him.

"I can't," he said, turning red again.

KNOCK KNOCK KNOCK.

"Come in," McCoy called.

"Specialist March reporting to the president of the board, Sergeant Major."

This was it—unknown territory. He had never made it this far before. "Knowledge is presentation," Mays had told him just before he knocked, and now he was presenting himself to four sergeants seated behind a table, three of whom were spitting tobacco juice into plastic cups. He saluted and held it. He presented his M-4 and, unlike the nervous soldier before him, didn't conk himself in the head with it. He was off to a good start.

"All right, March. There's a chair behind you. Go ahead and have a seat," McCoy said. "Go ahead and take a minute and tell us a little bit about yourself."

"My name is Jay March," he began, and it was at that point that his goggles began fogging up. "I was born July 23, 1986, in Ashtabula, Ohio . . ." Sweat beads were taking over his forehead. ". . . my near-term goals are to become a leader of soldiers . . ." His goggles were almost entirely fogged over now, but he ignored this and continued: ". . . and my long-term goal is to become a sergeant major."

"I see you've got an ARCOM and two AAMs already," McCoy said, looking over March's personnel report, which included his awards and medals. "And you've been in how long?"

"I've been in a little over two years, Sergeant Major," March said.

"That's pretty good. That's really good. To have that right now, with the time that you've got in, that's good," McCoy said. "All right. We'll get started with a little unit history. How many battle streamers does the Second Battalion, Sixteenth Infantry Regiment have?"

"Twenty-two, Sergeant Major," March said. His answer was quick and confident, and in no way betrayed the fact that he had no idea how many battle streamers the 2-16 had.

"*Second* battalion?" McCoy, who did know, said.

"Yes, Sergeant Major," March said.

"Okay," McCoy said, and moved on to the next question on his list, which was about the unfolding 2008 presidential election. "Current events. Tell us what's going on with the political race right now."

"Sir, right now, both Obama and Hillary Clinton are both trying to say they're advertising false information, and President McCain, er, no, McCain is the only one still with the Democrats, Sergeant Major," March said.

Again, confidence.

"Okay. Policies," McCoy said, moving on. "What's the standard for the PT uniform inside the gym?"

"You must have your shirt tucked in, shorts, no weapons allowed inside the gym, when you show up at the gym you must be in full PT uniform, when you get in there you can downgrade to tucked-in shirt, shorts, Sergeant Major," March said, nailing that one.

"All right," McCoy said, and passed the questioning on to the next sergeant. It was the sergeant who during inspection had told March to relax.

"Still a little nervous, I can see," he said, looking at March's goggles, forehead, and, now, his dripping neck.

"A little, First Sergeant."

"Just relax. We'll find out what you know. Okay? We'll start off with uniforms. What DA form is used to recommend or request an award?"

"I don't know, First Sergeant."

"Okay. When can soldiers begin wearing the fleece cap in theater?"

He got that one wrong, too. But then he began getting them right.

"What are the team-building stages?"

"Formation, enrichment, sustainment."

"What are the four common points for checking a pulse?"

"Throat, groin, wrist, and ankle."

Next sergeant.

"There are seven different types of ammunition for an M-4 rifle. Give me four."

He gave five.

"Good."

Next sergeant.

"Okay, let's go to army programs. What is the motto of ACS?"

"Self-help, service, and stability, First Sergeant."

"Hooah. What does BOSS stand for?"

"Better Opportunities for Single Soldiers, First Sergeant."

"Outstanding. Let's go on to Supply Economy. How long is a temporary hand receipt good for?"

"I don't know, First Sergeant."

"Okay. And what is supply economy?"

"Supply economy is all soldiers use it. It's neither haste nor waste of military equipment, First Sergeant."

"Okay. No more questions, Sergeant Major."

"All right," McCoy said to March. "You're dismissed," and that was that. In fourteen minutes, he had been asked thirty-seven questions. He had sweated, shaken, and fogged up his goggles, but after he walked out, McCoy, clearly impressed, said to the others, "He did pretty good."

Not that March heard that. He was already on his way back to the barracks, where some of the other soldiers were griping about what they had just endured.

"They kicked me out for a fucking grenade," one said.

"Stupid stuff," said another, whose dirty gun barrel had turned McCoy's pinky finger black. "Oil. I had oil."

"They were just looking to fuck people over," another said.

"I'm so happy it's over. Holy shit. I'm just so fucking happy it's over," March said, and then saw Swales walking back and ran to him.

"John! John! How'd you do?"

"I'm just glad it's over," Swales said and sighed. "Man."

"Hey, did your eyepro fog up?"

"No."

"Mine did."

"I was nervous. I forgot things," Swales said. "I forgot to mention my wife. I forgot to mention I was married."

Again and again Swales punched his right fist into his left hand as March, relaxed at last, started to laugh. "It's over," he kept saying, and Swales eventually relaxed, too. Tomorrow, they would learn the results. Neither of them would win, but neither of them would come in last, either. Of eleven soldiers, Swales would finish fifth, and March, not so fucking smart, would finish fourth. Not so fucking smart, but not so fucking dumb, either, and he wouldn't mind a bit, because of something that was happening now in the hallway of the barracks, where he stood in front of the rest of the platoon with his right hand in the air.

He had signed a contract a few days before, just after learning he would receive a bonus of $13,500. On such bonus money was the overstretched volunteer U.S. army staying afloat. His family wasn't happy with the idea, but it was like he told them: there weren't a lot of options waiting for him back in Ohio. "I, Jay March, do solemnly swear to come back to Iraq at least three more times in my career," he had joked about saying, but what he said now were the same words he had said before leaving Ohio, going to Fort Riley, and coming to Iraq as a soldier of the surge.

"Congratulations," said the lieutenant who administered the oath.

"I fucking reenlisted," March said, as if not quite believing the choice he had made to remain in the army until the year 2014. He wasn't shaking or blushing. He was just smiling. It was as Phillip Cantu, the dead recruiter, had once told him: there's nothing like the brotherhood when you deploy.

Those brothers now clapped for him, and then they surrounded him as he stood among them with his eyes momentarily closed.

Harrelson burning.

An Iraqi bleeding from a hole in his head.

A little girl looking at him.

And now there was another slide for his show—him as soldier of the moment and as happy as he had ever felt in his life.

It wasn't only him. As February ended and the deployment moved into its final months and then weeks, almost everyone was happier. They could sense the end now.

Because this was Iraq, not everything was satisfactory. The air still felt twitchy. The anxious hum was still there. If this had been the twelve-month deployment the soldiers were told at the beginning they would be headed into, they would be home by now, and that was one thing they thought about every time they climbed into their Humvees. Being dead was bad enough, but being dead when you were supposed to have been safely home and forever alive? One day the chaplain stopped in to tell Brent Cummings that six soldiers had come to him in the past few days saying they were burned out and didn't want to do this anymore. Over at the hospital, the physician assistant was hearing from soldiers who were headed home to broken marriages and bank accounts that had been cleaned out. At the chapel, there was a mandatory seminar on what to expect in the months ahead. It's normal to have flashbacks, the soldiers were told, normal to have trouble sleeping, normal to be angry, normal to be jumpy—and didn't that make everyone feel better. Also, the war continued. In February 2008, 29 U.S. soldiers died; in March there would be 39. In February, 216 were injured; in March it would be 327. On March 23 the total number of dead U.S. troops passed 4,000.

But still.

It was weeks now. A replacement battalion was on its way in. Soldiers were packing equipment in between missions and counting down the days, even though every one of them knew that to do so was the surest way to bring bad luck. Thirty days. Twenty-five days. Eighteen days.

"It's all good," Kauzlarich said one night, walking across a quiet FOB when there were no rocket smears in the sky and the air smelled not of trash or of sewage but just of air, and in this moment the words seemed right. The surge's counterinsurgency strategy seemed at long last to be working in the 2-16's favor. All the months of clearance operations, street patrols, arresting insurgents, building COPs, opening markets, starting adult literacy classes, and working with the National Police seemed to be paying off. In Kamaliyah, the sewer project was once again under way. In another part of New Baghdad, a community swimming pool was being built to help Iraqis fend for themselves in the coming summer heat. The National Police seemed to be trying ever harder, even after so many were killed in the lob bomb attack. At the gas stations, lines were down to fifteen minutes, and on some days even less, and on the lower part of Route Predators a new security tower was being built that stretched both physically and symbolically into the sky, as high as a minaret.

All throughout the 2-16's piece of eastern Baghdad, people seemed to be feeling safer—the very goal that the soldiers had been sent here to achieve.

"Sectarian violence now in Iraq is, I think, something in the past, and Iraqis are looking toward the future for peace and prosperity," Kauzlarich said on PEACE 106 FM, his voice floating out into that night. "So these different groups that are trying to create this chaos, it should be very evident to them now that they'll never be able to create that again."

Choices. Bush made his, the sergeants made theirs, Jay March made his. For fourteen months, Kauzlarich had been making his, and as of March 24, with just seventeen days to go, the insurgents seemed to have made theirs, too.

12

MARCH 29, 2008

And, yes, there's going to be violence, and that's sad. But this situation
needed to be dealt with, and it's now being dealt with.
—GEORGE W. BUSH, *March 28, 2008*

nd then, on March 25, with two weeks remaining in the 2-16's deployment, everything fell apart.

"Holy shit," a soldier said, watching images from surveillance cameras of Route Predators, which was shrouded in black smoke from burning tires.

"Fucking assholes. Fucking assholes. Fucking assholes," Brent Cummings said as report after report came in of EFPs, IEDs, explosions, gunfire, and, now, 140 rockets somewhere out there aimed at Rustamiyah.

"They say if this doesn't work, they will go to phase three," Kauzlarich said, telling his command staff about the latest intelligence that had come in of what the insurgents had been overheard saying, and then, shaking his head, he said, "I have no fucking idea what phase three is."

The situation that George W. Bush said "needed to be dealt with":

That was the situation.

"Good thing the surge is working," a soldier said bitterly.

But Kauzlarich saw it differently.

"This is war," he said of what fourteen months of counterinsurgency strategy had turned into, sounding almost eager. "This is what I do best. Oh my God."

Nate Showman

It had started that morning, way to the south, in the Shiite city of Basra. Since the American invasion five years and five days before, Basra had steadily descended into an awful place of executions, kidnappings, and some of the harshest interpretations of Islamic law in all of Iraq, carried out mostly by elements of Jaish al Mahdi, the militia of the cleric Muqtada al-Sadr. Even with the cease-fire that al-Sadr had imposed on his follow-ers in August 2007, Basra had continued to deteriorate violently, espe-cially after the British forces that were responsible for southern Iraq withdrew to Basra's fringes in December. Finally, Iraq's prime minister, Nouri al-Maliki, concluded enough was enough. Against the advice of U.S. officials who were urging him not to do anything that would tease apart the relative calm that had come to parts of Iraq, Maliki traveled to Basra to bring it under control and to show the world that Iraq was ca-pable of doing things on its own.

Things didn't quite work out that way. Over six days of fighting, the stories that emerged were of a thousand casualties, JAM fighters refusing to give up, water shortages, food shortages, and swarms of Iraqi Army deserters who looted stores and set fire to them as they ran. Eventually, U.S. and British forces began helping out with long-distance artillery barrages, and after that the fighting slowed, al-Sadr reinstated his cease-fire, both sides declared victory, a thousand funerals commenced, and the offensive fizzled out to an inconclusive ending.

That was what the world saw from various news reports, but what it didn't see was what happened in eastern Baghdad, beginning with a huge explosion on Route Predators late on the night of March 24.

"What the fuck?" a soldier said as he looked at surveillance images of where the new, mighty, just-completed security tower was supposed to be standing, but all he could see was a sad little pile of rubble.

It was gone, and by dawn, all of the 2-16's area, so vibrant just the day before, was a ghostly area of shuttered stores, emptied streets, and no people outside other than roaming groups of men who were carrying guns, planting bombs, and setting fires. The spasms of Basra had shivered their way north, straight into the 2-16's AO, and when al-Sadr lifted his cease-fire, it was as if the residents of Kamaliyah and Fedaliyah and Mashtal and Al-Amin and every other war-ruined patch of ground that the 2-16 had been trying to salvage had been waiting behind their closed doors, guns in one hand, EFPs in the other, for the chance to come out and attack.

There were reports that EFPs were being planted every five meters along parts of Route Predators.

There were reports that JAM members, dressed up as National Police, were taking over checkpoints.

The warning siren sounded: here came seven rockets, followed by seven explosions, just beyond the southern wall of the FOB.

"The key is to seize the initiative," Kauzlarich said now to his company commanders, who were crowded into his office, "and forget about how many days we have till we go home."

The company commanders nodded, but every one of them knew that wasn't going to happen. The schedule had been set, and every soldier was aware of it. The last full day of operations was to be March 30, a mere five days from now, after which it was all supposed to be about final inventory, final packing, final cleaning, and getting out. The flights out had been arranged: the first batch of soldiers was set to fly April 4, and by April 10, no one was supposed to be left.

"What are you guys thinking? What are your thoughts?" Kauzlarich asked, but before anyone could answer, Brent Cummings interrupted to say a route-clearance convoy in another battalion had been hit by an EFP on Predators.

"Anybody hurt?" Kauzlarich asked.

"Unknown," Cummings said.

"The thing I *don't* want is for the enemy to think they can do whatever the fuck they want whenever they want to do it," Kauzlarich said after a moment. "All right. Tomorrow, we gotta get out there."

Some of them already were out there, of course, on nervous patrols or bunkered down at COPs that were being hit with occasional gunfire and RPGs, and as the day went on, the threats against them kept increasing in ways that felt cruelly personal.

The school where the 2-16 had tried to develop adult literacy classes was now reportedly being stocked with weapons for an assault on the COP in Kamaliyah.

The swimming pool that was being built in New Baghdad was now filling not with water but with twenty armed men who had arrived in cars reportedly packed with bombs.

Now, near one of the COPs, a surveillance camera that had once tracked a suspicious man into a field where he proceeded to go to the bathroom now tracked another suspicious man, who squatted against a wall with a weapon and began firing. "So, he's shooting?" a soldier said. "Not shitting?"

And the answer was that everyone seemed to be shooting.

"Glad we're giving these people sewers," Cummings said at one point, when an exploding EFP missed a convoy but severed a water main, creating a giant water geyser that would soon flood parts of Kamaliyah, lead to water shortages, and soften the ground so much that some of the new sewer pipes would collapse. A year before, when Cummings had first seen Kamaliyah and peered into a hole in the ground at the cadaver named Bob, he had talked of the goodness here and the need to act morally. "Otherwise we're not human," he had said. Eight months before, when he had bent some rules to get Izzy's injured daughter into the aid station and had watched her smile as Izzy kissed her, he had said, "Man, I haven't felt this good since I got to this hellhole." Now, watching the water geyser, he simply said, "Stupid people. I hate 'em. Stupid fucking scumbags."

"This is the evolution of democracy, what's going on right now," Kauzlarich said at another point, late that night, searching for an explanation, and the following morning, as he and most of his soldiers prepared to go out to get things back under control, he was even more certain that his explanation was right. "This has to happen. This whole uprising has to happen. It's got to happen," he said as he got dressed. A year before, when he had tried to envision the moment he was now in, he had made a prediction. "Before we leave, I'm going to do a battalion run. A task force run. In running shorts and T-shirts," he had said, tracing a route on the map in his office that went from Route Pluto to Route Predators and back to the FOB. As it turned out, that route would be the route that he and his soldiers would follow today as they tried to restore some order, and as he covered himself with body armor and double-checked the ammunition in his gun, he said, "This is the last stand of the Shi'a populace.

That's what this is. This is Jaish al Mahdi's last stand, and that's why we gotta get 'em. Now is the time. Everybody has their last stand. The Japanese had their last stand. The Germans had their last stand. Everybody has their last stand. And now they're gonna die."

He walked out from his trailer and headed down the dirt road toward the operations center, where some soldiers who were part of his personal security detail were watching video images of roaming gangs and new tire fires along Route Predators. "This is where we're going?" one of them said. "This isn't fucking funny. This is what we're driving through?"

"Game on," Kauzlarich said as he approached them, and then he saw Izzy, who would be going, too, standing on the fringes, smoking a cigarette down to the filter.

"Izzy, how are you today? *As-Salamu Alaykum? Shaku maku?*"

"I don't know what the fuck is going on," Izzy said.

"What the fuck! What's wrong with your people? They're out of control," Kauzlarich said, and when he saw Izzy looking at him with a confused smile, he tried to reassure him. "Today will be a good day," he said. "You got earplugs?"

Izzy shook his head.

"You want some?" Kauzlarich said. "Save your hearing. Might need to."

He laughed and handed Izzy an extra pair he had, while one of his soldiers, Sergeant Barry Kitchen, watched from a distance.

"He thinks he's gonna change the country. He thinks he's gonna change all this. But he's not," Kitchen said. "I mean, it's good to believe, to a point, but when it comes to this? The whole country falling apart pretty much? One guy's not gonna fix it."

And off they went.

Up Route Pluto.

"I anticipate small-arms fire and possibly EFPs," Kauzlarich radioed in.

Onto Route Predators and toward the burning tires.

"I've got to piss. I'll put one out personally," he said now.

Around the burning tires and into a storm of gunfire.

"We're going to go ahead and turn around. We've taken a considerable amount of small-arms fire."

Onto another road and into an exploding EFP that passed between two vehicles.

"No worries. We're continuing movement."

Onto another road and into a second EFP explosion that went through the back of the Humvee directly in front of him, ruining it and just missing the soldiers in the rear seat.

"No casualties. The vehicle's jacked up. We are going to drag it out of here."

And on it went, not just for Kauzlarich, but for every convoy and at every COP. Gunfire. Mortars. RPGs. EFPs. "Our worst nightmare is coming true. We have two platoons in heavy contact," Cummings said at one point as he monitored radio transmissions that were at times inaudible because of all the gunfire. He tried to get some Apache gunships in to help. No luck. The 2-16 soldiers were on their own. They drove up streets and down streets. They got shot at, and they shot back. "Stay slow, stay low, and if you see someone with a weapon, fucking drop him. Don't even ask questions," had been Kauzlarich's instructions, and that was what they did: off of rooftops, in streets, behind buildings. But the Iraqis kept coming and coming. They shot at convoys and launched rockets at Rustamiyah, and when an Iraqi Army Humvee was hit and burst into flames, they swarmed it, reached into the fire, and ran off with whatever they could, even the portable stretcher.

"Wow," Kauzlarich said to Cummings when he finally made it back at sunset and walked into the operations center. He shook his head, unable to say anything more. He was furious. He and his soldiers had been in two firefights and had been hit with two EFPs. The soldiers who had been in the Humvee that was crippled in the second explosion, including Sergeant Kitchen, were at the aid station, being examined for signs of hearing damage and concussions. Izzy was there, too, with a terrible headache, looking sad and old, and so Kauzlarich found another interpreter to telephone a sheik who was one of the most powerful in Kamaliyah. "Tell him I'm going to blow up all the pump stations, and the sewage project will be no more," he said.

"Are you joking?" the interpreter asked.

"No. I am serious. Tell him I am going to destroy the Kamaliyah sewage project unless the people calm down. I will blow up your project and you will live in shit for the rest of your life."

He started to say more but was interrupted by the warning siren going off.

· Three rockets. Three explosions.

"We need to take a fucking knee," he said.

So, on March 27, they took a fucking knee, staying on the FOB or in COPs "to transition from Counterinsurgency Operations to High Intensity Combat Operations." That would be the wording in an official synopsis submitted afterward of all that had happened so far and would happen next. It was a lengthy document devoid of any emotion—making no mention, for instance, of the soldier who spent the day double-sandbagging the entrance to his room while saying over and over, "God, I hate this place," as if reciting a prayer—a document that boiled down to this: even though they were one day closer to being done, they weren't done yet. There was going to be more.

On the twenty-seventh, with the Americans mostly tucked away, the targets became the Iraqis who had worked most closely with them and now existed with the indelible taint of that contact. A call came in about Mr. Timimi, the civil manager. "JAM wants to burn down his house, and he wants help," the interpreter who took the call told Kauzlarich.

"We're not gonna protect his house. We don't do houses," Kauzlarich said.

Another call came, this one relaying a message from Colonel Qasim, who said most of his 550-member National Police battalion, known as the 1-4-1, were throwing down weapons, changing out of their uniforms, and defecting. He needed help, too.

"If One-four-one is going to surrender, no sense going in and saving their ass," Kauzlarich said.

Another call: Timimi again. "Mr. Timimi wants to say thank you," the interpreter told Kauzlarich.

"For what?"

"For letting JAM burn his house down."

Another call from Qasim: a mob was advancing on the District Area Council building, where his office was, and he was afraid. "He says they're almost at the fence and they will kill him."

"No. They won't kill him. Tell him he has to defend himself," Kauzlarich said. He then radioed Ricky Taylor, the commander of Alpha Company, to go to the DAC and rescue his friend forever who had given him a birthday party, and as a platoon of Taylor's soldiers shot their way toward Qasim, Kauzlarich made a new prediction: "The whole fucking city is going to erupt tomorrow."

But it was only the Shiite parts of Baghdad that continued to erupt. The morning of March 28 came with fresh fires and explosions, and after more than four hundred days here, there was a growing sense of bewilderment within the soldiers. What were they supposed to think of what was happening? How were they to make sense of it? How could they shape it into something understandable? Should it be by pure numbers? If so, the numbers added up to the most attacks on them ever, by far. Every convoy was being attacked now. It was June again, except doubled. Should it be by examples? Because if it was examples, here was one: a report just coming in that the Iraqi spokesman for the surge, a pleasant man who was often at press conferences with U.S. officials saying how well things were progressing, had been kidnapped by insurgents who had killed his bodyguards, burned down his house, and may have hidden him somewhere within the garbage piles and water buffalo herds of Fedaliyah.

Fedaliyah: once a shithole, always a shithole, and now a platoon was headed toward it to search for a spokesman of the surge. Kamaliyah: that was the shithole where the soldiers had tried the hardest and the violence was now the worst. Mashtal, Al-Amin, Mualameen: shithole, shithole, and shithole, all of them a warscape now, with streets so empty and life so hidden that, for a moment anyway, the most overwhelming thing about all of this was the silence it had brought. It was the silence of bending glass. It was the hush on a Kamaliyah rooftop just before Sergeant Emory received a bullet to his head. It was the quiet of a Kansas snowfall just before some soldiers began to cheer. It was silence just waiting to be broken, like the silence just before Joshua Reeves said, "Oh my God," like just before Duncan Crookston said, "I love my wife," and so it was broken now with explosion after explosion, all directed at Kauzlarich and his soldiers as they maneuvered under a sky speckled with high white clouds and spreading black ones beneath.

Almost everyone was out now, taking fire, dodging RPGs, finding IEDs and EFPs, and somehow, so far, not getting hurt. Kauzlarich was in a convoy headed toward Qasim, whose 550 police were now down to half that and dropping. Meanwhile, another National Police battalion that overlapped some of Kauzlarich's area was reportedly down to almost zero, and its defectors included the commander himself, whose last words, said in a departing rush, were something about JAM surrounding his house, his family was inside, he had to go, family first, apologies. Qasim, though, was hanging in, his fear gone, his defiance back, and ever so slowly, Kauzlarich and his convoy moved toward him. They found one EFP and detonated it. They received a report that another was hidden in a speed bump somewhere, and here came a speed bump. Here, now, around a corner, coming from the direction of Kamaliyah, careened a van with a coffin strapped to the top. Here, farther along, were a woman and three children, outside, unprotected, walking, crying their eyes out. Here came another speed bump. Here was another family—father, mother, two children—with filthy faces, in filthy clothing, huddled against a filthy wall on a filthy street, and was this the family Kauzlarich had in mind when he was still at Fort Riley talking about success? "The end state, in my opinion, the end state in Iraq would be that Iraqi children can go out on a soccer field and play safely. Parents can let their kids go out and play, and they don't have a concern in the world. Just like us," he had said, and then asked: "Is that possible?"

It was hope as a question, forgivably sweet, and yet even now, with the answer huddled in front of him against a wall, and now, at sunset, with more of the answer exploding around him in the form of a mortar attack that bloodied a few of his soldiers from flying shrapnel, and now, in the dark, as the attacks continued and he prepared to spend the night on Qasim's couch, he got on the radio and said to his company commanders, "Overall today, a very successful day out on the battlefield."

They were listening to him in COPs that were being mortared and fired upon, at checkpoints abandoned by Iraqis, where they were bracing for imminent attacks, and at the FOB, where the incoming sirens had been sounding all day. "Keep doing what you're doing," he continued. "Maintain vigilance. Remember the three Ps: patience, perseverance, and paranoia. There's a lot of bad guys out here that are trying to get some licks in on us. By the grace of God, today they weren't successful. We, on the other hand, were very successful, but our luck can run out. So just keep doing what you're doing and I have negative further. Over."

Over, and then out, and then one of the soldiers who had been listening said, "Well, this answers the question. They weren't attacking because one guy told them not to attack."

"If it wasn't for the cease-fire, it would have been like this the whole time," another soldier said.

"If the cease-fire hadn't been going on, all the surge would have meant is more soldiers to die," another said.

"The only thing the past few days have proved to me is that after a year they can still do whatever they please, whenever they please," another said.

But Kauzlarich remained adamant. The surge *was* working, and this, now, was the proof. "They wouldn't be fighting if we weren't winning," he had said in the worst of June. "They wouldn't have a reason to. It's a measure of effectiveness." He believed this even more stubbornly now, on March 29, as the fighting grew worse and he rose from Qasim's couch and ever so carefully picked his way through the depressing landscape of eastern Baghdad back to the FOB.

"I don't think they thought we were gonna do what we did," he said, in the operations center now, adding up the number of suspected insurgents his soldiers had killed in the past five days. "One hundred," he said, "one hundred twenty-five," and kept counting. On maps and by aerial surveillance imagery, he was also tracking the movement of his soldiers. A platoon led by Nate Showman was the latest out there, on a mission to bring fresh water and new radio codes to another platoon defending the DAC building. They had just found an EFP, but Showman, unfazed, had snipped the wires, and they were continuing on their way. Along Route Predators, other soldiers had found eleven EFPs and IEDs just in the past several hours. Sixteen other EFPs and IEDs had exploded on various convoys over the past twenty-four hours, but injuries had amounted to nothing worse than a few bloody cuts and concussions, and in every case the soldiers had continued to fight. The good soldiers. As far as Kauzlarich was concerned, they had become great soldiers.

Five fifteen p.m. now. Showman's platoon had made it to the DAC, unloaded, and was heading back to the COP. Predators was quiet. Pluto was quiet. The COPs were quiet. The FOB was quiet.

"It's all good," Kauzlarich said as the entire war seemed to go silent.

Five sixteen p.m.

Glass, bending.

Five seventeen.

Bending.

Five eighteen.

Bending.

Five nineteen.

boom.

The sound was tiny. The walls barely moved. No one seemed to have noticed, except for Kauzlarich.

"Shit," he said.

It took another second or so, but then someone was on the radio, screaming. One vehicle destroyed. Two medevac urgent. Air support needed, *now*. Ricky Taylor, the commander of Alpha Company, came on the radio for a moment, just long enough to say, "Not good, sir," and then dropped away. The camera on the aerostat balloon pivoted and found the war's newest column of rising smoke, and there, beneath it, was Nate Showman's platoon, and suddenly every piece of glass in the world seemed to be breaking, because they weren't even supposed to be here, that was the thing. They were supposed to be guarding convoys in western Iraq. They were supposed to have gone home after twelve months. They were supposed to be on the FOB, packing to leave a war that wasn't supposed to have ever needed a surge, and instead of any of that, they were running toward the ruined Humvee, and now gunfire could be heard over the radio, and now flashes were coming from a building just behind the DAC, and now they were piling into their own Humvees, and now they were barreling toward COP Cajimat, and now the phone in the operations center was ringing and Ricky Taylor was on the line and someone was handing the receiver to Kauzlarich.

"Hey, Ricky," he said.

He listened for a moment.

"Okay," he said.

"Roger," he said.

"All right, buddy. Hang in there. Standing by," he said.

"Thanks," he said and hung up.

"What'd he say, sir?" Cummings asked.

"Two KIA," he said.

His eyes filled with tears.

He dropped his head.

He stayed that way for a while, hands on his hips, eyes down, and when he was finally able to look up and resume the war, it was to request that the biggest bomb out there at the moment, not a missile on a helicopter, but a guided bomb attached to the underside of a jet, be sent into the building next to the DAC where the gunfire was coming from. After which there was nothing to do but wait.

Here came the first battle-roster number, over the radio.

"Bravo-seven-six-one-niner."

Fingers traced the manifest until they came to rest on B7619, next to which was the name of Durrell Bennett, and lots of heads dropped now. Everyone liked Bennett.

Now came the second number.

"Mike-seven-seven-two-two."

Again, fingers traced numbers until they stopped by the name of Patrick Miller.

"That's the new kid we just got," someone said, and everyone thought back to the new soldier who had arrived on the day in September when General Petraeus had visited and Joshua Reeves had died, the one who had been premed, who had run out of money, and whose smile seemed to light up the room.

Now came more details.

There had been five soldiers in the Humvee. The EFP had sliced open one soldier, who was bleeding internally; sliced off the hand of another; sliced off the arm of another; sliced off both of Bennett's legs; and gone through Miller's mouth, teeth, and jaw.

Now came the warning siren as another rocket attack began on Rusta-miyah. Now came a frantic call from Mr. Timimi to the interpreter: "He said they stole his car." Now came the scream of a low jet, followed by the satisfying sight on the video monitor of an exploding black blossom, somewhere inside of which was a building. "Enjoy your seventy-two virgins," Kauzlarich said as his soldiers, virgins, too, once, hollered and clapped, and then they got busy planning their very last mission on their very last day of full combat operations, bringing the two dead soldiers back to the FOB.

A convoy of three platoons and two body bags left at 3:22 a.m. By 3:40 a.m., the first IED had exploded and flattened some tires. By 3:45 a.m., the first gunfight was under way. By 3:55 a.m., soldiers had found and destroyed three EFPs. By 4:50 a.m., they were at the DAC, where the ruined Humvee had been taken. By 5:10 a.m., they were lifting and then scooping Bennett and Miller into the body bags. By 5:30 a.m., they were on their way to COP Cajimat to rendezvous with Nate Showman and his soldiers. By 5:47, they were in another gunfight. By 5:48, the vehicle leading the convoy was hit by some type of IED but was able to keep going. By 5:49, the same vehicle was hit with another IED but was still able to keep going. By 6:00 a.m., the convoy had made it to COP Cajimat. By 7:00 a.m., the soldiers were escorting Showman, his ruined platoon, the ruined Humvee, and the remains of Bennett and Miller to the FOB. By 7:55 a.m., everyone was back, and the mission was officially a success.

In the army, every event gets recorded on an "event storyboard," from which a kind of clarity can emerge. This was who. This was what. This was where. This was when. This was the task. This was the purpose. This was the time line. Pictures are included, and diagrams, and when a storyboard is finished, a narrative has formed that will forever make the event seem different from anything ever before it. An operation to get a soldier's remains becomes entirely different from another operation to get another soldier's remains. An EFP exploding from a trash pile is nothing like an EFP exploding from a water buffalo carcass. Every gunfight becomes unique. Every battle is original. All wars aren't actually all the same.

But by 7:55 a.m., even though another storyboard was being assembled about the successful mission to get Bennett and Miller, the war, the battles, the gunfights, the explosions, the events, had finally become a blur. Is war supposed to be linear? The movement from point A to point B? The odyssey from there to here? Because this wasn't any of that anymore. The blur was the linear becoming the circular.

The Humvee was unloaded at Vehicle Sanitization (there, hidden from view, photographs were taken of the damage, the holes in the door were measured and analyzed, and soldiers did their best to disinfect what was left of the Humvee with bottles of peroxide and Simple Green . . .).

The remains of Bennett and Miller were at Mortuary Affairs (being prepared for shipment behind the locked doors of the little stand-alone building in which there were sixteen storage compartments for bodies, a stack of vinyl body bags, a stack of new American flags, and two Mortuary Affairs soldiers whose job was to search the remains for anything personal that a soldier might have wanted with him while he was alive . . .).

And so on, from Cajimat forward to now. The air stank, the flies were swarming, and now Brent Cummings was walking across the FOB to see the Humvee. He looked at the holes in the door, and it was Joshua Reeves's Humvee and it was William Crow's Humvee. He crawled inside and looked at the gouges in the turret ring, where Bennett had been standing and gunning, and it was Gajdos and Payne and Craig and Shelton. He looked at the ruined rear seats, and that was where Miller had been sitting, and Crow, and Crookston. He looked at the dried blood on the floor. It smelled like iron. It smelled like iodine. It smelled like blood. It was Miller, Bennett, Doster, Reeves, Crookston, Shelton, Lane, Murray, Harrelson, Crow, Craig, Payne, Gajdos, and Cajimat. It was all of them. He thought he might vomit. He got out and walked away and cried and kicked rocks, and then he circled back to the operations center, where they were continuing to track the war, including, now, Kauzlarich's convoy, which was nearing Route Predators.

"I *gotta* go out," Kauzlarich had explained before leaving, "just to see how fucked up it is out there."

He'd waited until Bennett and Miller were back, and then he had gone. Battlefield circulation was what he called this kind of thing, and even though this was the last day of full operations, the battlefield was still out there and the war was still waiting to be won. The explosions continued, especially along Predators. The gunfire attacks continued on the COPs, the DAC, and the Iraqi-abandoned checkpoints, where his soldiers would remain until the replacement battalion could fully relieve them. He wanted to visit as many of the soldiers as possible, that was part of it, and he also simply wanted to be out there and in it. Counterinsurgency may have been the strategy he got, but who he was at heart was a soldier who wanted in, and in all likelihood, this would be his final trip out of the wire.

"Everyone's in the fight," he'd said. "Everyone." His intention was to go up Route Predators to Kamaliyah, and as he'd pulled away saying he'd be back in a few hours, it was hard not to think of a story he had related once about the nature of belief. He'd been at Fort Benning, Georgia, for some advanced coursework, and at the end of an exercise, as he and other soldiers waited outside for a ride, a visiting soldier from Sierra Leone explained how he had survived that country's various wars: "In my country, we put on a blouse. It is a magic blouse. When I wear it, I know bullets cannot harm me." The Sierra Leonean then rolled up a sleeve of the shirt he was wearing and said, "Give me a knife." Someone gave him a knife. "Watch," he said, and he then swung the knife toward his arm. It went through the skin. It went through muscle. It might have cut clean to the bone as far as Kauzlarich knew, but what he remembered more clearly was how for one belief-filled moment everyone was waiting for the magic, hoping for it, right up until blood began gushing and the Sierra Leonean looked at them in panic. "That's a form of belief," Kauzlarich would say of what he learned that day. "That's also a form of jackassery."

Now, as his convoy came to a stop on Route Pluto because of a possible EFP, the moment of the magic blouse seemed to have arrived again. "Can you squirt around to the right?" Kauzlarich radioed the lead vehicle. Or maybe it was a moment from the other story he liked to tell every so often, the heroic battle of Ia Drang.

They waited.

Over the radio came word that a route-clearance team ahead of them on Route Predators was in heavy contact and getting slammed.

A few minutes later came orders from the route clearance's battalion to turn back because Predators was too dangerous.

An EFP. A firefight. A road that had become so dangerous that other soldiers were being ordered to leave it. A convoy, paused, awaiting a leader's decision on what to do next.

The situation:

That was the situation.

It was the heroic situation that Kauzlarich had in various ways dreamed of since he was a boy who romanticized the idea of being a soldier: the final day of full combat, the final trip out of the wire, down to the bucket of old bullets, a final chance to prove greatness. Here was the moment of true belief, beyond which would be only victory.

"Trust your instincts," Hal Moore had said.

"I'll never forgive myself—that my men died, and I didn't," Mel Gibson had said.

"Tsk tsk," the Iraqi had said.

"Watch," the Sierra Leonean had said, swinging the knife.

"Bottom line," Kauzlarich said, and then came his heroic decision:

The 2-16 had given enough.

It would be jackassery to go up Route Predators, "absolute jackassery," and as relief spread through the soldiers in his convoy, who just wanted to go home, he guided them safely back to Rustamiyah and closed himself in his office to write his memorial speech.

In another part of the FOB, Nate Showman was writing, too.

"Rae baby," he wrote to his new wife.

He had come in at 7:55 a.m. with blood on his boots and a sadness so thorough that he'd been unable to speak, even when a few soldiers asked him how he was doing. His answer was to shake his head and stare at the ground. He had spent the rest of the day in isolation, and only now had he found some words he wanted to say, writing to his wife, "I'm gonna need some help when I get home."

He slept only a little that night, even though he was exhausted, and the next day, at Kauzlarich's request, he went reluctantly to the operations center for a debriefing. The two of them had always been able to talk more easily than most commanders and junior officers, maybe because Showman's self-confidence and methodical thinking in some ways reminded Kauzlarich of himself. "I'm just trying to figure out what the hell happened," Kauzlarich said now to Showman, getting right to it, and when Showman looked at him in silence, Kauzlarich said quietly, "If you would, just talk me through."

So Showman began by telling Kauzlarich about what Patrick Miller was doing just before he died, that he was standing outside of his Humvee eating a date that he'd been given by an Iraqi National policeman.

"The last thing I saw of Little Miller," is how he put it, and he didn't bother to explain that Miller was called Little Miller to differentiate him from Big Miller, a soldier with a back so hairy that there would be bets among soldiers over who would be brave enough to lick it. Or about the night his soldiers woke him up and there was Little Miller dancing in front of him, naked except for sunglasses, an M-4, a bandana, and a thong, and laughing hysterically as he chanted, "I'm ready to fight terrorists." All of the soldiers were laughing. He laughed, too. He had been crazy about Miller.

"Little Miller was putting a can of gas in the trunk. The National guy gave him a date," he said, and he didn't bother with the rest of it: that the reason the Iraqi gave him a date was out of gratitude; and the reason for the gratitude was that the Americans had come to save him; and the reason that the Americans had come to save him was because they had been trying to save him since 2003, when the number of dead American soldiers was zero and Patrick Miller was nineteen years old and about to start college and thinking that he was going to become a doctor. And instead:

"He took a date and ate it and gave the guy the thumbs-up and got back in the truck," Showman said, and then the truck took off on a route that Showman had just thought of, which led straight into an exploding EFP.

"We had two options," he explained to Kauzlarich, "either go back the exact same way we came, or try to get down Florida." He recounted a conversation he'd had with a soldier named Patrick Hanley, who was the truck commander in the lead vehicle and would typically be the one to choose the route.

"Hey, dude, we've got these two options," he'd said. "I'd like to try it on Florida because I don't think they'll be expecting it."

"All right," replied Hanley, who was about to give his entire left arm to the cause of freedom, as well as part of the left temporal lobe of his brain, which would leave him unconscious and nearly dead for five weeks, and with long-term memory loss, and dizziness so severe that for the next eight months he would throw up whenever he moved his head, and weight loss that would take him from 203 pounds down to 128. "Let's do it."

And so they did it.

Truck number one: Hanley was right front. A soldier named Robert Winegar, who was about to be broken open by shrapnel in his arm and his back, was driving. A soldier named Carl Reiher, who was about to lose one of his hands, was right rear. Bennett, up in the turret, was gunner. Miller, the taste of a date still fresh on his tongue, was left rear.

Truck number two: Showman was right front, watching truck number one through his windshield as it squeezed between some barriers and rolled over what seemed to be an old, rusted piece of a gate.

"Got through fine," Showman said to Kauzlarich.

Now Showman's Humvee rolled over the gate and lost a tire. "We were still rolling fine on the flat. I thought, 'We're a click and a half out. Fuck it.' Kept on rolling."

Now truck number one, moving along Route Florida, saw something suspicious and swerved.

"He took a real wide berth around it. All of the trucks did. Swung off the road, actually; went around and back on the road."

Got through fine.

Kept on rolling.

"Twenty meters up the road, right at the intersection, there's a little mud hut right there, off to the left, and then there's a light pole. They set it right in front of the light pole," he continued. "They must have camouflaged it real good because—"

"It's where those fuckers sell gas all the time?" Kauzlarich interrupted. "That mud hut?"

"Roger," Showman said.

"So it was on the ground, you think?"

"Roger," he repeated, and then stopped talking. Maybe he was seeing what was next.

"You guys did the battle drill," Kauzlarich said after a bit, trying to help him.

"I mean, I probably don't remember thirty seconds of this," Showman said. His voice had been getting quieter and quieter. Now he could barely be heard. "I was right on Hanley's ass. The next thing that I really do remember is the radio being in my hands, and I was hollering, 'Outlaw Six, we got hit at the intersection of Florida and Fedaliyah,' and then I told Mannix"—his driver—"to stomp the gas and haul ass. I couldn't see the truck at the time. The road ahead of me was clear back to the COP. We shot through the kill zone and then we got up just a little ways, probably thirty meters. The truck had rolled off the road to the left. There's like a garden and courtyard, and there's nothing past it, just a big dirt yard. The truck had pulled behind that courtyard. I told Mannix to pull up right alongside. We started taking heavy small-arms fire. I told Mannix to pull up. There was a house and the truck, and then just everything else."

Everything else:

"He was just white, with blood running down the side of his head, his eyes were vacant."

That was Winegar.

"I thought he was dead. Dead weight. Just completely unresponsive. Eyes were wide open. I grabbed his ass to boost him into the truck, and my hand just slipped away. It was covered with blood."

That was Reiher.

"And then Hanley?" Kauzlarich asked.

"Yeah. You could tell right away that it was severe head trauma because of the way his eyes were rolled back in his head, and he was foaming at the mouth," Showman said.

And Bennett?

And Miller?

"I told Outlaw Six we needed a medevac at COP Cajimat," Showman said of what he did next. He started to say something else, to explain why he hadn't directed the convoy to the FOB, where a medevac would have had an easier time landing, but his voice trailed off. "Because it was close," he said, and his voice trailed off again.

"It was the right call. It was the right call, Nate," Kauzlarich said. "And then the route you took—you had two choices. You picked the least of two evils, given the Ranger rule of never going out the same way you came in."

Showman looked at him, said nothing.

"It's fucked up. But you did the right thing," Kauzlarich said.

"The boys were still inside," Showman said.

"There's nothing you could do for them," Kauzlarich said.

"Yes, sir," Showman said, and that could have been the end of the conversation, confession made, forgiveness received, but for whatever reason, he needed to say it out loud.

"It took Little Miller's head right off," he said. "It went right through Bennett. When I opened that back door where those two were sitting . . ."

"They didn't know what hit them," Kauzlarich said.

But that wasn't the point. The point was that they had been hit.

Showman was looking at the floor now. Not at Kauzlarich. Not at the box of dust-covered soccer balls waiting to be given out. Not at the wall map of Iraq fucking itself. Just the floor.

The point was that he had thought of the route.

"So," he said, sighing.

Four hundred and twenty days before, when they were all about to leave for Iraq, a friend of Kauzlarich's had predicted what was going to happen. "You're going to see a good man disintegrate before your eyes," he'd said.

Four hundred and twenty days later, the only question left was how many of the eight hundred good men it was going to be.

On one end of the FOB, the soldier who had spent hours stacking sandbags until the entrance to his room was a tunnel pronounced himself ready for the next rocket attack.

In another part of the FOB, soldiers were learning that one of the rounds they had fired after being hit by two IEDs on their way to get Showman's platoon had gone through a window and into the head of an Iraqi girl, killing her as she and her family tried to hide.

In another part, a soldier was thinking about whatever a soldier thinks about after seeing a dog licking up a puddle of blood that was Winegar's, or Reiher's, or Hanley's, or Bennett's, or Miller's, and shooting the dog until it was dead.

The good soldiers.

They really were.

"The war's over for you, my friend," Kauzlarich said now to Showman, and of all the things he had ever said, nothing had ever seemed less true.

13

APRIL 10, 2008

I want to say a word to our troops and civilians in Iraq. You've performed with
incredible skill under demanding circumstances. The turnaround you have made
possible in Iraq is a brilliant achievement in American history. And while this
war is difficult, it is not endless. And we expect that as conditions on the ground
continue to improve, they will permit us to continue the policy of return on success.
The day will come when Iraq is a capable partner of the United States. The day will
come when Iraq is a stable democracy that helps fight our common enemies and promote
our common interests in the Middle East. And when that day arrives, you'll come home
with pride in your success and the gratitude of your whole nation. God bless you.
—GEORGE W. BUSH, *April 10, 2008*

You know what I love? Baby carrots. Baby carrots and Ranch dress-
ing," a soldier said. "I think I'm going to be eating some baby
carrots when I get home."

"Shhh," another soldier said, eyes shut. "I'm on a pontoon boat
right now."

They were done. They were all done. It was April 4. In a few hours,
once it was dark, some Chinook helicopters would cut across the night
shadows toward Rustamiyah. Soon after that, the first 235 of them would
be on their way out, and by April 10, all of them would be gone.

Rustamiyah to the Baghdad airport.

Baghdad to Kuwait.

Kuwait to Budapest.

Budapest to Shannon, Ireland.

Shannon to Goose Bay, Canada.

263

Mortuary Affairs

Goose Bay to Rockford, Illinois.

Rockford to Topeka, Kansas.

Topeka to Fort Riley, by bus.

And then a welcome-home ceremony from a grateful nation in a small, half-filled gym.

It had been difficult getting everyone ready to go. Muqtada al-Sadr had reinstated his cease-fire as April began, but the attackers kept attacking anyway, which meant that even though full combat operations were over, the soldiers still out of the wire at COPs and checkpoints had to fight their way back to the FOB. At one point, in the operations center, where the movements were being coordinated, several soldiers watched incredulously on a video monitor as an Iraqi with an AK-47 jumped out from behind a building and began firing Rambo-style on a convoy. "Die, monkey, die!" Brent Cummings hollered for some reason, and the others began hollering it, too, laughing and chanting right up until the moment an Apache helicopter swooped in and blasted the monkey to smithereens, at which point they broke into cheers. At another point, they were monitoring a route-clearance team from another battalion that was moving up Predators toward some 2-16 soldiers at an abandoned Iraqi checkpoint. All of a sudden the screen went black, and when it cleared, the lead vehicle was curving off the road and accelerating through a field, the result of an EFP explosion that had decapitated the driver but left his foot in place on the gas pedal. All night long, Cummings continued to see that vehicle curving ever so gracefully into the field, and meanwhile Kauzlarich had his own images to contend with in the form of another dream. This one had been about mortars. They were exploding everywhere. In front of him. Behind him. They kept coming, the bracketing bringing them closer and closer until the entire world was only noise and rising fire, at which point he had awakened and realized he was fine. He was absolutely fine.

"You are happy? Because you are leaving?" an interpreter asked Kauzlarich now as she placed a call for him on a cell phone. She was substituting for Izzy, who had gone home to see if his family was safe.

"I don't know," he said.

"Okay. Qasim. Ringing. You want to talk to him?" she said.

Kauzlarich took the phone. *"Shlonek?"* he said ("How are you?"). And so it was that a few days later, Colonel Qasim and Mr. Timimi came to Rustamiyah to say goodbye to Muqaddam K.

"Kamaliyah?" Qasim said as they waited for an interpreter.

"No problem," Kauzlarich said.

Qasim made a whooshing sound. Maybe he was trying to say missile. Maybe he was trying to say RPG. Maybe it was the sound of 420 of his 550 men deserting.

"Marfood. Fucking guys," Kauzlarich said.

"Hut hut hut hut hut," Qasim said, imitating one of the expressions he had learned from Kauzlarich.

The interpreter arrived, giving Timimi the chance to tell Kauzlarich what had happened when Kauzlarich didn't come to his rescue. "They burned everything," he said. "Like savages, the things they did." He was a humble man with a wife and two daughters, he said, and now he and his wife and daughters had nothing other than the clothes they were wearing. No house. No car. No furniture. Not even a pair of slippers, he said. He leaned closer to Kauzlarich. "I want just one thing from you," he said in English. "If you can help me with money." Then, moving away, as if being too close would make him seem like a beggar rather than a powerful administrator with an ornate desk and a cuckoo clock on a wall, he switched back to Arabic and asked for something else. "A letter saying he was working with you," the interpreter said. "In case he goes anywhere for political asylum."

Qasim's turn. He, too, leaned toward Kauzlarich, but before he could ask for anything, Kauzlarich said he had something to give him and handed him a box. It didn't say "Crispy" on top. There was no pizza inside. Instead, there was an old, polished pistol.

"From World War One," Kauzlarich said.

"Thank you," Qasim said.

He then handed Qasim another gift: a new switchblade knife.

"Thank you," Qasim said again.

And a third gift: a photograph in a frame. It was of the two of them.

"Thank you, thank you, thank you," Qasim said, ducking his head and hiding his eyes. He excused himself, went to a bathroom and splashed water onto his face, and on the way out of the FOB, he reached for Kauzlarich's hand and held it as they walked. Kauzlarich held onto Qasim's hand, too. "Anything you need, I will be only seven thousand miles away," he said to Qasim when they reached the main gate, and Qasim laughed for a moment, and then he stopped laughing, and then he and Timimi disappeared down a long corridor of blast walls and concertina wire.

It was the same a few days later, when Izzy returned to say goodbye. Kauzlarich gave him a watch as a gift and also handed him a letter saying that if Izzy were ever to make it to the United States as a refugee, he would be willing to be Izzy's sponsor. "It would be my honor," he had written.

"Thank you very much, sir," Izzy said.

"And do you smoke cigars?" Kauzlarich asked.

"Sometimes," Izzy said.

"My brother," Kauzlarich said.

"Thank you, sir," Izzy said.

"Forever," Kauzlarich said, and away Izzy went with a letter and a watch and a cigar. Outside, he paused to light it, but the wind was up, blowing flour into the thorn bushes, and so he lit a cigarette instead and walked by himself past the soldiers he had become friends with, who were now busy packing to leave.

It was an astonishing amount of work, leaving a war. Everything had to go somewhere, either back to Fort Riley, over to another battalion, or into the trash. Every unused bullet had to be inventoried. Every grenade had to be accounted for. Every weapon. Every gas mask. Every atropine injector. Every pressure bandage. Every tourniquet.

The dusty counterinsurgency manual on Cummings's desk had to be packed, as did the battalion flag, and the American flag, and the poster of Muqtada al-Sadr that hung upside down outside Kauzlarich's office.

The fly swatters would go in the trash. So would any leftover junk food that had been sent by Americans who wanted to support the troops, as well as the toothpaste they had sent, the deodorant, and the odd stack of *Glamour* magazines that had come from an Arkansas middle school, along with a hand-drawn card that read, "Show Dem Arabs Who's Boss. Nuke em. Happy Thanksgiving."

The photographs of twelve dead soldiers nailed to a plywood wall— there hadn't been time to include Bennett and Miller—had to be packed, as did the other thing nailed to a wall, a sign intended to remind anyone who remembered to look at it why they were there. MISSION: TO CREATE A BALANCED, SECURE, AND SELF-SUFFICIENT ENVIRONMENT FOR THE IRAQI PEOPLE, it read.

All of it had to go. Every soccer ball that hadn't been pushed out of a Humvee window to neutralize the insurgency. All of the pencils that hadn't been handed out to keep a five-year-old with a rock in his hand from becoming a future EFP emplacer. Everything in every corner, down to the football that Brent Cummings's high school class had sent to him when they realized why he'd be missing their twentieth reunion. "You're my hero!" someone had written on the football. "Kill some towell heads," someone else had written. So that had to go, along with the good-luck charms soldiers carried, the love letters they had received, the divorce papers they had been sent, the photographs of family and cars and un-dressed women they had taped to walls, the books they had read, the video games they had played, and finally their computers, on one of which Cummings now scanned the last of his e-mails before shutting it down.

"Subject: Human Remains Pouches. Please send me your on hand quantities of human remains pouches. In addition, I need to know if you need more and quantities. Thanks."

Human remains pouches. They had to be packed, too. At least they were already folded.

April 4 now. Two hundred and thirty-five soldiers headed home.

April 5. One hundred and eighty more headed home.

April 6. The one-year anniversary of the death of Jay Cajimat, and here came the mortar attack Kauzlarich had dreamed of. Fourteen soldiers on the FOB were injured. Five had to be evacuated. One died. But none was Kauzlarich's, and none was Kauzlarich himself. The closest call was to Brent Cummings, who was standing in line outside of the laundry when the explosions began. He flung himself to the ground. The mortars came closer and closer, and finally were so close that the concussions felt like they were lifting him into the air, scaring him as much as he'd ever been scared in his life, but he was fine. He was fine.

April 7. Another death—this one a soldier in the battalion replacing the 2-16 who was out on his first patrol and was shot through the mouth. He was the battalion's first KIA, their Jay Cajimat. "A heart the size of the entire state," was how he was going to be remembered in his hometown paper, and meanwhile, Kauzlarich was in his office staring at a photograph he had just received. It was of the inside of the Humvee in which Bennett and Miller had died, and even though he needed to pack, he kept staring at the photograph.

April 8. Almost everything was packed now. One of the TVs was still working, though, and on it was General Petraeus, back in Washington, once again testifying before Congress about the success of the surge. "I'm not suggesting that we yank all our troops out all the way," a senator was saying to him. "I'm trying to get to an end point. That's what all of us have been trying to get to." This was Barack Obama, but the soldiers were more interested in a report, just coming in over the radio, that the COP they had built in Kamaliyah had been mortared and was at that moment on fire and burning to the ground.

April 9. Most of the remaining soldiers headed home. Only eighty or so were left. Late at night, Kauzlarich finished his work, realized he had nothing more to do, and walked down the dark road to the trailer where a year and three days before he had been awakened by a knock on his door. "What the fuck?" he had said then, opening his eyes.

April 10 now.

Time to go.

Past the operations center, which was back to being an empty building with cracked walls.

Past the DFAC, where during their last meal they'd heard a whistle, followed by a massive explosion, which sent them diving to the floor.

Past the road to the hospital, with the little room at the top of a chipped stone stairway where Kauzlarich had gone for the final time the other night, just before Bennett and Miller's memorial service, to say into the microphone of PEACE 106 FM, "Thank you, Mohammed. This will probably be my last show, so to all your listeners, I would just like to say, *shukran jazilan*."

Through a small gate and into an open field, where, with the help of the dim light of a rising dented moon, eighty soldiers scanned a very dark sky for the final rocket that would kill them, or the final mortar that would kill them, or the helicopters that would take them away.

They were in the wide, unprotected open. There were some old bleachers to take cover beneath, and a bomb shelter that would hold five or six of them, but that was it. The helicopters would come when they could. There was no telling when. That was the best the war could do for them, so they waited. They wore their body armor and eye protection and gloves. They smoked cigarettes and ground them out into the cracked, weedy asphalt where the helicopters would land. An hour went by. Another hour went by. They calculated the odds of a rocket attack. It had been two days, one of them said. No, there was the one the night before, by the DFAC. But that wasn't a rocket. Yes, it was. No, it wasn't. Well, whatever it was, it roared down and shook the building. Okay, a day, then. It had been a day. Yeah, but so what? So it had been a day! Yeah, but that doesn't mean anything if a rocket comes right now! They talked of home and the first thing they wanted to do, and the second thing they wanted to do, and they kept searching the sky, and standing among them, Kauzlarich kept searching the sky, too.

Two months from now, in early June, he would gather them as a battalion for the final time at an event called the Ranger Ball. It would be held in a hotel banquet hall on the outskirts of Fort Riley, and it would be the last chance for the soldiers to get together before they went away to new battalions and new assignments.

Not all of them would come to the ball. Adam Schumann, for instance, who lived just up the street from the hotel, would stay home that night. He had flown away from the war in a medical helicopter, and when he came home he had been loaded up with antidepressant medication, and anti-anxiety medication, and anti-panic medication, and narcotics for back pain, and something else to help him stop smoking, and something else for the impotence that had developed from all of the medications, until finally his wife mentioned that he was turning into a zombie and their marriage was dying. On his own, he had stopped taking most of the medications after that, and only reluctantly continued to see the social worker he'd been assigned to, who had listened to him describe his dreams and had said that bad dreams in returning soldiers were quite normal. The key was to relax, the social worker had said, and so Schumann would try to relax. He would go fishing. He would walk around a golf course and think it might be a good place to work after the army discharged him. He would grill up some fresh walleye in his backyard, where he had planted some rosebushes. But the war seemed to want to continue. On the day of the Ranger Ball, he would cut some roses to bring inside for his wife, and when a thorn pricked his finger he would think of the firefights, and when he tasted the blood, as he licked it away, he would think of Sergeant Emory, and by the time of the ball he would decide it would be best to stay home.

Hundreds of soldiers would go, though, including Nate Showman, who by then would no longer be trying to see through every trash pile as he drove around Kansas, but at the Ranger Ball would jump from his chair when a waiter dropped a tray of dishes on the far side of the room. Jay March would be there, too, pleased that he would soon be a sergeant, disappointed that the girl who said she'd be at the airport waiting for him when he came home hadn't been there, and wishing that he was one of the soldiers this night who would be receiving a medal. Sergeant Gietz, who would be receiving a medal, and who would soon be diagnosed with PTSD, and a second condition called traumatic brain injury from being around so many explosions, and a third condition that he would refer to as "survivor guilt, whatever the hell that is," would also be there. "I feel dirty about all of this. I ask myself, am I going to be forgiven?" he would say beforehand, and then he would receive a Bronze Star Medal with Valor for all of the soldiers he had helped rescue in June. Joshua Atchley, one of those rescued soldiers, would be there, too, and upon hearing his name being called and the applause of hundreds of soldiers, would pop out his fake eye and thrust it high in the air. Eight seriously wounded soldiers in all would be there, including Sergeant Emory, who upon hearing his name called would gather every bit of strength he had gained since being shot in Kamaliyah in order to push himself out of his wheelchair and up onto his feet. Trembling, up he would go. His posture would be lopsided. His left arm would be quivering. His head would still be misshapen. His speech would still be slurred. His memory would still be hazy. His thoughts would still be the thoughts of a man who had once decided to bring his wrists to his teeth and bite. But for one minute he would stand on his own and try not to lose his balance as the rest of the soldiers, one after another, rose to their feet, too.

It would be that kind of night. There would be some speeches, some food, some music, and a lot of drinking, and at its craziest, Joe Mixson, the only survivor from the explosion of September 4, would roll in his wheelchair onto the dance floor and start spinning around. The wheelchair would have a large American flag on a pole attached to the back, but even more noticeable would be Mixson himself: stripped of all clothing except for his underwear and a bow tie and clean bandages over his stumps. Back among his fellow soldiers, he would be the real deal this night, no fake legs, no bionics, no microchips, no Wounded Warrior, just a wounded warrior with two stumps, up high, spinning faster and faster in underpants and a bow tie until the American flag was swinging around behind him as he screamed at the top of his lungs in the 2-16's very last hours:

"Thank you, Colonel K!

"Thank you, Colonel K!

"Thank you, Colonel K!"

"They're coming," Brent Cummings said now on the tarmac.

Everyone looked where he was looking, toward the horizon well beyond Rustamiyah, until they saw them, too. Two shadows. They came in fast, and as they settled with spinning rotors onto the tarmac and dropped open their rear hatches, they gave the soldiers a final coating of foul-smelling Rustamiyah dust.

This place.

The fucking dust.

The fucking stink.

The fucking all of it.

This fucking place.

"Well, here are the differences," George W. Bush had said on January 10, 2007. Fifteen months later to the day, the differences were done. Up rose the helicopters with their hatches still open, allowing Kauzlarich a last perfect view of the surge. Instead of opening his eyes, though, he closed them. They had won. He was sure of it. They *were* the difference. It *was* all good. But he had seen enough.

APPENDIX

The 2-16 Roster of Soldiers

LIBORIO ACOSTA, JR.

BRYAN AGOSTOORTIZ

TAUSOLO AIETI*

HOSEA AILOLO

TORRI KAAHA AKUNA

ROBERT ALANIZ

CASEY ALEXANDER

COSTA ALLEN

NICHOLAS AMANN

TYLER ANDERSEN

CHRISTOPHER ANDERSON

DARRELL ANDERSON

DEANE ANDERSON, JR.

MICHAEL ANDERSON

PATRICK ANDERSON

RICHARD ANDRUS

SHANNON ANTONIO

CHRISTOPHER APPIAH

DANIEL AQUINO

ROGER ARNOLD III

JESSE ARRIOLA

APOLLO ARTSON

ZACHERY ASH

CHRISTOPHER ASHWELL

JOSHUA ATCHLEY*

COSTEL BACIU

YONATHAN BAEZ*

ERIC BAGGETT

JOHN BAILEY

JUSTIN BAILEY

MICHAEL BAILEY, JR.

TIMOTHY BAINTER

ALPHANSO BANTON*

JEFFERY BARKDULL*

DARREN BARKER

ASHER BARNES

CHRISTOPHER BARNES

DEREK BAROLET

ROBERT BARTOLOMEO

KURTISS BAUMGARTNER

BRANDON BEAR

TROY BEARDEN

BRIAN BEAUMONT*

CHRISTOPHER BEEM

DALE BEHEE

DURRELL BENNETT*

JOSHUA BERLONGIERI

WHITNEY BERNARD

JERMAINE BILLIE

BRENTYN BISHOP*

EVERARDA BLANCO

LOWELL BLANDING

TERRY BLESSING, JR.*

BRIAN BLOW

DUSTIN BLUM

RYAN BOATWRIGHT

EDWARD BOLAND

DOUGLAS BOLLSCHWEILER

CHRISTOPHER BORNEMANN

FREDERICK BORRELL

HENRY BOSHART

WILLIAM BOSO

JOSEPH BOTKA

CHRISTOPHER BOUTEN*

MARIO BOWEN*

MATTHEW BOYDEN

FRED BOYER*

JORDAN BRACKETT*

MELISSA BRASKO

APPENDIX

CHRISTOPHER BRAUTIGAM

GREGORY BRAY

ANGELO BRELAND II

MARCO BRETTMAN

GERALD BRIGHT

RONALD BROCK

MARK BRODZINSKI

CALVIN BROWN, JR.

MATTHEW BROWN

CHRIS BROWNE

TYLER BRUMMOND

GREGORY BRUNSWICK

ALAN BRUTUS

WILLIAM BRYANT IV

MILTON BUNCH

KYLE BUNKER

KORY BUNTEN

JESSICA BURGE

BRANYN BURKHART

PAULA BURNS

ERIC BURRISS

JUSTIN BUSHONG

ZACHARY BUTLER

BRANDON BYBEE*

PHARRISH BYRD

JASON CAIN

JAY CAJIMAT*

BRANDEAUX CAMPBELL*

DANIEL CAMPBELL

WILLIAM CANNON

MATTHEW CARDELLINO

WILLIAM CAREW

BRIAN CASEY*

MARK CASHMAN*

BRANDON CASSAUBON

PHILIP CASTANEDA

JOHNNY CASTILLO, JR.*

JORDAN CASWELL

TONY CEVILLE

GARY CHAFFINS

WILLIAM CHANDLER

ANGKEAREASEY CHHOEUN

STEWART CHIEF

AARON CHONKO

STEPHEN CHU

PAUL CINKAN

ROY CLARK

CHRISTOPHER CLAUSS

JOHNATHAN CLIFTON

DANIEL CLINGMAN

BRIAN CLONINGER

DENTON CLOWSER

DERECK COBB

TIMOTHY COBLE

SAMUEL COCHRAN

JOSHUA COHEN

BRIAN COLLVER

JASON COMMANDER

MANUEL CONTRERAS

JAMES COOPER

JUSTIN COOPER

CLARENCE COPELAND

JERRID COPPEDGE

RAY CORCOLES, SR.

DAVID COREY

MICHAEL CORNETT

HOWARD COVEY, JR.

ANDRE CRAIG, JR.*

KEVIN CRATON

MICHAEL CRAYTON, JR.

DUNCAN CROOKSTON*

WILLIAM CROW, JR.*

JOEL CRUZ

JOSE CRUZPELLOT

GERY BRENT CUMMINGS

THOMAS CUMMINGS

WAYNE CUNNINGHAM

MARCUS DAERR

GREGORY DAILEY

JIMMIE DALE, JR.

JASON DANCE

JACOB DAVIS

NICK DAVIS*

JAMES DAVISON

ROBERT DEAN

ANDREW DEARDEN

BRIAN DEATON

CHRISTOPHER DECH

DAVID DEFENDALL

CHRISTIAN DEGUZMAN

ALBERT DE LA GARZA

ENRIQUE DELAMORA, JR.

MATTHEW DELAY

OTERRIAN DEMMING

NICOLAS DENINNO

STEVEN DENNISON II

REGINALD DENTON

BENJAMIN JO DERRICK

YURY DESANTOS

LEO DEVINE

IVAN DIAZ, JR.*

JOSE DIAZ, JR.

JOSEPH DIAZ

KEVIN DOLLENS

CASEY DONAHUE

APPENDIX

JAMES DOOLITTLE

JAMES DOSTER*

SKYLER DROLL

DERRICK DUER

DANE DUNHAM

MARK DUNN

MICHAEL DUNN*

SEAN DUSESOISEDILLO

DENNIS DUSTIN, JR.

CHARLES DYBO

KEVIN DYE

MENSAH DZEDIKU

FLETCHER EATON

FRANK EDDLEMAN

DREW EDWARDS*

RICHARD EICHBAUER

MATHEW ELKINS

MATTHEW ELLCESSOR

ANDREW ELLIOTT, JR.

ALFRED ELLIS

BRIAN EMERSON*

MICHAEL EMORY*

ARTHUR ENRIQUEZ

GREGORY ESCOBAR

ADRIAN ESPADAS

RYAN ESTRADA

JUSTIN FAAFITI

DOUGLAS FAZEKAS

EDDIE FELICIANO

CODY FERLICKA

DOUGLAS FERNANDEZ*

JOSEPH FIGERT

MICHAEL FIGUEROA

NICHOLAS FOGLE

GERALD FOLK, JR.

FRANK FORD

DAVID FORSHA

ROBERT FOXWORTHY

MICHAEL FRADERA*

BENJAMIN FRENETTE

ANDREW FUKUZAWA*

JOSHUA FULTONBARKER

EDWARD FURLONG

SHAWN GAJDOS*

SETH GARCI

ABRAN GARCIA

JON GARCIA

CHARMAINE GARON

JUSTIN GARRISON

ALFREDO GARZA

NICHOLAS GASKINS

RICHARD GASS, JR.

MARQUEZ GIBSON, JR.

STEPHEN GIESER

FRANCISCO GIETZ*

PERCY GILES

ANDREW GILLESPIE

JOSHUA GIST

JASON GLADWELL

GLENN GOAD, JR.

DAVID GOETZE

CHRISTOPHER GOLEMBE

ABELINO GOMEZ*

RYAN GOMEZ

RAUL GONZALEZ, JR.

THOMAS GONZALEZ

CHRISTOPHE GOODRICH

DUSTIN GORMAN

JASON GRAHAM

SEAN GREALISH

ALLEN GREBAS

JOHNATHAN GREGORY

MATTHEW GRIFFIN

TYLER GROS

BRIAN GRUESSER

JEREMY GUE

ARTHUR GUERRA

KYLE GULDEN

JESSE GUNNELS

ELMAR GUSEYNZADE

ZACHARY GUTHRIE

MICHAEL GUTIERREZ

JOSE GUZMAN

JAMES HALE

BO HALL

JAMES HALL

THOMAS HALL

ZACHARY HALL

JOSHUA HALSTEAD

JARED HAMBY

RYAN HAMEL

CHARLES HAMMOND

JERMAINE HAMPTON

MICKELL HAMWEY

ERIK HANCOCK

PATRICK HANLEY*

CODY HANNSZ

JARED HANSEN

ANDREW HANSON

JACOB HARBIN*

STEVEN HARDEMAN

FRANK HARDIN

JAMES HARRELSON*

DANELLE HARRIS

MICHAEL HARRIS

BENJAMIN HART

FREDERICK HARVEY

RAHIM HASIRBAF

EDWARD HASKINS, JR.

JAMES HAWLEY II

BRYSON HAYDEN

BENJAMIN HAYES

BRETT HAYES

DONALD HENDERSON, JR.

PEDRO HENRIQUEZ

TIMMOTHY HENRY

JOSEPH HENSON

JOHN HERMAN III

JARED HERMANN

GREGORY HERNANDEZ

MARIO HERNANDEZ*

LEE HETZLER

FRANK HICKMAN IV

MATTHEW HICKOK

JEWITT HILL

MATTHEW HILL

RICKY HILL

BRANDON HIPOL

TATWING HO

CHRISTOPHER HOFFMAN

NEIL HOLMES II

CHRISTIPHER HOLUB*

DARRYL HONICK, JR.

SHAUN HOOFARD

WILLIAM HOPPER

LUCAS HORN

HOWARD HORTON III

SHARON HORTON

LEONARD HOWARD

WAYNE HOWARD

JAY HOWELL

ROBERT HUBERTZ

KANIEL HUFF

JONATHAN HUGHES

JOSHUA HUNSUCKER

DONOVAN HURLEY

RAYMOND HYMAN, JR.

RYAN IMMEL

JASON INGRAM

JAIME INIGUEZ

RONALD IRVING, JR.

LAJUANE ISLAND

CHRISTOPHER IVERSEN

FRANK JACCARD

JOSEPH JACENKO

DANIEL JACKSON

JEFFREY JAGER

TAD JAMES

DAVID JANIS

JEFFREY JARAMILLO

JASON JEAN

BROCK JENSEN

EBENS JEREMIE

JOSE JEROME

DARRYL JEWELL

CODY JIMENEZ

BENJAMIN JOHNSON*

CHRISTOPHER L. JOHNSON

CHRISTOPHER W. JOHNSON

FREDRICK JOHNSON

JAN JOHNSON

JEFFREY JOHNSON

MEGAIL JOHNSON

WILLIAM JOHNSON

BO JOINES

BOBBY JONES

BRIAN JONES

JOHN JONES

KYLE JONES

RENNESS JONES

TIMOTHY JONES

PAUL JOWERS, JR.

PAUL JUBINVILLE, JR.

ROBERT JURIC

MICHAEL JURICK, JR.

DOUGLAS KAMM

BRENT KATCHATAG

RALPH KAUZLARICH

BILL KEARNEY

JERMAINE KELLEY

DARRIAN KELLY

WILLIAM KELLY

DANIEL KELSO

WILLIAM KEMPTER

JASON KENT

MARTHA KEY

RICHARD KIM

COREY KING

JOHN KIRBY*

DONALD KIRKLEY

BARRY KITCHEN

SCOTT KLEIN

JOSHUA KNUTSON

JAMES KOLKY

JASON KOUIS

KYLE KUMBIER

WILLIAM LAFLIN

CLARKE LAM

JEREMY LAMBERT

ROBERT LAMBERT

APPENDIX

LEROY LANCASTER*

JAEL LANDAVERDE

DAVID LANE*

TRENT LARSON*

TERRANCE LAVALLIE, JR.

KASEY LEA

JAMES LEACH

ALEXANDER LEE

SEUNG LEE

STEVE LEE

JOSHUA LEHMAN

DARTH LENZ

JOHN LEONARD

KEVIN LEONARD

WILLIAM LESIAK III.

JOSHUA LEVERE

SHAWN LEVERINGTON

JEREMIAH LEWIS

NATHANIEL LINK

ANDREW LIVERMORE

LOREN LONGIE

ANDREW LOONEY

NICHOLAS LOONEY*

FERNANDO LOPEZ, JR.

GREGORY LOPEZ

ALBERTO LORAROMERO

CHRISTOPHER LOVE

JEREMIAH LOVELADY

JUSTIN LOWE

MICHAEL LUKOW*

MARIONCIANO LUNA

SHAWN LYNCH

RAYMOND MCALLISTER II

SEAN MCALPINE

NATHANIEL MCCLURE*

JOE MCCOLLUM

WARREN MCCONNELL

ETHAN MCCORD

ZANE MCCOSKER

MICHAEL MCCOY

ALLEN MCDANIEL

BARRY MCDONALD, JR.*

ROBERT MCDONOUGH

LUKE MCDOWELL

DEVIN MCDUFFIE

CHAD MCGARVEY

JASON MCGARVEY

NATHANIEL MCGEE

NICHOLAS MCGINNIS

FREDRICK MCKELVIN

JAMIE MCPHERSON

MATTHEW MCWHORTER

MICHAEL MAEKER

MIKAEL MAGNUSON

MICHAEL MAHAR

ANDREW MAJEWSKIQUEALE

CHARLES MANARANG

RYAN MANN

SEAN MANNIX

JAY MARCH

ANTHONY MARIE

PATRICK MARRILL

JOHN MARTIN

JOSE MARTINEZ, JR.

SANTOS MARTINEZ

TIMOTHY MASON

BRETT MATHEU

MICHAEL MATHIEUS

WAYNE MATHIS

PHILIP MATRO

ERIC MATTSON

JUSTIN MAVITY

DONALD MAYS, JR.

PHILLIP MAYS, JR.

MELISSA MEDEL

STEPHEN MEDER

DARIO MEDINA

STEPHEN MENDES

BRIAN MENNIG

MATTHEW MERGELE*

ANTHONY MERLINO

GLEN MESA

KYLE MIDKIFF

PIOTR MIKOLAJEWSKI

BRET MILLER

JOSEPH MILLER*

NICHOLAS A. MILLER

NICHOLAS M. MILLER

PATRICK MILLER*

ROY MILLER

SHAWN MILLER

JEREMY MITCHELL

SATONYA MITCHELL

JOSEPH MIXSON*

THOMAS MOHART

ROBERT MONTEZ

COLIN MONTGOMERY

KRISTOPHER MONTI

JOSHUA MORAN

DAVID MORENO

EFREN MORENO

RASHAN MORRIS

JEFFERY MOSS

RICHARD MOSS, JR.

CARROLL MOULDEN, JR.

RAYMOND MOUNGEY	CHRISTOPHER PATTERSON	JAMES QUACKENBUSH
OLIVER MULLINS	THOMAS PATTERSON	THOMAS RACHELS
MATTHEW MURPHY II	CAMERON PAYNE*	JAMES RAGAN
JOEL MURRAY*	EDWARD PAYNE III	ENRICO RAY
JEFFREY MUSIL	JARETH PAYNE*	CHARLES REED
ERIC MYERS	DARRELL PEEBLES, SR.	WHITNEY REED
ELVIN NAEA	ANTHONY PELLECCHIA*	JOSHUA REEVES*
GRANT NAUGHTON	THOMAS PENDLETON	CARL REIHER*
ARNULFO NAVARRO, JR.	TIMOTHY PENN	GARRETT REILMANN
WILLIAM NEDDO	MARK PEREZ, JR.	ANDREW REINKE
MATTHEW NELSON	TRUONG VU PHAN	LAWRENCE REISINGER
ANDREW NETHKEN	ALBERT PHILLIPS	DARYL REVEL
MATHEW NEYLAND	CHRISTOPHER PICARD	BOBBY REX
KAITH KHANH NGUYEN	MELVIN PIERCE	THOMAS RICE
PHAT NGUYEN	NICOLAS PINA	THOMAS RICHARDSON
RYAN NIEDERT	MICHAEL PING	WELBY RICHARDSON
BENJAMIN NIEDZWEICKI	ANDREW PIPER	KJANAI RILEY
SHANE NORDRUM	CHRISTITUTO PITCHFORD	ERIK RILLERA
JUAN NUNEZ	JOSHUA POLING	JOSEPH RINEHART
OSCAR NUNEZ	RODY POLOJAC	JOHNNY RIVERA
RYAN NYHUS	DARIN POTT	ANGEL ROBLES
JUSTIN OAKS	MICHAEL POTTEBAUM	ISAAC RODGERS
JOSEPH OGNIBENE	BENNY POTTER	ARMANDO RODRIGUEZ
JEFFREY O'HARA	MITCHELL POTVIN	JOE RODRIGUEZ
STEVEN OLIVAREZ	BILLY POULSEN*	LUIS RODRIGUEZ
MICHAEL OLSON	KENNEDY POWELL	NICHOLAS RODRIGUEZ
JOSE OLVERA	DANIEL PREISSNER	RUBEN RODRIGUEZ
JORGE ORELLANA	CHRISTOPHER PREMORE	RUBIN RODRIGUEZ
CESAR ORNELASSILVA	DONALD PRESTLEY	MICHAEL RODRIGUEZTORO
TIMOTHY ORR	DANIEL PRICE*	HENRY ROJASAMPUDIA
RANDALL PACKER	JACOB PRICE	KIPP ROLLASON
RICHARD PARK	GORDON PRICKETT, JR.	JAMES ROSS III
VICTOR PARKER	JOHNATHAN PRITCHETT	BARACH ROULEAU
ROBERT PARSONS	CHRISTOPHER PROFET	WILLIAM ROY
DUSTIN PATRICK	ANDREW PUCEK	TRISTAN RUARK

ROBERT RYDER	MICHAEL SHORTLIDGE	JARED STEVENS*
PATRICK SALENTINE	NATHAN SHOWMAN	CHAD STEWARD
COLE SAMMONS	JOSHUA SICKLES	ALLEN STEWART
JONATHAN SANDERS	THOMAS SIMMONS	JOSHUA STIEBER
LARRY SANDERS II	TIJERA SLACK	SHAUN STILLWELL
JOSHUA SANDLIN	JUSTIN SLAGLE	DERRICK STINNETT*
STEVEN SANTAMARIA	JEREMY SLATER	BENJAMIN STORM
JONATHAN SANTEE	JEFFREY SLAVENS	TRENTON STORM
ROBERTO SANTIAGO, JR.	CHARLES SMITH II	LARRY STREEPER, JR.
RICKY SARRINGAR	DANIEL SMITH	STEVEN STRICKLAND
STEVEN SARTOR	DEONTA SMITH	TYREE STRICKLAND
LUCAS SASSMAN*	HOWARD SMITH	GILLIAN STUMBO
TERELL SAULS	JASON H. SMITH	JONATHON STUREK
LOUIS SCARINGELLA	JASON M. SMITH	DANIEL STYLES
CHRISTOPHER SCHAIRER	JEREMY SMITH*	JOHN SWALES
JUSTIN SCHAUER	JUSTIN SMITH	JONATHAN SWAN
ALLEN SCHLITTLER, JR.	RICHARD SMITH	MICHAEL SWANEY
ADAM SCHUMANN	ROBERT SMITH	RICHARD TACKETT
JAMES SCHUTT	SETH SMITH	BRANDON TALSMA
WENDELL SCOTT	SKYLER SMITH	PETERO TAUFAGU
SCOTT SCUTARI	THOMAS P. SMITH	RICHARD TAYLOR
ADAM SEIBOLD	THOMAS R. SMITH	MATTHEW TEBEEST
JOSEPH SEMTAK	THOMAS R. SMITH	DAVID TEDROW
ROBERT SENSIBAUGH	WESLEY SMITH	IAKOPO TEI
WALTER SEPULVADO	JARED SPARKS	ALEXANDER TELLEZ
EMIR SERRANO	BILLY SPEEDY	NATHAN TENNEY
ROSADA SERRANO	DONALD SPENCER*	ALEXANDER TEUSAW
WESLEY SETZER	GARETT STACKPOLE	ANTONIO THOMPSON
JEREMIAH SHAFER	JOHN STAHMAN	DEREK THOMPSON
ADAM SHAW	ERIK STANCIL	JUSTIN THOMPSON
KELLAN SHEELY	CLINTON STAUB	LELAND THOMPSON*
ALEXANDER SHELTON	RAYNELL STEELE	NICHOLAS THOMPSON
RANDOL SHELTON*	RYNE STEGURA	TROY THOMPSON
JOHNNY SHERFIELD	DAVID STERLING	TIMOTHY THOMSON
TRUMAN SHIMKANIN	MATTHEW STERN	ANDREW THORNBERRY

APPENDIX

CHRISTOPHER TINGLE

RUDY TOIA

CHRISTOPHER TORIX

ROBERT TRUEX

CHARLES TRUNNELL III

JARRAD TRUOG

DEAN TUBBS

KYUNG TURNER

PATRICK TUTWILER*

ASILA UME

MICHAEL VACANTI

GEORGE VALENCIA

RAFAEL VALENTIN, JR.

BRANDON VALENTINE

ALLAN VALTIERRA*

IGNACIO VALVERDE, JR.

JASON VAN GUNDY

JAMES VAN ZYTVELD

CHARLES VASQUEZ, JR.

JAIME VASQUEZ

SHAWN VENTURA

JOSE VERA*

WILLIAM VIAN

BENJAMIN VILLASENOR

JOHN VIOLA

RANDY WADDELL

CHARLES WADE, JR.

JEROD WADE

ERIC WAGNER

NICHOLAS WAGNER

SETH WAHL

REBECCA WAINNER

WILLIAM WALDEN

JOSEPH WALKER, JR.

WILLIAM WALKER

WILLIAM WALLACE

ANDREW WALLER

ALBERT WALSH

MICHAEL WAPELHORST

MICHAEL WARD

PRESTON WARD

THOMAS WARTH

RYAN WATERS

ERIC WATSON

CHRISTOPHER WATTS*

MICHAEL WEAKLEY

WILLIAM WEBB

ORIS WEBSTER

SAMUEL WEISSMAN

HOWARD WEITZMAN

JOSHUA WELBORN

DANIEL WENZEL

JACK WHEELER, JR.

CHARLES WHITE

NICHOLAS WHITE

ALLEN WICK

JAMES WIDENER

MATTHEW WILES

AMANDA WILLIAMS

BRANDON WILLIAMS

CARL WILLIAMS

JAMES WILLIAMS

KENNETH WILLIAMS

TIMOTHY WILLIAMS*

MICHAEL WILLIFORD

CRAIG WILSON

JAMES WILSON

JEFFREY WILSON

KRYSTAL WILSON

RYAN WILSON*

MICHAEL WINCHESTER

ROBERT WINEGAR, JR.*

ANDREW WINKLER

SHANE WINN

SCOTT WINTER

BRANDON WISE

LEONARD WISNIEWSKI

MATTHEW WITTE

JOSHUA WOLD*

BRANDON WOOD

RYAN WOOD

JASON WOODBURY

TREVOR WOODS

DARRIN WOOLF

WILLIAM WORTHINGTON

JOSEPH WRIGHT

MATTHEW WRIGHT

RICHARD WRIGHT

THOMAS YANNELLI

ADAM YOUNG

DAVID YOUNG

JUAN ZAMBRANO, JR.

EDGAR ZAMORA

WILLIAM ZAPPA*

DIONICIO ZARRABAL

STEVEN ZEBROWSKI

TODD ZIEGLER

VANCE ZIMMER

RUSTY ZIMMERMAN

ALLEN ZURENKO

BRIAN ZWEIBOHMER

ABRAM ZYNDA

Information courtesy of the 2-16. List includes original deployers and mid-tour replacements. Asterisks signify Purple Heart recipients.

The 2-16 Soldiers Who Died

Jay Cajimat, April 6, 2007

Shawn Gajdos, June 6, 2007

Cameron Payne, June 11, 2007

Andre Craig, Jr., June 25, 2007

William Crow, Jr., June 28, 2007

James Harrelson, July 17, 2007

Joel Murray, September 4, 2007

David Lane, September 4, 2007

Randol Shelton, September 4, 2007

Joshua Reeves, September 22, 2007

James Doster, September 29, 2007

Duncan Crookston, January 25, 2008

Durrell Bennett, March 29, 2008

Patrick Miller, March 29, 2008

A NOTE ON SOURCES AND METHODS

Most of this book is based on events I personally observed between January 2007, when I first met the 2-16, and June 2008, the month of the Ranger Ball. I spent a total of eight months with the 2-16 in Iraq and made additional reporting trips to Fort Riley, in Kansas; Brooke Army Medical Center, in San Antonio, Texas; the National Naval Medical Center, in Bethesda, Maryland; and Walter Reed Army Medical Center, in Washington, D.C.

The book also contains some scenes for which I wasn't present. In those instances, the details, descriptions, and dialogue used in the book were verified through internal army reports, photographs, videos, after-the-fact observation, and interviews with as many participants as conditions would permit. All of the people described and quoted in the book knew that I was a journalist and that everything I was seeing and hearing was on the record.

It is to the army's credit, I believe, that during the length of my reporting, there were only two times that I was asked to treat something as off the record. Both requests involved classified technological applications in use by the soldiers, the revealing of which could conceivably put subsequent soldiers using the applications at increased risk, and I agreed to do so.

And it is to the 2-16 soldiers' credit that they tolerated a journalist being among them, and in almost all cases welcomed me with their trust. From the beginning, I explained to them that my intent was to document their corner of the war, without agenda. This book, then, is that corner, unshaded. I feel privileged to have been its witness, and to write the story of what happened.

ACKNOWLEDGMENTS

There are many people I want to acknowledge and thank, beginning with the soldiers of the 2-16, every one of them.

I want to thank Sarah Crichton, of Farrar, Straus and Giroux.

I want to thank Melanie Jackson, my literary agent.

At *The Washington Post*, I want to thank Don Graham, Leonard Downie, Jr., Mary Ann Werner, Rick Atkinson, Bill Hamilton, David Hoffman, Dana Priest, Sudarsan Raghavan and the heroic Baghdad bureau, Tom Ricks, Liz Spayd, Julie Tate, Karl Vick, the foreign desk, and everyone in Benefits.

At the Woodrow Wilson International Center for Scholars, I want to thank Lee Hamilton, Michael Van Dusen, Lucy Jilka, Janet Spikes, and especially Margaret Paxson.

At Stanford University, I want to thank the Hoover Institution.

Thank you to my parents.

Thank you, Bob Barnes.

Thank you, Lucian Perkins.

Thank you, John Nagl.

Thank you, Katherine Boo.

Thank you, Anne Hull.

Thank you, Phil Bennett.

Thank you, Steve Coll.

Thank you, Julia, Lauren, and, most of all, Lisa. You are the home I got to come home to.

A NOTE ABOUT THE AUTHOR

David Finkel is the National Enterprise Editor of *The Washington Post*. He joined the *Post* in 1990 and has worked for the paper's national, foreign, and magazine staffs. He has reported from Africa, Asia, Central America, Europe, and throughout the United States, and was part of the *Post*'s war coverage in Iraq, Afghanistan, and Kosovo.

Among Finkel's journalism honors are a Pulitzer Prize for explanatory reporting in 2006 for a series of stories about U.S.-funded democracy efforts in Yemen. He has been a Pulitzer finalist three other times, for both explanatory reporting and feature writing.

A 1977 graduate of the University of Florida, Finkel is married, has two daughters, and lives in Silver Spring, Maryland.